Indigeneity, Globalization, and African Literature

AFRICAN HISTORIES AND MODERNITIES

Series Editors

Toyin Falola, University of Texas at Austin
Matthew M. Heaton, Virginia Tech

Editorial Board

Aderonke Adesanya, Art History, James Madison University
Kwabena Akurang-Parry, History, Shippensburg University
Nana Amponsah, History, University of North Carolina, Wilmington
Tyler Fleming, History, University of Louisville
Barbara Harlow, English and Comparative Literature, University of Texas at Austin
Emmanuel Mbah, History, College of Staten Island
Akin Ogundiran, Africana Studies, University of North Carolina, Charlotte

This book series serves as a scholarly forum on African contributions to and nego-
tiations of diverse modernities over time and space, with a particular emphasis on
historical developments. Specifically, it aims to refute the hegemonic conception of
a singular modernity, Western in origin, spreading out to encompass the globe over
the last several decades. Indeed, rather than reinforcing conceptual boundaries or
parameters, the series instead looks to receive and respond to changing perspectives
on an important but inherently nebulous idea, deliberately creating a space in which
multiple modernities can interact, overlap, and conflict. While privileging works that
emphasize historical change over time, the series will also feature scholarship that
blurs the lines between the historical and the contemporary, recognizing the ways in
which our changing understandings of modernity in the present have the capacity to
affect the way we think about African and global histories.

Published in the series

Contemporary Africa: Challenges and Opportunities (2014)
Edited by Toyin Falola and Emmanuel M. Mbah

African Postcolonial Modernity: Informal Subjectivities and the Democratic Consensus
(2014)
By Sanya Osha

Building the Ghanaian State: Kwame Nkrumah's Symbolic Nationalism (2014)
By Harcourt Fuller

*Prisoners of Rhodesia: Inmates and Detainees in the Struggle for Zimbabwean
Liberation, 1960–1980* (2014)
By Munyaradzi B. Munochiveyi

Mugabeism? History, Politics, and Power in Zimbabwe (2015)
Edited by Sabelo J. Ndlovu-Gatsheni

Indigeneity, Globalization, and African Literature: Personally Speaking (2015)
By Tanure Ojaide

Indigeneity, Globalization, and African Literature

Personally Speaking

Tanure Ojaide

INDIGENEITY, GLOBALIZATION, AND AFRICAN LITERATURE

First published 2015 by
PALGRAVE MACMILLAN

The author has asserted their right to be identified as the author of this work in accordance with the Copyright, Designs and Patents Act 1988.

Palgrave Macmillan in the UK is an imprint of Macmillan Publishers Limited, registered in England, company number 785998, of Houndmills, Basingstoke, Hampshire, RG21 6XS.

Palgrave Macmillan in the US is a division of Nature America, Inc., One New York Plaza, Suite 4500, New York, NY 10004-1562.

Palgrave Macmillan is the global academic imprint of the above companies and has companies and representatives throughout the world.

Hardback ISBN: 978–1–137–54220–5
E-PUB ISBN: 978–1–137–56002–5
E-PDF ISBN: 978–1–137–56003–2
DOI: 10.1057/9781137560032

Distribution in the UK, Europe and the rest of the world is by Palgrave Macmillan®, a division of Macmillan Publishers Limited, registered in England, company number 785998, of Houndmills, Basingstoke, Hampshire RG21 6XS.

Library of Congress Cataloging-in-Publication Data

Ojaide, Tanure, 1948– author.
    Indigeneity, globalization, and African literature : personally speaking / Tanure Ojaide, Ph.D.
        pages cm. —(African histories and modernities)
    ISBN 978–1–137–54220–5 (hardback : alk. paper)
        1. African literature—20th century—History and criticism. 2. African literature—21st century—History and criticism. 3. Politics in literature. 4. Africa—Politics and government—1960– 5. Africa—Intellectual life. I. Title. II. Series: African histories and modernities.
PL8010.O3295 2015
809'.8896—dc23   2015013927

A catalogue record of the book is available from the British Library.

CONTENTS

Introduction

As a creative writer and a literary scholar, I am very concerned about the direction of African literature in its production and interpretation. Since literature is a cultural production, and so an aspect of culture that is dynamic, it is bound to be dynamic too. This means that literature will continue to change with time or history and according to the context, place, or nation in which it is produced. Each period of history, call it generation, has its own zeitgeist or intellectual climate that affects the inspiration of creative works. After all, the writer is an antenna of society and responds to what is happening around him or her. As history is always moving forward inexorably, the happenings are set in place. Place in its widest meaning of nation, homeland, and geography, among many other aspects of setting, becomes where humans act out their experiences at particular times. Since writers live in a place and gain their experiences from what is happening around them, they are rooted somewhere. As they are based somewhere, they can feel what is happening near and far and respond to those happenings according to their own set-out missions of what they want to achieve with their writings. It is from the land or place that the fiction writer and dramatist frame their characters that act out a vision. The poet, on the other hand, experiences from the interaction with human and nonhuman beings and the world around.

Each culture changes as a result of internal and external factors. Often there are stresses from within about what things people no longer find relevant or cumbersome and so abandon. As there are changes informed by internal factors, so also are changes brought about by external factors. A people may find some new things relevant and so absorb them into their culture. That is why there is the continuous dynamism of culture as history marches on resulting in changes in the way of life of a people.

Modernity has brought changes that have turned traditional modes in Africa into a new dispensation. From the nonliterate societies of precolonial times emerged literate societies. Similarly, changes came in the political, economic, and social spheres in the lives of Africans. While the oral still exists, the written has taken its place in Africa's modernity. The new literature has merged African traditional and oral methods with European modern writing traditions into a modern African literature. Africa has had a lot to contend with in modernity: colonization, struggle for political independence, self-rule, and managing political independence. In all, it has been a difficult history transiting from foreign rule to self-government. The modern state has posed a problem for Africans. The experience of political independence has not been as positive as expected. Civil wars, military dictatorship, corruption, and lack of good leadership have bedeviled many African states. It is not Uhuru yet in most African states where there is poverty, ethnic conflicts, insecurity, poor health, and other afflictions that have placed most African states at the bottom of human development in the world.

The cultural producers of literature live in these societies and respond to them in their respective individual ways. This is because the situation in each country is different and so the national experience is somehow unique. Even there is diversity within the national experience as a result of many factors within the state. For example, it makes a difference if one lives in Francophone or Anglophone Cameroon as in North or South Cote d'Ivoire or Nigeria. It matters if one is from one region or the other within a country. However, nationhood tends to be a cohesive factor for a country's citizens. But despite the uniqueness of each nation's experiences, there are some general or rather continental similarities; hence without writers not meeting to form groups or associations they still tend to express the same sentiments, especially on political, economic, and social issues that many African nations share. Thus, each generation is influenced by its zeitgeist to which it responds. Let me give an example with what I call the second generation of African poets. Kofi Anyidoho and Abena Busia of Ghana, Odia Ofeimun, Niyi Osundare, and Chimalum Nwankwo of Nigeria, Jack Mapanje, Frank Chipasula, and Lupenga Mphande of Malawi seem to demonstrate that as generations form in each African country, they spread across the continent. In *The New African Poetry: An Anthology*, Tijan M.Sallah and I have assembled poems from across Africa. These poems seem to express comparable themes with similar techniques; hence we call the works "the new African poetry." Thus, while there are individual writers and nations, African people still share similarities in their postcolonial, modern, and contemporary realities.

My angst is that much as cultures worldwide change, some seem to influence others with their values and ways without a reciprocal change in them from interactions with others. There is a Western canon of literature and there is no dispute about its Greco-Roman origins. Similarly, Western values have Judeo-Christian origins and Westerners talk of "our values." African oral literature is generally seen as functional and the early generations of African writers seem to have carried the functionality on. The positions of many African writers have affirmed the importance of literature beyond its entertainment value. For instance, Chinua Achebe sees the writer as a teacher. Sembene Ousmane and Ngugi wa Thiongo see writers as at the vanguard of their people's struggle. Many other African writers also fashion their respective visions to improve their societies.

In this work I interrogate modern and contemporary African literature, especially since the 1980s, to see how the cultural production of literature is faring. Of course, this has to be in the context of history. Since modern African literature seems to parallel the history of the continent and realities of the people at particular times, I have to talk about how politics has shaped the African creative vision. And that brings me directly to what is African in literary works produced by Africans who are in the flux. With globalization, which has led to accelerated communication and migration, Africa and what is African are changing fast. Universal attention has been drawn to so many issues by globalization—democracy, human rights, climate change, sex and sexuality, and many more. Africans have migrated outside to mainly North America and Europe for economic and other reasons and advantages in stable societies. The liberal attitudes in the West and developed publishing tradition have attracted many African writers. As discussed in the book, there are now African writers in diaspora and African writers at home, a condition that is complicating the African literary tradition. What I have noticed is that because Africans have migrated a lot outside their cultural region, unlike Westerners, African literature is undergoing a crisis of cultural identity. While globalization is ongoing and strong, there is still a move for indigeneity to retain Africanness despite changes. This tension between indigeneity and globalization seems to be driving contemporary African literature.

As I stated earlier, I am both a cultural producer and interpreter. I have attempted to "interprete" modern and contemporary African literature from my writer-scholar position. I have thus interrogated the general trend of African literature while at the same time doing a reading of particular writers, especially poets. I have also looked at the intersection of culture, society, economics, and other aspects of contemporary African reality in the literature. I have devoted a section to my own experience of writing; hence my research in oral poetic performance, self-profile, and "personally speaking" on a particular poetry collection of mine to give some background to my production.

I have divided the work into four sections, each with related chapters. Section I takes on my major angst of "The Perils of a Culture-less African Literature in the Age of Globalization" as well as "Contemporary Africa and the Politics in Literature," and "Homecoming: African Literature and Human Development." This section also deals with the emerging Niger Delta literature in Nigeria as well as critiquing Chinua Achebe's *Things Fall Apart* as a world literature text. These latter two chapters of the first section illustrate how contemporary African literature is growing especially in the areas of environmental and human rights as well as showing how a literary work set in a specific place and time, an Igbo village in a period of transition, has universal validation.

Section II focuses on poetry in the dynamics of African history and reality. Starting with Wole Soyinka's poetic output since he won the Nobel Prize for Literature in 1986, I examine three poets whose respective works deserve more critical attention than they have received: "An Unusual Growth: The Development of Tijan M. Sallah's Poetry," "An Insider Testimony: Odia Ofeimun and His Generation of Nigerian Poets," and "Traditional Izon Court and Modern Poetry: Christian Otobotekere's Contribution." The last chapter of this section, framed as an "argument," seeks ways to revive modern African poetry that appears to have lost not only its vitality but also its preeminent position in literature to fiction. One has to bear in mind that poetry was the genre of choice of many of the early exponents of modern African literature, be they the Negritude writers or the group cormprising of Lenrie Peters, Kofi Awoonor, Christopher Okigbo, J. P. Clark, Wole Soyinka, and Dennis Brutus.

Section III goes to more general issues in African literature and strategies that seem to make literary works successful. There is "The Imperative of Experience in Poetry: An African Perspective" and "Indigenous Knowledge and Its Expression in the Folklore of Africa." This chapter on folklore gives some background to many literary works be they drama, fiction, or poetry. Folklore provides the indigeneity that continues to give African literature its cultural identity but which some younger contemporary writers seem to avoid. "Policy Studies, Activist Literature, and Pitching for the Masses in Nigeria" provides a continuation of the functional nature of modern African literature. The last chapter of this section, "The Politics of African Literature: Production, Publishing, and Reception," returns to the stress between globalization and indigeneity as well as the condition of African literature with many renowned writers outside the continent. I must state it matters not where one lives and writes but it depends on the perspective one propagates on literature that makes one an African writer.

The final section—IV—is more personal, hence "personally speaking." Here, I have used my personal writing career to give an example of who I am, what made me what I am, and experiences and realities behind my literary work. Though personal, it is meant to reflect how to understand many African writers and their works. I have thus included my address to a conference on my work, "Inviting the World into the House of Words: The Writer, His Place, People, and Audience" and an invitation to talk on one of my poetry books, "Personally Speaking: On *The Beauty I Have Seen*" at The University of North Carolina at Charlotte. Both "Revisiting an African Oral Poetic Performance Tradition: *Udje* Today" and "Performance, the New African Poetry, and My Poetry: A Commentary" point to my indebtedness to the oral poetic performance of *udje* that I have spent time researching in the manner of Kofi Awoonor on Ewe oral poetry, Wole Soyinka on Yoruba traditional drama, J. P. Clark on "udje dance poetry," Jack Mapanje on Chewa oral traditions, and Kofi Anyidoho on Ewe poetry. The last chapter is my personal tribute to two writers I respect who have recently died: "Two Tributes: Chinua Achebe and Kofi Awoonor."

Though different chapters of this book might have been written at different times, I have always had this book project in mind as I reflected on indigeneity and globalization in African literature. As stated in chapter 12 and a few other places, many African writers are very conversant with their indigenous folklores which in their writings become "a means of cultural resistance." There is always that stress between indigeneity in the form of using the traditional folklore to inform the expression of contemporary thought and feeling and the globalization, which includes expression irrespective of the language used but avoids specific folklores or oral traditions and indigenous location. It appears using folklore brings to bear on the writings a sense of cultural and place location, which further marks the literary work as African. From the contemporary state of African literature, it is likely the tension between indigeneity and globalization will persist and how it is managed will determine the future of African literature as it evolves.

It is my ardent hope that this book's content will stir a discussion among writers and critics/scholars on the direction of African literature toward making it strong, diverse, and relevant to the African reality.

SECTION I

CHAPTER 1

The Perils of a Culture-less African Literature in the Age of Globalization

Introduction

By now I have been associated with the idea that a writer is not an air-plant but someone rooted in a specific place or environment and time. Place and time are respectively geography and history and they form the bedrock of human experience. The two factors have bearing on culture. An intrinsic aspect of a place or environment is the culture which has evolved over time as the inhabitants attempt to reconcile their ways to the physical world and reality they face on a daily basis. This means that the writer is born into, if not raised in, lives or appropriates a culture that feeds his or her creative impulse. The culture of a people gives grounding to an artistic creation with its aesthetics, which impels the artist to have at the back of his or her mind the function of the work being created and the anticipated pleasure to the audience—the society for whom the work is created. Certain criteria might therefore exist in the creation of an artistic work within a culture. As such, those who are masters or judges of the artistic creations can say, "This is the way it is done so that it will be this when completed."

Rootedness also places the writer in a tradition, which (s)he can develop, interrogate, expand, disrupt, or even mock or abandon but which stands as the basis or touchstone of the very artistic medium. This phenomenon exists in every culture: the tradition that the individual artist has to confront in the artistic creative process. T. S. Eliot affirmed the obvious in every artistic tradition in "Tradition and the Individual Talent." There is an established tradition that the individual poet or writer attempts through talent and craft to redefine in an artistic fashion with his or her created works.

Culture is never static but always dynamic and it should not be seen as a limiting factor or constraint in creativity; it changes with time as well as individual or communal interrogation. In Chinua Achebe's *Things Fall Apart*, Okonkwo's Umuofia was already changing before the coming of the European colonialists from adjustments made to punishment to those who violated the Week of Peace from being dragged to death to a stipulated fine. Other examples in other creative works or real life exist to show this dynamic march of culture. As far as literature is concerned, it is a people's culture that sets up a canon that promotes its classics or models that artists endeavor to attain or raise higher to an ever more sophisticated stature for adoration. From the foregoing it can be seen that literature is a cultural production and any literary work should make the most meaning in the cultural tradition that inspired its creation.

A common humanity does not necessarily beget a common culture or way of life. To me, culture is a form of adornment to humanity. As humans, we all become hungry and eat but we do not eat the same foods, nor do we prepare them or eat in the same manner. We feel hot or cold and need clothing but do not wear the same clothes or even sew them the same way. We have our desires and make love but not the same manner. Culture is thus the ornamentation to our humanity in different ways. It is the culmination of a people's or group's ways of life with their beliefs, lifestyle, and manner of dealing with their human condition and practical realities. There is thus one common humanity—we are born, grow old, and eventually die—but we have a diversity of cultures as each group of people have rites of passage that differ from place to place and people to people.

Culture has the geography of the place and the history of the people feeding it in a continuum of self-renewal. This process involves abandoning some aspects that are no longer relevant and appropriating some new things that could come from outside. A culture always has a past and present but what is important is that the present reality is bound with time to change. There are both internal and external dynamics at play in every culture which continues to evolve. Words enter the lexicon from outside such as *kwashiorkor* into English, even though originally Akan, and recently *vuvuzela*, the Zulu trumpet used to exhort players in a contest. Neologisms are part of the dynamic growth of every language and many African languages have a plethora of neologisms, especially resulting from technological inventions abroad. It is in the context of this broad definition of culture that I look at the state of modern African literature and explore how writers who are conscious of their indigenous cultures have gained literary strength while those who ignore their cultural origins even in the age of globalization have done so at their own peril.

GLOBALIZATION

This discourse of literature and culture is done in the context of globalization and migration which have dispersed Africans to other parts of the world, especially Europe and North America. Whether out of the Mother Continent or in it, there is a free flow of ideas of globalization which appear to be influencing many African writers and many other Africans who are not writers.

From colonial and imperial discourses, Africa and Africans have been at the periphery of world civilization and stand outside the dominant Western/European culture. Westerners justified slavery and later colonialism with the argument of Africa having no history and no culture, a tabula rasa that they had to fill with civilization. Many European philosophers and scholars, including G. W. F. Hegel and Hugh Trevor-Roper, opined that Africa had no history and culture before European exploration and colonization of the continent. Africa was labeled the "Other," as opposed to them, in a binary world of white and black, cultured and savage, and so forth (Mudimbe 1994; Bhabha 1994). These Western stereotypes prevail in their literatures before the current age of globalization. It should be realized that globalization is "the expansionist takeover of the present-day developing countries by the Western economic system" (qtd. in Donkor 29). Thus, globalization is another form of Western domination of the world in political, economic, and cultural terms. It is an effort to promote homogeneity that is Western and absorbs the once "Other" into the hegemonic West.

Let me dispose of the spurious counter discourse that modern African literature by its written nature is foreign anyway and so the argument of a cultural identity is not tenable. Others also argue that globalization has made African culture irrelevant as if Westerners and Asians, for instance, say the same of their own respective cultures. As long as there are a people, they have a culture and a literature in the forms of their song/poetry, performance/drama, and narrative/ fiction. One may argue about the development of a specific literature that places it higher in its currency because of the advantage of promotion as the literatures of imperial powers whose mediocre works could be praised and foisted upon subject people as great works. Today, I can say with a measure of experience and authority that many British writers that I was compelled to study about in high school and in my undergraduate years, do not qualify by any measure as more than mediocre authors. I remember some of the sonneteers, metaphysical poets, satirists of the Augustan Age, Pre-Raphaelites, and Victorian writers we studied in school and they do not measure up when compared to many African writers whose works do not have the advantage of imperial promotion. The point then is that there is always a literature as part of a people's culture.

Once a people become literate, whether it is part of imperialism, colonization, or the natural growth of that civilization, their literature is bound to move into a new medium. Oral or written, literature always carries the experiences, history, sensibility, worldview, and realities of a people. Whether people become cosmopolitan or globalized, it is from the standpoint of their individual reality that they express their feelings and thoughts. Even when a writer's experience is private, that experience is still inseparable from individual response to society and the culture. The literary creation derives from within the matrix of the writer's society. The saying attributed to the late Jewish American writer, Saul Bellow, that the Zulu people or any African ethnic group do not have a literature of a high standard is an arrogant racist statement that should be dismissed for its ignorance when you think of Zulu izibongo, Yoruba ijala and oriki, Urhobo *udje*, Ewe *halo*, and the great epics of *Sunjata*, *Ozidi*, and *Mwindo*, among so many other forms of literature in the continent. There are many works of American or British literature that are anthologized or studied that do not rise to the stature of many of the African literary works mentioned here.

Art and Artifice

Let me make some comparisons to clarify the thrust of this argument. Those African writers who argue that culture is not or no longer significant in literature can be compared to a phenomenon which is unfolding before our very eyes. There are singers/musicians who sing with their voices and are acknowledged for that—great divas such as Whitney Houston and Adele. There are others who cannot sing and call themselves studio artists and mix sounds in the studio to sell in DVDs. The latter type of musical artists do not go on concerts to play live because they can't just sing. The same phenomenon is going on in the visual arts. There are artists who paint wonderfully with brushes and oil or acrylic colors and there are others who use the computer to generate images and can be called artists or graphic designers. Similarly, literature is coming to the same thing. There are those for whom the creative work is no longer the amalgam of the culture and used to express feelings and ideas from the historical and cultural experiences of the people. On the other hand, there are those who see a literary creation as a mere form, almost devoid of the laughter and sorrows, trials and triumphs of the people, but meant to play a game of words for commercial success.

How does one argue that culture is not relevant to a literary work? What will the writer express if he or she discountenances the indigenous culture in its fluidity? As stated earlier, we may share a common humanity but do not share a common culture. If history, geography, worldview, sensibility, and reality are ingrained in the culture of a people, will such an African writer argue that there was no slave trade, no colonialism, and no imperialism and neocolonialism in whatever guise the political powers frame them? On what side of the situation of slavery and colonialism is the writer, the oppressor and exploiter or the oppressed and exploited? Will such a writer wipe out from memory the flora and fauna that formed his or her landscape both without and within?

A writer can imagine what is outside his place but that imagining has to be comprehensible to his anticipated audience. Whatever we say about Joseph Conrad of *Heart of Darkness*, as a sailor he was said to have sailed through the coast of the Congo where he set his novel in. A writer can encompass through travels other landscapes in his imaginative field to express his individual or public experiences. The 2009 Nobel Laureate for Literature, Herta Muller, comes to mind. He used his experiences of residency in Eastern Nigeria in his writing and that is fine. Similarly, Wole Soyinka summons "seasons of an alien land," where he was when the civil disturbances that led to the Nigerian Civil War broke out, in his *Idanre*. In a similar vein Gabriel Okara writes a poem on snow flakes, which he might not have seen then or just imagined. In "Piano and Drums" the poet expresses himself in diverse symbolic musical instruments. The tenor here is stronger than when talking about snowflakes that are very alien to his tropical Niger Delta environment.

It is pertinent to note that Westerners trace their civilization to Greco-Roman times. They seem to claim monopoly of democracy, which they say they have practiced from Ancient Greek times. Often they describe their tradition as Judeo-Christian whose values they hold dear. It is this ancient origin that they trace their culture to, irrespective of the so many changes that have taken place and continue to take place in their culture. Why should the African be so accepting of other people's ways, whether it is Christianity, Islam, language, and other things and why are other people not accepting of African ways? Why do Africans change to other people's image, especially the Western, and not vice versa?

Language and Folklore in Literature

Rather than single out writers deeply rooted in their cultures and those positing a culture-less type of writing, it is important to examine the place of language and folklore in the lives of a people and their literary and other artistic creations. Language carries the culture and the thought patterns of a people. It is the storehouse of their wisdom, mores, worldview, sensibility, and what identifies them as a people. According to Edward Sapir,

> The fact of the matter is that the "real world" is to a large extent unconsciously built up on the language habits of the group...We see and hear and otherwise experience very largely as we do because the language habits of our community predispose certain choices of interpretation. (Whorf 134)

Edward Sapir also says, "The content of every culture is expressible in its language" (7). He goes on to say of a people's language that "its forms predetermine for us certain modes of observation and interpretation" (10). The phenomenon of language creates a complex window for the African writer: his/her mother tongue and the adopted foreign European language. Can the African writer who is steeped in the language of his people use a European language without a subtext of the indigenous African culture? To me, an emphatic No! We cannot forget the "language we cry in." There is always a subtext in the English, French, or Portuguese the African writes. A people's language also bears their folklore. For the African writer, the use of an adopted foreign/European language is often informed by the native African language and its folklore, symbols, and other embedded nuances. If language is the vehicle of a people's civilization, ideas, and folklore, incorporating indigenous African culture into our writings in adopted foreign languages goes to give profundity to the literary works and reflect the postcolonial condition of the African.

It is clear therefore why the pioneer/first generation poets of Africa are seen as "apprentice poets." It is because of their being very imitative of foreign literary artists, especially of Pre-Raphaelite and Victorian poets. While some of these poets praise the foreign ways without reservations, most did not affirm faith in their culture in their works. Why are the next generation of writers, novelists, poets, and dramatists canonical? It is because they are deeply anchored in their roots. Examples of cultural roots in literary production can be seen in Chinua Achebe's *Things Fall Apart* and *Arrow of God*, Wole Soyinka's *Ogun Abibiman* and *Death and the King's Horseman*, Ngugi wa Thiongo's *Petals of Blood* and *The Trial of Dedan Kimathi*, J. P. Clark's *Song of a Goat* and *The Biroroa Plays*, and Kofi Awoonor's *Songs of Sorrow*. Among this generation, it is on record that Soyinka received a fellowship to research into Yoruba folk drama in the early 1960s, Clark taped not only the Ozidi Saga but also Urhobo *udje* dance songs published in *Nigeria Magazine* (1964), and Awoonor collected Ewe poets in *Guardians of the Sacred Word*. This affirmation of faith in their indigenous cultures gives their works a cultural identity. Despite Christopher Okigbo's eclecticism and modernist influence, it is to Mother Idoto that the initiate goes for cleansing and his highly incantatory sequence of "Poems Prophesying War" is informed by traditional African rhythms.

Let me use Wole Soyinka as an exemplary African writer who has used his Yoruba culture for maximum benefit to art. Even with his modernist influences, Soyinka's deployment of Ogun into his poetry in *Idanre*, fiction in *The Interpreters*, and drama in *The Road*, among so many texts, tells his incorporation of Yoruba folklore into his works. In an interview with Ulli Beier in 1997, Soyinka tells his interviewer of his views on Yoruba religion:

> I had this rather comparative sense and I wrote in *"Ake"* that I used to look at the images on the stained glass windows of the church: Henry Townsend, the Rev. Hinderer and then the image that was supposed to be St. Peter. In my very imaginative mind, it didn't seem to me that they were very different from the *Egungun*.
>
> So one was surrounded by all these different images which easily flowed into one another. I was never frightened of the *Egungun*. I was fascinated by them. Of course, I talked to some of my colleagues, like *Osiki*, who donned the masquerade himself, from time to time.
>
> The *Igbale* was nothing sinister to me: it signified to me a mystery, a place of transformation. You went into *Igbale* to put on your masquerade. Then when the *Egungun* came out, it seemed that all they did was blessing the community and beg a little bit for alms here and there. Occasionally there were disciplinary outings: they terrorized everybody and we ran away from them but then, some distance away

you stopped and regathered…maybe my dramatic bent saw this right from the beginning as part of the drama of life.

I never went through a phase, when I believed that traditional religion or ceremonies were evil. I believed that there were witches—I was convinced of that—but at the same time there were good apparitions. And of course I found the songs and the drumming very exciting.

In another section of the interview, there is this question and the response to it:

> *Beier: Now the Ogun you created in "A Dance of the Forests" stresses particularly the creative aspect. He is not merely the warrior, he is also the creator!*
>
> Soyinka: This was for me very obvious, because the instrument of sculpture belongs to *Ogun*; many sculptors are his followers and so is the blacksmith, again a very creative person, not just an artisan. And then of course there is the *Ijala* – he is therefore by implication the father of poetry. All this made me delve more into the complexity of *Ogun* and given my own creative bent, I explored that a lot more. And also given my own acknowledged combative strain, I found a fine partner in *Ogun*. It was a kind of liberation for me, having grown up in a narrow form of Christianity. (*Isokan Yoruba Magazine* Summer 1997, volume III, no. III)

I have deliberately quoted copiously from Soyinka to show the writer's sophistication, his absorptive personality that garners the energy of his people's folklore to make his writing superbly African.

The next generation of African writers, especially the poets, learned from their literary elders the power of culture in a people's literary tradition. That is why they took that aspect of their writing but shed the use of what has come to be described a la Chinweizu as "euro-modernist Hopskins disease." I think this second (sometimes called third) generation took over from where the second generation stopped. Copious examples can be found in the writings of Jack Mapanje studying Chewa oral literature, Kofi Anyidoho doggedly sticking to Ewe orature, Ojaide researching into Urhobo *udje* dance song tradition, and the knowledge of other poets, especially Niyi Osundare, Ademola Dasylva, Remi-Raji Oyelade, and Akeem Lasisi of Yoruba folklore, and Chimalum Nwankwo and Hyginus Ekwazi of Igbo folklore. This is the poetry that the late South African poet laureate, Mazisi Kunene, referred to as "heavy" and is deep, unlike the culture-less poetry that is light and shallow. In fact, what makes the second generation to flourish is its ability to be steeped in poetic content and form derived from the oral traditions of the poets. In fiction, Nega Mezlekia, Zakes Mda, Chimamanda Ngozi Adichie, among others, show a rootedness in their culture and that gives so much depth to their thematic articulation. And similarly, in drama, Femi Osofisan has a Yoruba cultural stamp on his plays.

African Globalists

For those who fear that works based on African culture will not be circulated to readers outside Africa, they should know that translation is always there. Achebe's *Things Fall Apart* has been translated into more than thirty languages. Ngugi wa Thiongo, since the early 1980s, has been an advocate of works written in indigenous African languages. Whether African writers write in indigenous languages or foreign ones, their works should reflect their African reality and culture.

I remember the Gambian poet, Lenrie Peters, writing that the "universe is my book." If he means that he is an internationalist poet and not a Gambian of Aku ethnicity, then the same volume of poems *Katchikali* contradicts him. It is interesting that the rooted title poem carries more passion and traction than the poet's other rootless poems. One may say that Syl Cheney-Coker does not flaunt any ethnicity as other African poets of his generation do. However, he does present his experiences through his Creole origin, an example which shows the diversity of the African experience. His poetry and his *The Last Harmattan of Alusin Dunbar* are deeply rooted in the Sierra Leonean Creole tradition that he mocks and elevates. The African culture undergirds them toward reliability and those that are "global" are inconsequential.

Teju Cole, author of *Every Day Is for the Thief* and *Open City*, has called himself an internationalist writer. But he does this with caution because of his favorite writers that are outside the African literature tradition. Born of Nigerian and European parents in Michigan and having an Indian-born wife, he is described as a Nigerian-American. He tells Emma Brockes on Saturday, June 21, 2014: "I'm an African kid. I'm not going to go straight into writing." And in an answer to a question, he says:

As for faith: I don't believe in the Christian god, or the Muslim one, or the Jewish one. I'm sentimentally attached to some of the Yoruba and Greek gods—the stories are too good, too insightful, for a wholesale rejection—though I don't ask them for favors (Aleksandar Hemon on Teju Cole).

Cole thus acknowledges his roots and identity in admitting his location of place and culture.

I have often given the examples of European writers in Africa appropriating African names to gain validity in their writings set in Africa. The cases of Ulli Beier as Obotunde Ijimere to project Yoruba reality and John Haynes as Idi Bukar to express Hausa reality show the way even outsiders see the place of culture in literary creation. With names that make meaning in the Yoruba cultural context, the Austrian-born Beier claims authority to write *The Imprisonment of Obatala*. Similarly, while in Zaria, Northern Nigeria, in the 1970s the British born John Haynes used the pseudonym of Idi Bukar to publish his collection of poems, *The Desert Came and Then the Toturer* (Zaria: RAG, 1986).

Despite globalization and internationalization, many writers know the importance of location in place and culture to their literary works. While there is World Literature, which has its own standards, there is no global or international literature as such. World Literature, as is discussed in another chapter, may have its global and international qualities but there is no class of literature at the present that is grouped as international. Literature appears to remain national, regional, and cultural and there seems to be no place for a literature that does not fall within such locations.

PERILS OF CULTURE-LESS AFRICAN WRITINGS

Why are African poetry and other literary writings flat if they do not pay attention to the people's culture? Ben Okri's *The Famished Road, Dangerous Love,* and short story collections such as *Stars of the Curfew* and *Incidents at the Shrine* even with their magical realism have a different impact on me than *StarBook* and his millennium poetry collection. The difference to me is that those works anchored on African mythology, especially *The Famished Road*, have substance or content that *StarBook* does not possess. The latter work, in spite of its mythic nature, is an artificial creation that is not rooted in African culture. Ben Okri wants his books shelved with British ones in a bookstore but is he going to be taught as a British writer? Perhaps only as a British immigrant writer! Is Chris Abani an American or Western writer with his newer novels that include *The Secret History of Las Vegas*? Will any of these be admitted into the Western canon that critics such as Stanley Fish and Harold Bloom define and write about? These questions are meant to interrogate the futility of "rootless" African writers who write works that are not identifiably African in content and form. It is the culture that calls you its own but not you forcing yourself into a specific culture or tradition! It is not just the butterfly saying it is a bird but one has to be a real bird to be a bird! Every African has a right to write the way he or she likes. But is that writer part of the African tradition of writing/literature?

The Third Generation and Globalization

There are mixed signals in African literature coming out from a newer generation that Pius Adesanmi has described as the third generation, especially in Nigerian literature. Some of the members such as Remi-Raji Oyelade and Ademola DaSylva are very conversant with Yoruba mythology but may use it differently from older poets like Wole Soyinka and Niyi Osundare. In any case, I want to quote copiously from Adesanmi on being global and yet being rooted. One should not confuse being rooted in place and culture as being global. This is what Adesanmi has to say:

> Using mainly the poetry of Emman Shehu, Harry Garuba has described the aesthetic departure of the third generation from the practices of preceding generations in terms of a decentering of the mytho-ritualistic bases from which the first two generations imagined project nationhood. Here, nobody is going to make Ogun or any of the weird characters in *A Dance of the Forests* the organizing principle of an imagined nationhood; nobody is going to invoke the matricial or nativist essence of mother Idoto as a pathway to personal and national becoming; nobody is going to expect a new Nigerian nation to say yes so that her Chi may echo yes in return.
>
> Even in the context of SAP and military despotism, the evacuation of the mytho-ritualistic centre as the basis of engaging and imagining project nationhood led to textual adventurism and thematic daring on a scale previously absent from the Nigerian imagination. Nigeria could now be imagined as a postmodern force-field of play in which other emotions, other psychologies, other realities beyond the admonitions of history and culture could be summoned to feed the psychic will and desire of the patriotic self for anchorage in a hostile national space. Consider the difference in the use of laughter as a motif in the poetry of Niyi Osundare and Remi Raji. Osundare's laughter is bitter, the sort of ironic laughter which is said to be worse than crying in Yoruba lore. The reality of the homeland that Osundare is engaging calls precisely for such a deployment of laughter. Laughter in Remi Raji's poetry does not serve the purpose of lamentation. It is indicative of the poet's ability to find spaces of love for a scorched and scorching homeland.

But Remi Raji is not alone. Freedom from the mytho-ritualistic imperative is what accounts for one of the most powerful enactments of patriotic attachment to fatherland in Nigerian poetry. Who could have thought that this could happen outside of a cultural-nationalist praxis involving the salute of a mytho-ritualistic source? But Olu Oguibe pulled it off. "I am bound to this land by blood" announces the poet persona of his great poem of the same title with considerable gusto. And with this anthem-poem – arguably the most famous poem of my generation – inaugurated what you could call a poetics of love as the predominant ritual of relating to fatherland in Nigerian letters. In previous traditions, love took the indirect route of admonition, reproach, and chastisement for the errors of the rendering; chastisement for the roads not taken. With my generation, a poetics of boundless love was unleashed.

And here comes the crux and problematic side of Adesanmi's lecture and defining of his third generation of Nigerian, albeit African, writers:

Harry Garuba opines that the extension of Nigeria as a self into the self of the global and the transnational begins in the poetry of Emman Shehu. I think a similar claim can be made for Uche Nduka. After the chronicle of the life of my generation that he offered in the cinematic clip strategy of *Chiaroscuro*, it is safe to say that Uche went on to embrace the world, fashioning a poetics unmoored in immediately localizable national anchors. The embrace of the world. The transnational imagination. The Afropolitan persona. If you move beyond what Uche Nduka has been writing and publishing after Chiaroscuro – consider his poem, "Aquacade in Amsterdam"; if you move beyond the Toronto peregrinations of the poet persona in Amatoritsero Ede's "Globetrotter", if you move beyond the imaginative transnational crossings of Chris Abani's Elvis in *Graceland*, if you move beyond Sarah Ladipo Manyika's attempt to reproduce the London errantry of earlier generations in *In Dependence*, you encounter a new generation that must grapple with the identity politics of Afropolitanism and the attendant contradictions of trying to imagine a new Nigeria in an existential context which daily reminds them that the world is now their playground.

My challenge: is it only Nigerian/African writers that see their homelands in "an existential context"? If the world is "now their playground," has African new migration erased the homeland from memory for migrants to think only of their existence outside? And most important of all, is this trend in European, American, South American, and Asian literatures or just unique to African literature?

My angst is that the African wants to have the world as "playground" while others outside Africa want their homelands to be the "world."

SPECIFIC LOCATION IN THE GLOBAL

There is nothing wrong in being global or incorporating its elements. However, there should still be location, a specific portion of the earth, so to say, from which one should respond to the global. This portion of the earth has geography, history, culture, society, nation, and other components that make it distinct from other portions of the same earth it shares with so many other groups. It is from this location that some kind of specificity is inscribed into the global where the existential issues of, for instance, human rights, social justice, gender and sexuality, environment, and many others can be interrogated. I don't mind the concept of culture being replaced by the nation, as Pius Adesanmi attempts to espouse in his post-centenary Nigerian literature lecture at Minna, Nigeria, concerning the third generation of writers, mainly poets. Nation is itself a location which invokes other locations such as geography, history, folklore, culture, society, and others. However, newness without specificity of location could be problematic because experiences, realities, or existential issues whether of love, justice, human rights, and a clean environment still have to be contextualized rather than be seen in the abstract or in an amorphous state.

The African should not accept the global and transnational in a non-specific sense. After all, to the American or European, especially English, German, or French, the global is not defined in the form of assimilating with "others" but rather of highlighting the self in the globe. The European may even be ready to subsume aspects of the nation in the European Union but the sense of place or a shared Western civilization with values that both the Union, NATO, and individual European nations want the non-Western world to accept and pursue—issues of democracy, human rights, gender and sexuality, climate change and environment, and others.

Admittedly, there is a newer generation of African writers who do not know their indigenous cultures as older writers do. Some of them do not care to know or learn as the first two generations did through conscious study of their specific folklores. The younger writers are likely to write poems, novels, or plays that may not likely include elements of their folklore or culture found in the works of their modern predecessors. Has globalization robbed Africans of their culture? I would say that the way of life now has been shaped for the young by social media and many elements of globalization. Still, being rooted somewhere will give them some identity rather than a global identity that has more of the Western than anything African in it.

The Imperative of Strong Critics of African Literature

A new crop of African critics of African literature should work hard to awaken younger writers and African immigrant writers to the perils of ignoring their culture. A situation in which some Euro-American or Western critics, without knowledge of what they are talking about, pontificate on good African literature is injurious to African literature. What do these foreigners know about the background of these works? From what worldview and experience are they talking about African literature? Do they acknowledge an African aesthetic tradition which they use in judging these works or they are using Western aesthetics which they feel is universal (and perhaps as superior) and so applicable to African literature too. Their position often places Western literature on top and African or postcolonial literatures below or inferior. That is despite the fact that since the mid-1980s some of the best writers in the world have been African or of the African world—the likes of Wole Soyinka, Chinua Achebe, Toni Morrison, and Derek Walcott! Judging one literature with the criteria of others is always injurious to the literature. This is true whether the critic is Western or African. There is the example of Sunday Anozie in his Structuralist approach to African literature which screwed up the African literary works he interpreted. It is revealing that the once America-based critic of African literature recanted his writings when he returned to Nigeria in his old age. The challenge is for new African critics to emerge and theorize African literature from the African experience, which involves the ever-changing culture.

Conclusion

It should not be that once Africans, wherever they are, whatever they write, and whatever manner they write, they should be seen as writing African literature. If Africa is defined by its experiences, history, culture, and reality, among others, then African writers have to be informed by the African condition, sensibility, and paradigms. One may ask, will Obotunde Ijimere's (Ulli Beier's) *Not Even God is Ripe Enough* written in English but from the Yoruba worldview be called German literature because the writer is German? Surely not! I am not arguing against borrowing what could strengthen one's artistic creation from outside one's cultural world; I am arguing against denying the existence of and the jettisoning of one's culture and its aesthetics and still claiming to be a part of that culture. As such, one who denies African culture should not be seen as an African writer!

So those who accept a Western canon but are averse to essentialism in other cultures should be ignored. I argue that we need some essentialism if others hold on to theirs. An African writer needs to project Africanity to remain an identifiable personality in a world of many cultures despite claims of cosmopolitanism or globalism. One can be African and share with others the African as others should share their cultural contributions with the rest of the world. We will be stupid if we continue ceding our values to others who do not cede any part of theirs to us.

In conclusion, I repeat what I said in an earlier book, *Contemporary African Literature: New Approaches*:

> It goes without saying that since literature is a cultural production and is dynamic like the culture that carries it, the notion of an African literary canon is fluid and not cast in stone. The canon is not calcified, but evolving within the shared experiences of Africans, rooted in their known reality, and forever tapping into their changing consciousness. However, despite the diversity and the expanding content and style of modern African literature arising from the dynamic experience of the people and continent, African literature will remain that literature that responds to the concerns and expresses the sensibility and aspirations and ideals of African people in a form and manner that they see as part of their living reality.

CHAPTER 2

Contemporary Africa and the Politics in Literature

INTRODUCTION

Contemporary Africa conflates the literary works of three major generations of writers that include the first generation of Sembene Ousmane, Chinua Achebe, Christopher Okigbo, Wole Soyinka, Kofi Awoonor, Ngugi wa Thiongo, Ama Ata Aidoo, and J. P. Clark; the second generation comprising Niyi Osundare, Jack Mapanje, Nurudin Farar, Isidore Okpewho, Festus Iyayi, Femi Osofisan, Jack Mapanje, Frank Chipasula, Mandla Langa, and Tanure Ojaide; and the third generation consisting of Chimamanda Ngozi Adichie, Sefi Atta, Vonani Bila, and other younger writers. This generational periodization is not rigid because it tends to take into consideration when a group of writers are in vogue and not when the writers stopped writing at some specific times. Some of the first generation African writers are still writing and many in the second group are as prolific as those in the third generation. These writers come from different countries such as Senegal, Morocco, Egypt, Ghana, Malawi, Nigeria, Kenya, Zimbabwe, and South Africa, among others. As such, modern African literature comprises a range of writers with some dead, many others ageing and also the younger ones of different age-groups from a variety of countries in the African continent. Never before has Africa had as much quantity and diversity of literary works of writers from different generations. This phenomenon affords the literary scholar of contemporary African literature the rare opportunity to evaluate the many writers' appropriation of politics into their respective works and understand how politics has affected the literary works themselves in terms of themes, form, and techniques.

African political experience is almost, if not totally, synonymous with the historical experience. Hence, one cannot talk about the writers' appropriation of politics into their writings without recourse to knowing how history has influenced the African experience. In fact, history could be said to be a major determinant of African politics or vice versa, more so in its colonial and postcolonial conditions. Africa suffered from both the Atlantic and Arab slave trades, both of which dispersed black Africans not only to the Americas (North and South) and the Caribbean but also to Europe and Asia. That memory would ever haunt blacks in Africa and elsewhere and African writers would refer to its trauma hundreds of years after the end of slavery. Then there was Western colonization of Africa starting with the Berlin Conference (1884–85) when European powers, especially Britain, France, Belgium, and Portugal, shared Africa among themselves for economic and political exploitation by whatever name they called their actions. Many African writers were born, raised, and lived a great part of their lives in colonial times and have written much on the period. Then came the period of postindependence in which there was still some tele-guiding from the Western powers, a period of neocolonialism, in which France and Britain in particular still wielded much influence in their former colonies. Now we live in a period of globalization where the entire world is linked by communication. One can see the different periods of history as having a kind of political power play that affects the lives of Africans. African politics therefore has always been determined by history. Also politics in Africa, as seen with its historicity, intersects with the culture, society, economy, and other aspects of the people's lives. One can say with a measure of modesty that the African experience is in one way or the other a political experience or a politically inspired experience. Or, put differently, the historical and the political scenarios determine the African experience to a large extent. It is on the basis of this interrelatedness of politics, history, and human experience that there can be no meaningful discussion of African literature without these three factors that are the bedrock of the writers' attention.

Africa's checkered history has resulted in its checkered politics that the writers address. With the exception of Spanish Sahara seized by Morocco, Africa has completely shed colonialism for political independence at various times. The gaining of independence started from the late 1950s with Ghana and Guinea Conakry blazing the trail. In the 1960s a majority of African countries including Congo DR, Kenya, Nigeria, and Senegal became independent. The 1970s saw the independence of Portuguese-ruled Mozambique and Angola. Then

Zimbabwe became independent after the collapse of the Ian Smith Unilateral Declaration of Independence (UDI) by the minority white population. Later it was South Africa's turn with the collapse of apartheid and the election of Nelson Mandela as the country's first black president in 1994. The more recently independent countries are Eritrea and South Sudan, both of which broke out of Ethiopia and Sudan respectively. African countries, now numbering about 54, are members of the African Union (AU), which is a contemporary transformation (2002) of the Organization of African Unity (OAU) founded in 1961.

Africa is a highly diverse continent with the Arab-influenced Muslim North leaning more toward the Arab world culturally and also politically toward the Arab League currently headquartered in Cairo, Egypt, while maintaining political affiliations with Africa through the African Union. Africa is thus not only a geographical expression but also more of a political and cultural expression. Sub-Saharan Africa is apparently more cohesive in the black population despite the multiracial nature of South Africa and Zimbabwe which have minority white populations in those two countries. Despite the similarity in cultural terms of sub-Saharan Africa, there are differences that make almost every ethnic group or nation unique in some ways. However, overall, sub-Saharan Africa exhibits so much in common culturally and politically that it is seen socioculturally as belonging to a world region.

This chapter deals with how African writers have dealt with the contemporary African experience conditioned by politics. This will involve how writers have responded to the sociopolitical, cultural, economic, and other conditions affecting human development in Africa in recent times. Politics will be used in its broadest possible meaning to involve all the multifarious aspects of human experience in the African continent as expressed in the written literature. Politics is so pervasive that there is barely any sphere of life that cannot be linked to it. It is necessary from the start to draw parallels between human and national experiences arising from the history of colonialism, political independence, developing country status, culture, economic and social issues that contemporary African countries share. It is from these common experiences that writers draw not only their materials but also express their feelings and thoughts and project their respective visions with the background of their respective national and individual particularities. After all, the writers are responding to their times and places, and these multifarious responses broadly reflect the politics of their continent and respective nations and the historical periods in which they find themselves.

One's place and time, otherwise known as location and history, set in motion the dynamics of one's participation or involvement in politics. A writer is rooted and/or nurtured in a specific place. A writer's nativity is important but what is more important is where he or she lives at the time of writing. That Nurridin Farah is Somalian but writes in Nigeria and South Africa has political implications. That a self-declared Marxist such as Ngugi lives and writes in the capitalist United States of America should give the literary critic some food for thought. The same question should be asked of so many writers whether they write in their home countries or in Western countries. Irrespective of whether the writer has a personal reason for his or her location, migration, or exile, there are always political implications involved. There are plenty of examples from all three generations, with Chinua Achebe, Ezekiel Mphalele, Dennis Brutus, and Wole Soyinka, as also of Ben Okri, Jack Mapanje, Frank Chipasula, Niyi Osundare, Tanure Ojaide, Zakes Mda and many others. This phenomenon is equally true of Chimamanda Adichie, Sefi Atta, and others of their generation. Staying in the homeland and migrating have political implications too in the production of literary works by Africans as discussed later. One obvious example is that the liberal societies of the West have encouraged some African writers to delve into thematic explorations as of sexuality that they would not have dealt with in their African homelands. A necessary political issue to appraise in contemporary African literature is the access to foreign publishers who promote literary works and their authors.

Contemporary African literature contends with the sociopolitical, cultural, and economic issues from which African writers draw inspiration to project their views and feelings through imaginative writings that include poetry, fiction, nonfiction, and drama. It is an aggregate of so many creative works of varying qualities that draw upon the African experience as lived or imagined in contemporary times.

At this point there needs to be some demarcation of the term "contemporary" to refer to either works published since the 1980s or experiences of that particular period that have been dealt with in the literature. While this is an elastic, or rather arbitrary, definition of the word "contemporary," the period coincides not only with the New World Order which later became globalization but also the African renaissance as proclaimed by Thabo Mbeki, who succeeded Nelson Mandela as president of South Africa in the 1990s. With the Organization of African Unity becoming the African Union, with NEPAD refocusing African attention on priorities of economic development, and globalization in full swing, there appears to be similar historical and political experiences shared by many African countries. While the genocide in Rwanda took place early in the period, the civil wars in both Liberia and Sierra Leone, and the war in Congo DR also fall within the period. However, now there appears to be a relative calm in Africa with countries having civilian governments and focused on economic development more than other issues, unlike as experienced in the 1960s and 1970s.

Writers are sensitive human beings who are like the antennae of the society; hence they respond to what is happening in Africa during the period. They are involved in, touched by, or observe happenings in their respective societies to which they respond through their literary works. They are concerned about the underprivileged in the society, the excessive use of power by most of the politicians, and the impact of world phenomena such as migration, globalization, and climate change, among others, on their national and local communities. They attempt to address these phenomena by drawing attention to critical issues so that they can be discussed and resolved for the amelioration of people's lives. They pay attention to the changes taking place in their respective cultures, societies, economies, and political practices. They often write "applied art" by providing in their works viewpoints that help to change the society for the better. Nevertheless, they have different viewpoints in their approaches. Their engagement of issues is often political in the sense that they choose what to highlight and what to be silent about. What is significant is that while they are the voices articulating private and public experiences, their respective stands could be said to be political in its broadest definition of strategizing power relationships and protecting and advocating what is of interest to them.

POLITICAL PLURALISM

African writers deal with the political pluralism that has emerged in most countries in the continent. In these countries, elections, however flawed they may be, are held and many parties contest these elections at national, state, and local levels. In place of military regimes of the late 1960s, 1970s, and early 1980s are now found civilian regimes as the world community now frowns at military coups in order to promote democratic principles. The problem in most African countries is no longer the military versus the people but political competition among various parties. Military dictatorship has gone and especially since the 1990s all forms of autocratic governments appear to be disappearing. In fact, through NEPAD African governments now watch each other's manner of governance. The NEPAD Council is a non-political and independent nonprofit organization that was founded to support the New Partnership for Africa's Development, a strategic framework for Pan-African socioeconomic development. The attention it pays to agriculture and food security, climate change, human development, economic and corporate governance, and issues of gender, ICT, and capacity development gives each African government a focal point to work with to improve the lots of its people. While each country is a sovereign state, this practice itself shows the long way African nations have gone; they have abandoned autocracy in theory and principle and are now determined in furthering democratic principles in their respective countries.

That there is political pluralism does not mean that in countries such as Cameroon, Kenya, Nigeria, and Zimbabwe there is no sabotaging of the democratic process through election rigging and other electoral malpractices. Also in Equatorial Guinea there is almost a one-man show type of government run by Sasso Ngueso. Often the ruling party attempts to stay in power by marginalizing other parties and in a recent election in Mauritania (November 23, 2013), the opposition parties boycotting the legislative election describe the process as "election masquerade." African countries generally have acceded to Western demands for democratization which though now thrives in the continent is beset with many problems.

One can say that the competition for the sharing of natural resources in mineral-endowed countries such as Liberia, Sierra Leone, and Congo DR has led to civil wars in which atrocities were perpetrated toward domination of the economic wealth of the country by a group or party. The diamonds in Liberia and Sierra Leone as in the Congo have led to civil wars in which even children are recruited to fight for warlords. Autobiographies have documented the Sierra Leonean and Liberian civil wars such as Ishmael Beah's *A Long Way Gone: Memoir of a Boy Soldier*. Uzodinma Iweala's *Beasts of No Nation* deals with child soldiers with the protagonist growing up and leaving the military at a point to go to school and be like an ordinary child. A work such as Emmanuel Dongala's *Johnny Mad Dog* reflects the Congolese civil war and the involvement of children in the civil war in the two major characters of Laokole and Johnny Mad Dog.

CORRUPTION AND ETHNIC CONFLICTS

Perhaps the most endemic problems facing contemporary Africa are corruption manifesting in a multiplicity of ways and ethnic conflicts that result in violence and deaths. Corruption takes many forms in Africa—political, economic, and other ways that retard the political and economic growth of Africa. Most states have enough resources that, if fairly distributed, would uplift drastically the standard of living of their people. However, lack of the rule of law or lack of its enforcement allows corruption to thwart economic development as in Nigeria, Cameroon, and Kenya. The law enforcement agencies are generally corrupt and do not carry out their duties as designated in their national constitutions. Bribery, nepotism, and doing things for selfish remunerations against the general and public good are common practices. There is so much disparity between the resources available and the dire plight of the people who should have benefited from a corruption-free government and society in countries such as Congo DR, Nigeria, and Equatorial Guinea.

African writers expose and protest against corruption in all the literary genres available to them. The objective of the satire is to embarrass the culprits so that they would be deterred from further bad behavior. There is barely a novel, play, or collection of poems without reference to corruption.

National Literatures

The nation is a political entity and those who claim it as birthplace, homeland, or its citizenship are bound by a political reality. Citizens or residents of a country respond to its governance and the national direction, identity, and problems. One can go as far as saying that the nation for its citizens or residents is a mark of political identity. Whether one is a patriot or critic of one's nation, that person is acting politically.

One can already talk of national literatures in the sense that there are features that distinguish them, for instance, South African literature from Malawian literature as of Nigerian from Senegalese literature. Each country with its history, national experience, politics, and topography provides not only the setting of the writings but also becomes a repository of materials from which writers draw their allusions and visions. Each country has its own ethnic folklores which the writers draw from to express themselves. For instance, there is so much drawing from the fauna and flora in such a unique way that many Nigerian writers such as Wole Soyinka, Chinua Achebe, and Tanure Ojaide, among many others, use the iroko, the eagle, and the tortoise which have symbolic meaning in various folklores of the country. Ghanaians have figures such as Ananse and Sankofa to draw from to express their contemporary thoughts and feelings as Benjamin Kwakye does of Sankofa in *The Crucifix*. Thus, the writer's nationality or nationhood becomes a political as well as cultural marker of identity that impinges on the writing from the folkloric allusions and use of topography as setting.

Modern African literature has become more local and national than at its early stage in the 1950s, 1960s, and 1970s. There was a time when African writers, be it Leopold Sedar Senghor of Senegal, Chinua Achebe of Nigeria, Lenrie Peters of The Gambia, and many in their generation wrote as if for all blacks in Africa or worldwide and not with an immediate specific local audience in mind. In his poems "In Memoriam," "New York," and "Femme Noir," among others, the Senegalese poet writes to showcase the African reality. In "In Memoriam," he writes about ancestors as a means of differentiating the African reality from the Western reality. The dead ancestors have their presence among the living as they are invisible but everywhere and they guard and guide the living. The reality he addresses is applicable to blacks in sub-Saharan Africa and the African diaspora. Similarly, in "New York," the speaker of the poem talks of the natural in Africa as contrasted with the artificial in the West. To the poet, Manhattan, which symbolizes the white race, needs to be complemented by Harlem, representing the black world that is sensuous and bubbling with life. And in "Femme Noir," he pays tribute to the black woman the poet sees as different from women of other races. In none of these poems does the poet think of his field of imagination as limited to Senegal nor does he anticipate only a Senegalese audience. The same could be said of Chinua Achebe who sees the European colonization of Africa as damaging to the African psyche and exposes, especially in *Things Fall Apart* and *Arrow of God*, the inhumanity and savagery of the so-called civilized white man. His assertion that Africans did not learn about culture for the first time from Europeans but had theirs is a strong indictment of European greed expressed in their colonization of weaker people.

If one were to "fast forward" and look at the works of, for instance, Chimamanda Adichie and Frank Chipasula, the poetic field has narrowed to the nation as the center of experience and no longer the black world of Senghor and Achebe during whose times in the pre-independence and the period immediately following independence in most African countries there was cultural conflict raging between Africans and Europeans because of the western denigration of African culture. Senghor, like Aime Cesaire and Leon Damas, and other Negritude literary artists from Africa and the Caribbean set out to showcase African culture as a valid way of life compared to the European.

On the other hand, Adichie's contemporary *Purple Hibiscus* and *Half of a Yellow Sun* are limited, so to say, to interrogating the Nigerian nation at different times—during a period of the military and the latter during the Nigerian Civil War (1967–70). With *Purple Hibiscus* apparently set in the Sani Abacha military regime period, there is the denial of human rights of the people by the military. Editors of newspapers are detained for publishing sensitive issues. At a point the military leader dies in the manner that Sani Abacha is rumored to have died—eating an apple offered him by Indian prostitutes! Similarly, if one should look at Malawian literature, Jack Mapanje and Frank Chipasula write with the Dr. Hastings Kamuzu Banda's autocratic regime as the background to their poetic writings. In fact, Chipasula's *Whispers on the Wings* and Mapanje *Mikuyu Prison* poems are focused on the political happenings in Malawi during the idiosyncratic rule of Kamuzu Banda. The arbitrary arrests and detentions point to an autocratic regime in which people have to live according to the whims and caprices of a senile dictatorial leader.

There are other examples from Ghana and Eritrea, for example, in the works of Kofi Awoonor as *The House by the Sea* and Haile Reesom's *We Invented the Wheels*. Both works are respectively inspired by Awoonor's being detained after a failed coup attempt in which he was accused of abetting a culprit and Reesom's experience after Eritrea fought a war of independence from Ethiopia. Though set in limited national spaces, the poetic, dramatic, or fictional works address human and universal problems. Contemporary African literature has no doubt narrowed its field of political interrogation to the nation and immediate societies of the writers as it deepens the probing of human problems as they affect the common man.

The zeroing in on socioeconomic issues starting from the 1980s has made the African writer generally more myopic in his political vision. Though myopic, the writer often looks deeply at local sociopolitical, economic, and cultural issues within the continent. The writers generally are conscious of the great class divide between the haves and have-nots. So in place of the cultural conflict that Senghor and Achebe portrayed, many contemporary writers see conflict in the Marxist class divide. In most cases, as in many Nigerian writers of the second generation such as Niyi Osundare in *Song of the Marketplace* or Festus Iyayi in *Violence*, there is a thorough analysis of the class conflict within the Nigerian society. This phenomenon is surely a reflection of the times which impose new necessities to be addressed on the writers.

Changes in National Literatures: The Case of South African Literature

There is a noticeable change even within national literatures as a result of political happenings that affect other aspects of the national experience. The respective histories of African countries appear to have brought about this phenomenon. Though the focus here is on South African literature, it is similar to the literature of Nigeria, Ghana, Congo (Brazzaville), and other countries that had histories of coups and military regimes in the 1960s to the 1980s and are now having democratically elected governments. The post-military literatures of these countries offer something different but comparable to the South African experience to be discussed.

South Africa's antiapartheid literature dominates the years of apartheid. Dennis Brutus, Peter Abrahams, Eski'a Mphalele, and others expressed the inhumanity of the apartheid system on black people in South Africa. The apartheid regime treated blacks as subhuman and meted indignities, humiliation, and physical and psychological tortures on the majority black population who had to carry passes to travel within their own country. At a point in the apartheid system, black homelands were created that limited every black to a homeland (Bantustan). It was inevitable for blacks to fight against apartheid for their human rights and to regain control of their country. A later generation during the apartheid regime would be influenced by the Black Consciousness Movement (BCM) of the 1970s and a writer such as Mbulelo Mzamane wrote stories which reflect the Black Students' Manifesto "that the Black man must build up his value systems, see himself as self-determined and not determined by others" (qtd. in Lokaganka Losambe, *Dictionary of Literary Biography* 360, 184).

Mandla Langa has used his fiction to interrogate the apartheid experience as well as the return from exile when freedom came with the presidency of Nelson Mandela in 1994. According to Sam Raditlhalo, "Langa's novels deal with the themes of commitment, betrayal, love, and loss; the characters emerge imbued not with revolutionary zeal but a dogged and dour determination to succeed" (*DLB* 360, 154). In *Naked Song and Other Stories*, according to Raditlhalo, "Three of the stories make a seminal contribution to South African writing by examining the tortured souls who returned 'home' from exile" (136).

However, since the end of apartheid and the ascendancy of Black majority rule starting with President Nelson Mandela, the changed political landscape has drawn attention to more socioeconomic issues that relate to the common man who seems to be still struggling to eke out a living. There are problems of housing in the shanty towns and recent mine strikes in which many black strikers were shot dead tell the story of the economic struggle that continues in South Africa after the demise of apartheid.

The case of South Africa is a good example of how our gaze turns to some other things once there is political change. Sandile Dikeni is reflective of how poetry changes with the times. Though relatively young, he saw the last days of apartheid in which he was very active and suffered detention for four months in 1986. His attitude to postapartheid or the "new" South Africa is ambivalent. As Mncedisi Mashigoane puts it, "Rebellious language is evident in his refusal to celebrate the dawn of democracy without reservations" (Ojaide, *DLB* 360, 85). His postapartheid poem, "Way Back Home," tells this ambivalence:

> do not scoff when I spit at the fruits of freedom
> because maybe, my bongo
> has the sound of a wail
> and my voice, the anger of distance. (from *Telegraph to the Sky*, 2000)

Once apartheid collapsed, there was internal conflict within the African National Congress between the fighters and the returned exiles. Dikeni expresses a lot of irony in "A Long Story" as his friends killed his grandmother after "they sucked her breasts dry" for her to burn well. Further divisions will occur between the veteran ANC members and the youth wing and it will be a matter of time for this to be reflected in the literary production of the time.

Sandile Dikeni represents the "new" postapartheid literature, especially the poetry. He inherited the *izibongo* tradition and chants his poetry in the manner of Lesego Rampolekeng and Gcina Mhlophe. And like the postapartheid writers, he expresses himself in a simple language to be understood by the common people for whom he struggles and writes. His idea of poetry is a functional one, whether during apartheid or after, and that shows a marked difference from western art for art's sake type of writing.

MIGRATION AND GLOBALIZATION

Contemporary African writers, especially in fiction, have been dealing with the issues of migration and globalization. In Chris Abani's *GraceLand* as in Chimamanda Ngozi Adichie's *Purple Hibiscus*, major characters are on the verge of leaving Africa for the United States. In *Purple Hibiscus*, for instance, things have become so harrowing for Ifeoma that she has to leave Nsukka for the United States to avoid further harassment by the military men under instructions from the university authorities and also to avoid being fired and losing her only means of livelihood. On the other hand, in Zakes Mda's *Heart of Redness* and Tanure Ojaide's *The Activist*, the protagonists are returnees from exile in the United States to their native African homelands. It is interesting that Adichie's *Americanah* and Chika Unigwe's *Black Sisters*, more recent works, also deal with Africans who migrate to the North (Europe and North America) and return of their own volition or forced to repatriate to their native African homelands.

In a recent collection, *The Sahara Testament*, that won the prestigious Nigerian Liquified Natural Gas (NLNG) Literary Prize (Poetry), Tade Ipadeola describes the plight of Africans escaping to Europe through the Sahara and the Mediterranean for a better life in the North. Of course, in the perilous journey, most lose their lives. Those that survive the Sahara desert with its heat and the extortion of North Africans fall foul of the Mediterranean Sea and their corpses are recovered at the island of Lampedusa, Italy. A few other poets, including the writer, have also addressed the phenomenon of African migrants facing great risks to escape their difficult lives in Africa to reach developed countries as in Tanure Ojaide's *Waiting for the Hatching of a Cockerel*.

The writers deal with issues of citizenship and nationality and the practice is described by Arjun Appadurai in *Modernity at Large: Cultural Dimensions of Globalization* as "place polygamy." Often there is hope that going abroad would solve all personal, especially economic, problems. However, as in the case of Adichie's *Purple Hibiscus*, migrating to a developed country as the United States involves paying a price. Amaka, daughter of the affable Ifeoma, the beleaguered lecturer at the University of Nigeria at Nsukka, who emigrated to the United States with her children, says "There is water...but we don't laugh anymore." Thus, one is trading off some psychological and emotional comfort at home for economic and social comfort abroad. Exile thus has a price to pay on both sides; hence some exiles have to return home to uncertain prospects in their homelands. Similarly in

Chika Unigwe's *Black Sisters*, the ladies that emigrate to Europe pay a heavy price—they are forced to become prostitutes and encounter many problems to make a living and in the end some return to Nigeria and another is killed as she attempts to free herself from the bondage in which she is kept by the person who facilitated her going to Europe. In Europe the ladies face alienation, lack of free movement, and a kind of modern slavery. Sisi's effort to free herself costs her her dear life.

Globalization and Indigeneity

Much as globalization has taken possession of the world and no place is an island unto itself, there is also the cry for indigeneity in Africa. There is an oppositional pull to either side by different advocates on what they feel is beneficial to Africa. Should Africa open itself to the rest of the world or maintain its own indigeneity? Often globalization appears to be masking Westernization and at present looks more of a one-way traffic than the two-way traffic that it should be in ideal terms. In Zakes Mda's *Heart of Redness* the protagonist, Cumago, advocates ecotourism in which the indigenous folks prepare indigenous materials, primarily crafts, to be sold to foreign tourists to make money while at the same time keeping the environment as healthy as it possibly can be. Mda strikes a delicate balance between maintaining the environment and at the same time acceding to the call for development. He thus says that the environment does not need to be destroyed for the sake of development but a balance can be struck to protect the environment and still develop economically. By his proposed solution, Mda resolves the long history of antagonism between the Believers and the non-Believers. In Ojaide's *The Activist*, the protagonist enters the state political process and when he becomes a state governor, he deploys those who are sympathetic to the environment to take charge. These are indigenes of the Niger Delta who have seen their farmlands and rivers polluted by the unbridled activities of the multinational oil corporations. Such people have farmers and fishermen and women as parents or uncles and know how important a healthy environment is to their people. He also deploys such a sympathetic foreigner as Erika to save the Niger Delta environment. In this manner, the Activist saves the environment from rampant degradation caused by the multinational oil companies who think only of the profit margins and do not care at all about the environment that gives the local communities a source of livelihood in their fishing and farming, and ensures health needs.

CLIMATE CHANGE, ENVIRONMENT, AND ECOLOGICAL ISSUES

Politics, as noted earlier, permeates all aspects of life in the nation and society. The issues of climate change, environment, and ecology are very political at global and local levels. There have been many world conferences held, including one in Rio de Janeiro, Brazil, in the 1990s to address climate change. So it is a major political issue especially between the developed and developing countries. At the same time, it is both national and local in Nigeria where oil exploitation and its consequences are major political subjects of debate as to the sharing formula of national revenue and other economic matters.

Contemporary African writers have seized upon global issues that have a local impact on their societies. These global issues are very political and one's response depends on one's ideology. In the developed countries, especially in the United States, there are a majority who believe strongly in climate change and a few conservative groups that do not believe in it. However, there is overwhelming scientific evidence to back climate change. In Africa the educated and the writers are aware of global trends and the debates going on. However, there is no universal involvement in the climate change and environmental issues in Africa as in the Western world. This is understandable because though climate change is a global issue, a majority of Africans have more immediate economic issues to contend with and that has not allowed as much attention to the environment as desired.

While there are works relating to the environment such as Osundare's poetry collection, *The Eye of the Earth*, Zakes Mda's novel, *The Heart of Redness*, and Tanure Ojaide's poetry collection and novel, *The Tale of the Harmattan* and *The Activist*, there is a plethora of works on Nigeria's Niger Delta environment. What has stoked the literature of the Niger Delta is the intersection of multinational capital enterprises and exploitation of local communities by the oil and gas companies. See chapter 4 on "Defining Niger Delta Literature: A Preliminary Perspective on an Emerging Literature." In the case of the Niger Delta, literature is able to integrate politics at local and national levels, the environment, issues of exploitation, economic and political marginalization, and cultural genocide into a holistic experience through the prism of oil exploitation and its consequences in literature. The writers expose the callousness of the foreign oil companies that are abetted by despotic military regimes to exploit the local communities who suffer immensely on so many aspects from the exploration and exploitation of oil. That has turned the local communities, especially the youth, into what Al Gedicks calls "resource rebels." Called "militants" in Nigeria, the youths have been able to force the hands of the Federal Nigerian Government and the oil companies to pay attention to the needs of the local communities in the establishment of the Niger Delta Development Corporation (NDDC) and the Ministry of the Niger Delta. Most Nigerians believe that the election of Dr. Goodluck Jonathan is a concession to the oil-producing Niger Delta whose oil forms about 95 percent of the national revenue.

The struggle for environmental justice is documented in poems, novels, and plays set in the Niger Delta as in Ahmed Yerima's play, *Hard Ground*, Isidore Okpewho's novel, *Tides*, and so many poetry collections. Politics is at stake in the Niger Delta from the struggle for minority rights and eco justice. In fact, Ken Saro-Wiwa promoted the case of the Niger Delta and the nonchalant manner that the oil companies amassed profits without spending a fraction of their profits on taking care of the damages to the environment that their exploitation had caused. He was framed for treason and hanged by the Sani Abacha military dictatorship in 1995. As Gedicks observes, it is where you have indigenous people with little or no political power that the multinationals operate with impunity as done in the Amazon Basin and some other parts of South America. The environmental struggle in Nigeria's Niger Delta also involves the use of indigenous languages, political marginalization, and the rights of a people to the resources in their lands. Both the Ogoni Bill of Rights and the Kaiama Declaration show how political the exploitation of oil is in Nigeria. Niger Delta writers experience the reality of the environmental degradation as well as the politicization of natural resources in Nigeria whose federal system takes all monies and shares according to population with very little regard for the local communities who suffer the brunt of the hazardous consequences of oil and gas exploitation from their area.

Sociocultural Changes in Africa

Africa is a dynamic continent and the literature keeps pace in reflecting its changing nature in all its ramifications. Religion and spirituality are basic aspects of a people's culture. Africans are losing their traditional culture, spirituality, and values to new religions and material greed. As a result of the overwhelming economic plight of many people, many new churches promise prosperity and they have large congregations of prosperity-seekers. It appears as if the daunting problems in life which make life difficult have made it look like it is only miracles that could provide what the people want. And so many folks who are non-Christians and those from older traditional churches get converted into or "born again" in the new churches. Africans appear to be caught up in a bind—though believing in the supernatural, many still believe in witchcraft or the ability of evil forces to hurt them mystically. Such people who feel haunted and hunted by so-called demons also flock to the new churches where the pastors promise to destroy the demons and deliver them from negative forces.

A keen observer sees the rapid growth and influence of Pentecostal churches which have transformational influence on indigenous African cultures and the societies at large. In recent times in Nigeria, traditional rulers who are supposed to be the custodians of traditional culture and mores have attempted to shirk that responsibility and become "born-again." Two of such cases in Delta State of Nigeria, the Ovie of Agbarha Kingdom and the Olu of Warri, caused uproars and the traditional rulers were asked to abdicate if they would no longer be comfortable with exercising their traditional spiritual roles. In the end, they stayed as traditional rulers to perform those traditional duties and rituals they now see as "Satanic" or unchristian! Many writers are lamenting the erosion of traditional African culture and values by the new wave of Pentecostal evangelism. Tope Folarin's "Miracle" was the winner of the Caine Short Story Prize in 2013. Set in a Nigerian evangelical church in Texas in the United States, the congregation gathers to witness the healing powers of a blind pastor-prophet. There is the exploitation of the people's plight by new religions and their gullibility and credulity predispose them to embracing fanatical faiths. In the story a young boy volunteers to be healed and believes that a miracle will be performed for him.

What is apparent is that there is less use of traditional folklore in the poetry of contemporary younger African writers and the older writers appear to have reduced using traditional folklore to express themselves. Gone are the days of Christopher Okigbo whose "Heavensgate" begins with "Before you / Mother Idoto / Naked I stand" and Wole Soyinka's "Idanre" on the god Ogun in *Idanre and Other Poems* and *Ogun Abibiman* focused on the Yoruba god of iron and creativity and the Zulu king Shaka. Mda's *Heart of Redness* uses Xhosa folklore copiously. So also has Nega Mezlekia written copiously on Abyssinian/Ethiopian folklore in *The God Who Begat a Jackal*. The Nigerian poet Chimalum Nwankwo uses Igbo folklore about the *udala* tree in his *The Womb in the Heart*.

The current state could be that younger writers do not know the folklores of their people or do not care about them but look for new ways to express themselves in their poetry and drama that used to rely much on traditional African folklore. This is not to say that contemporary African writers no longer incorporate the folklore or orature of their people in their works but it appears not as profuse as before recent times. The Nigerian Okinba Launko (Femi Osofisan) in his recent *Seven Stations Up the Tray's Way* uses the Opon Ifa of Orunmila to compose a poetry sequence that is exhilarating. As the poet explains, "The tray is—of course—the tray of Ifa" (vi), which has to do with the complex divination system of the Yoruba people. Many Yoruba-originating poets such as Damola Dasylva, Akeem Lasisi, and Remi-Raji Oyelade still use the folklore of their people. A good guess is that there are some ethnic groups as the Yoruba, Ewe, and Zulu whose traditions are still effectively affecting the literary works as lives of their people. On the paucity of younger writers with folkloric background to their writings, one can only guess that globalization is giving them the impression that the ethnic group no longer matters in a global world of a universal culture. Time will tell whether they are right or wrong in abandoning cultural identity. See chapter 12 "Indigenous Knowledge and Its Expression in the Folklore of Africa and the African Diaspora."

Personal, Private, and Public Issues

Africa is fast becoming liberalized and receptive in the sense of the people's acceptance of Western lifestyles. This is primarily by the educated elite in the urban areas. With growing urbanization, there is generally less attachment to what used to be tribal/ethnic codes of conduct for a more individualized lifestyle. This is reinforced by globalization through which process it really does not matter where one lives because even the rural areas have become more accepting of Western and town lifestyles and values than before. There is a lot of conurbation as former villages have become parts of ever-growing cities exploding with new migrants seeking jobs and better incomes that they think are found in the cities.

Issues of love and individual freedom are constantly interrogated by writers in their works. Such issues involve sexuality. Homosexual and lesbian characters are unabashedly portrayed in contemporary African fictional and dramatic works. There are copious examples in literature published since the early 1990s. Tess Onwueme's epic play, *Tell It to Women,* features a housewife having a lesbian partner and the husband may not be aware of his wife's true bisexual nature. Chris Abani's novel, *GraceLand,* presents homosexual practice in traditional Igbo society. Calixthe Beyala, a Cameroonian living in Paris, France, has novels that deal explicitly with sex. Other African writers in one way or another in their poetry, fiction, and plays deal with sex and issues of sexuality.

Women writers are no longer inhibited in expressing themselves. Naana Banyinwa Horne in her poems in *Sunkwa* speaks without any cultural inhibition of the male and female private parts. Many female and male writers describe sex graphically. The writers are no longer shy to describe what everybody knows happens in society. What is noticeable is that North America and Europe-based African writers tend to be more open in describing sex than those based in Africa. This is understandable because of the liberal and tolerant societies in which they live and write.

One can align the portrayal of sex and sexuality with the blooming of feminism in Africa. There is more sensitivity to women and issues concerning them in the still overwhelmingly patriarchal African societies. In addition to more female literary artists writing, many male writers are getting more aware of female sensibilities in their works. In South Africa and Nigeria in particular, female novelists and poets are thriving and almost dominating the literary scene. One cannot imagine contemporary Nigerian fiction without Chimamanda Ngozi Adichie, Sefi Atta, Akachi Ezeigbo, Chika Unigwe, and other female writers whose works are almost defining the new literary landscape. Thus, it was only a matter of time for female writers to catch up with and possibly overtake male writers since women now embrace Western education with the same zeal as men in most African societies. In most universities in Africa there appears to be more female students than male students and that has translated to also many women writers.

OTHER LITERARY TRENDS IN CONTEMPORARY AFRICAN LITERATURE

As already emphasized, Africa is a big continent and is very diverse. Writers respond to the African reality based on their location and individual experiences and dispositions. Many writers use their genres to write about human experiences of love, friendship, betrayal, family relationships, and so on. That trend holds across the continent. What is significant is that these human aspects could be linked to the politics of the place or time. In many countries, politics interferes with the private lives of people. For instance, while South Africa may be more liberal on gay lifestyle, Zimbabwe, Nigeria, and Uganda, for instance, are conservative and in some cases passing legislations against homosexual practice. This is bound to affect some people and should be seen as part of the intolerant African society.

In any case, many experiences center on the family and basic human needs of people. One has seen Dikeni Sandile write about his grandmother's murder by his fellow African National Congress friends. He expresses love for his granny and a sense of betrayal by his fellow ANC comrades. Writers take on the family and there are explorations of human relationships in many novels, especially set in patriarchal societies. Mandla Langa, like Zakes Mda in *The Heart of Redness*, writes about the position of those who returned from exile after the collapse of apartheid—those who did not know the "new dance"! This is similar to the Activist in Ojaide's *The Activist* who on his return from the United States to Nigeria was laughed at and spited by his relatives and colleagues and it took courage and persistence to withstand that psychological attack and make meaningful contribution to the nation.

Literary Implications of Politics in Literature

There is no doubt that the incorporation of politics into contemporary African literature has literary implications for that tradition of literature in terms of themes, form, and techniques. There is the obvious implication that if contemporary African literature is a reflection of the history and politics, it means that this literature renews itself much as history does with each era highlighting certain themes relevant to the time. And the themes condition the forms and techniques used in expressing them. In contemporary African literature, the themes have continued to shift in emphases according to the political moment. As Africa engages itself at the local, national, social, and global levels, the writers interrogate their national destinies or paths in comparison to some other nations within or outside Africa toward improving on the human condition. Nigerian and South African literatures are good examples of how politics aligning with history brings to the forefront different facets of the people's lives. Military dictatorship, just like apartheid, generated a plethora of literary works critical of those phenomena in the two respective countries. These are condemnations of the inhumanity and the violation of human rights in both countries.

However, the shift in history to civilian or freedom again has generated another type of literature with its own preoccupations. There
is much use of satire and irony as writers question the new political
dispensations. In Nigeria, there is satirizing of the democratic process
which is highly corrupted. G. 'Ebinwo Ogbowei's *The Heedless Ballot
Box* (2006), a collection of poems, deals with the exposure of the
irregularities of the electoral system that was meant to make people
freely express themselves but that is not the reality in which elections
are rigged and people do not make their choices in elected positions.
In South Africa, there is "freedom" but at the same time no freedom
and not much change in the economic condition of the common people. There is satire, parody, burlesque, and irony in confronting the
current history with the earlier expectations of what the future under
different circumstances would bring. In the South African case, freedom does not necessarily advance economic progress as one expected
or done at too slow a pace.

The apparently more liberalized environment has broadened the
landscape of writers, especially as they express their private experiences as in poetry. There is an escalation of love poetry as female and
male writers express themselves without inhibitions. Okinba Launko
(Femi Osofisan) in *Seven Stations Up the Tray's Way*, Tanure Ojaide's
Love Gifts, and Tony Afejuku's *A Spring of Sweets* are examples of love
poetry that are so revealing of individual experiences. Already mentioned is the fact that the African women resident in the West seem to
exercise more courage than those living in the continent in expressing
their private feelings. The Ghanaian Naana Bayinwa Horne living in
the United States is a good example in her poetry.

To avoid duplication of materials even though the themes sometimes intersect, here are some of the major thematic preoccupations
in contemporary African politics which its connectedness to the rest
of the world has given rise to in literary works. The new issues of history such as climate change and the environment have triggered new
areas of inspiration in the eco literary works arising from the intersection of history, politics, and the environment in Nigeria's Niger Delta
region. A group of writers have focused on the economic and political
exploitation of their area.

There are works on women's liberation that relate to self-actualization and sexuality as in Lola Shoneyin's *The Secret Lives of Baba Segi's
Wives*. Other works, especially in fiction, have to do with migration
for economic comfort in a globalized world. It is not that contemporary literary works are the first to deal with this issue but this is from

a different perspective. While *Ambiguous Adventure* dealt with this in the 1960s, it was more of the cultural clash between the West and Africa. Now migration has more to do with economic opportunities in the developed countries of Europe and North America as in Adichie's *Purple Hibiscus* and Abani's *GraceLand*. Migration in some literary works has become a kind of quest and when it does not work, there could be repatriation. Thus, there are migrations and reverse migrations. While many Africans are flocking to the developed countries, others are tired of their stay abroad and return to Africa as in Mda's *The Heart of Redness*, Tanure Ojaide's *The Activist*, Adichie's *Americanah*, and Chika Unigwe's *On Black Sisters' Street*, among others.

Exile or residence abroad involves issues of cultural identity that are still there in contemporary works but framed on the basis of an economic migrant in the process of searching for opportunities. Amaka's lamentation in *Purple Hibiscus* indicates the part lost culturally, psychologically, and emotionally in seeking economic well-being abroad.

As globalization facilitates migration on the one hand, on another there is resistance to globalization. Often some writers pitch indigeneity against globalization or try to make the local global or the global local. This has been mentioned in the protagonists of Mda's *The Heart of Redness* and Ojaide's *The Activist*. However, there is another level of indigenous or local resistance to globalization. That is in the area of using folklore to establish the local or ethnic roots of the writer's experience. Older writers, as already indicated, tend to do this the more. Mda gives a detailed Xhosa historiography, folklore, and political conflicts in the Believers and the non-Believers in a struggle for keeping the culture pristine or accepting development at any cost.

Another theme that has been fairly common is the reflection of the diaspora in literary works. Two novels that easily come to mind are Isidore Okpewho's *Call Me by My Rightful Name* and Benjamin Kwakye's *The Crucifix*. In Okpewho's novel, the African American goes to Africa to reconnect with his origins. This is a step further from Alex Hailey's *Roots* because the protagonist goes to Yoruba land in Nigeria to live the life of his ancestral origin. In Kwakye's novel, the African protagonist interacts with and has a series of African American female friends. There is the effort in African writers in the diaspora to express sociocultural solidarity with their black brothers and sisters. Usually space in diaspora literature is wide as the characters live out their lives in the United States or the Caribbean and Africa. Again, this turns out to be another kind of journey or search for cultural or emotional balance.

Perhaps the greatest loss in contemporary literature is the absence of lyrical poetry as poets and other writers focus on attacking the prevailing socioeconomic and political situations in their respective environment. Other writers lament failed national aspirations. Gone are the days when writers reflect on nature and describe the serenity of the environment as in J. P. Clark's poem, "Night Rain." Many are now more likely to criticize the environmental degradation and how the environment and its resources have become politicized and wasted by the politically powerful at the expense of the local communities as in the Niger Delta area.

Conclusion

Contemporary Africa's political direction in the New Millennium has not attracted as much literary forays as those periods of African history that had to do with nationalist struggle, postindependence, apartheid, corrupt civilian leadership, coups and military dictatorship, civil war, and civilian autocracies. Turbulent or bad periods of history tend to elicit creative works as during the military regimes in Nigeria and Ghana and the apartheid in South Africa with a lot of satirical works in all the genres. There are periods in the history of nations and people when writers protest what they see as inhuman rule. One can see the flourishing of poetry during Stalin's time in Russia with the poetry of Anna Akhmatova, Boris Pasternak, Osip Mandelstam, and others of that generation. The same happened during the dictatorship in Modern Greece. Apartheid provided black and colored writers the avenue to attack its inhuman system that kept blacks in a subhuman condition. That resonant voice in the poetry of Dennis Brutus as in "The sounds begin again" and other poems in *Letters to Martha* has not been matched in recent South African poetry. Military dictatorship was similarly a rallying point for many writers who lived in such countries where the military denied citizens basic human rights. It seems as if periods of pain accentuate the poetic tone just like the case of literature against apartheid.

Africa is in a flux and so are the culture and literature. Since literature is a cultural production, the stresses on Africa resulting from globalization and wave of Pentecostal religious groups are being reflected in the literature. On a broad picture, it is the politics of globalization that has given rise to these stresses that are affecting the literary production of many works published and promoted in the West while local African productions are not widely circulated and not promoted with the same ardor as the capitalist trade publishers do in North America and Europe. Politics has come to intersect with the culture, economy, society, religion/spirituality, and other major segments of the African experience. Thus, contemporary African literature is a reflection of the politics and history of the continent.

CHAPTER 3

Homecoming: African Literature and Human Development

Literature has a place in the society and culture in which and for which it is produced. Writers can be public intellectuals who address the sociopolitical happenings around them. Even introspective writings on deeply personal topics may be political in their interrogation of the human condition. For a literary artist to set works in a society, culture, or environment and to not help raise the consciousness of the people about their problems is unconscionable. There needs to be a "homecoming" so as to make literature matter in our societies and cultures, more so because of the developing nation and continent we live in or belong to. Writers should re-establish themselves as a uniquely imaginative, activist, and alternative voice in a country with so many problems. This means they should respond to the reality that the place and moment require of them as writers to act in a constructive manner.

An honest appraisal of countries and regions worldwide indicates Africa's backwardness compared to other continents in human development. This low United Nations' ranking also reflects the continent's low-level of social and economic development. The human development index of a country or any region of the world comprises primarily the health/life expectancy, education, and living standards/income of its people. Countries are ranked very high, high, medium, or low in human development. It is pertinent to know that in 2010 of all 192 countries then in the world, only a few African countries were in the medium group and most, including Nigeria (ranked hundred and forty-second), were on the low-level of human development. Sub-Saharan Africa was at the bottom of all regions of the world, scoring 0.389 where the regions and countries with the very high rankings scored close to the maximum 1. Life expectancy in sub-Saharan Africa was 52.7 and the mean years of schooling merely 4.5.

In addition to health, education, and income, human development also includes the rate of inequality, poverty, gender gap, and human security. Nigeria ranks very low in all of these indices.

But that is not all about human development, which also involves having a sense of corporate existence, selflessness, honesty, generosity, and integrity. The aforementioned virtues are aspects of an individual's character that indicate the level of human development and can be attained through education. Coincidentally, the countries and regions of the world that have these qualities and values also rank the highest when it comes to issues of health, education, and living standards. It follows therefore that a country or region that is very corrupt and with a lot of undisciplined, self-centered, and ignorant folks and rife with injustice is very low in human development.

In many literate cultures, it is the writers who project a vision in the form of ideas that later materialize into creative inventions. Jules Verne's *Around the World in Eighty Days* (1873) was written at a time when it would realistically take half a year or more time to travel round the world. Today we know what that literary vision or creative dream of conquering long distance has brought about through the story of a wager for 20,000 pounds not only to Britain and France or Europe but also to the entire world: airplanes and spacecrafts that can now go round the world in a matter of a few hours! Literature can be a catalyst for human development by inspiring people to stretch their imaginative potentials for physical development and the well-being of people. In fact, without human development there can be no industrial or other forms of development. That is why there must be a "homecoming" for all African writers, not merely a call for those in exile or the diaspora to come home but an inward-looking exploration for literary strategies and fresh visions to drastically improve the African condition in the areas of health, education, and standard of living as well as in eliminating the rate of inequality, poverty, gender gap, and human insecurity. In a global age it may no longer matter where you live but African literature needs "homecoming" physically, spiritually, and metaphorically to be relevant to the people of the continent.

Literature is a cultural artistic production that deals with the totality of a people's experience; hence it incorporates sociocultural, politico-economic, and other issues as of gender, class, marginalization, and justice that confront a people. African literature, therefore, whether traditional or modern, is a cultural production expressing African sensibilities, aesthetics, and material reality. At the same time, African literature, like the other arts such as the visual arts and music, is traditionally primarily utilitarian. In the oral tradition, folktales are didactic and are meant to educate the young ones to grow into responsible citizens of their respective communities. Since there are no formal schools, the folktales and the myths (etiological tales) are geared toward moral and ethical development of young ones, while the legends and epics create a sense of patriotism, group responsibility, and commitment to one's group. This notion of a unitary ethos does not exclude some form of diversity, which the modern state tends to expedite by giving "rebels" like the Nwoyes of Umuofia a place in the sun. Growing up, therefore, in the traditional community nobody tells one not to be selfish; rather the tale of the tortoise whose inordinate greed and self-centeredness alienate it from the rest of the animal community is told to reflect the human society. The small or weak live on their wits among the strong that harass and often want to exploit, oppress, or destroy them. On the other hand, the proverbs, riddles, and tongue-twisters deal with language skills and help to sharpen the human intellect.

Song/poetry is very significant in traditional African societies. A few examples show the importance of some types of songs. The satiric *udje* of Nigeria's Urhobo people and the *halo* of the Ewe of Ghana and Togo are composed and performed to use laughter to regulate the behavior of people in a community. The songs attack negative social practices such as stealing, laziness, indebtedness, selfishness, greed, and other vices or disruptive modes of behavior that can cause disharmony in society. These satiric songs have an important social function, for they maintain a delicate balance between the general good of the society whose ethos must be upheld and respect for the law-abiding individual. Thus, they do not promote unquestioning following of the communal ethos to the extent of stifling individuality. Similarly, the Yoruba *ijala* and the Zulu and Xhosa *izibongo* sing or chant praises of people who exhibit the virtues of courage, generosity, and honesty, among others.

African oral literature, therefore, plays a major role in human development. Literature, in the African tradition, is thus deployed toward drawing attention to and attempting to solve the problems and issues of the society so as to enhance the creation of a healthy social ethos. It aims at harmony, justice, fairness, selflessness, communality, sensitivity, kindness, and other values and virtues that the generality of the people hold dear and extol so as to be emulated, while the negative ones are satirized in songs and narratives. Literary composition thus imposes a responsibility on artists in their creations as traditional literature appears to have generally inculcated the virtues of selflessness and discipline on the people. But can the same be said now of modern literature in Africa, where one person can embezzle wealth that could bring improvement to millions of people without any form of literary reproach? What is literature doing to curb the excesses of today's politicians who are so greedy that one person can steal forty billion naira or even more? What are writers in countries with "sit-tight" presidents doing about the governance of their states? Have writers not become too timid in the face of power, too soft and distracted by other considerations to speak truth to power? Contemporary African writers have to responsibly create texts that advance the vision and ideals of their respective communities. Modern African writers have generally imbibed the didactic aspects of orature into their writings, making their works not merely art for art's sake like most Western artistic productions but tools to advance society's progress. But the results have not been the same as with the oral tradition's impact in the area of human development.

The state of contemporary African literature gives one cause for anxiety. Older writers appear to be focused on the role of the writer in society. To Wole Soyinka, African artists are the "critical prods and guides of the societies. The artist has always functioned in African society as the record of the mores and experience of his society and as the voice of vision in his time" (20). To Chinua Achebe, the writer is a teacher involved in the education and regeneration of his people (45). Their respective *Death and the King's Horseman* and *Things Fall Apart* fulfill these sentiments of the role of literature in society.

However, today things have changed. Some recent developments in African literature intensify my angst. Some younger writers, especially those residing in North America and Europe, in interviews go as far as questioning the existence of any writing that could be called African literature. It is also interesting to note that two recent winners of the Caine Prize for African Writing (Nigerian E. C. Osondu and Sierra Leonean Olufemi Terry) are lukewarm to the idea of African literature. There is the Western literary canon which nobody seems to dispute. There is no interrogation of the notion of "American," "British," "Russian," or "Indian" literature as is currently being done of "African" literature or any of its national subsets. As Dr. Joseph Obi puts it, "To the extent that ethnicity, nation states, and continents are realities, there will perforce be ethnic, national, and continental literatures. Creative consciousnesses and products gel within these matrices and it would be foolhardy to discount them in favor of some ill-defined universalism." That said, according to him, one can detect a looser and more elastic category which might be considered national or continental "writing." In this sense, a putative African author could produce a work which does not reflect (or at best is only tenuously informed by) African sensibilities, aesthetics, and material reality. The "Africanness" of these works is self-referential to the extent that they are simply written by Africans on some subject in or about Africa. This kind of writing does not consciously model itself on any storehouse of aesthetics. Rather it is fluid and pragmatic. Some writers may not know or may not want to be constrained by the cultural silos that predate them.

With this in mind, the title of the Caine Prize for African *Writing* (not *Literature*) is instructive. So also was the inaugural Penguin Prize for African *Writing* in fiction and nonfiction in 2010. It is revealing also to note the description of the kinds of works that the Nigerian National Liquified Natural Gas (NLNG) literary award committee says it will not consider ("low moral thresholds, junk reads, thrillers") as recognition of the distinction that has set in between African *literature* and African *writing*. It may seem faddish though for some writers to give dubious answers to questions about the reality of African literature in the hope that their writings might attract global interests and even prizes, but they run the risk of being lost in a vast grey market with no long-term value. Canada-based Amatoritsero Ede describes the kinds of art of such writers without a tissue of conscience and having a "huge moral hole" as "*Sunday distractions for somnambulist petit bourgeoisie; transient art, which like bubble gum, is chewed, enjoyed, and spat out*" (emphasis mine).

Mazizi Kunene, the late South African poet laureate, has extolled the ethical development of Africa, as opposed to the material development of Europe and the Western world. He is of the view in *The Ancestors and the Sacred Mountain* that "the earliest act of civilization was...the establishment of a cooperative, interactive, human community" (xvi). He sees African literary works that do not aim at human development as "light" and irrelevant. Pursuing the ethical orientation of modern African literature involves more than an imaginary home return from the diaspora as done in Zakes Mda's *The Heart of Redness* and my *Activist* in which the respective protagonists, Cumago and the Activist, return with experiences of their foreign sojourns to do some concrete projects in their African homelands. True, an ambassador should return home to contribute to the building of his or her own homeland.

On a more practical level, there is the ethical obligation of a writer's "homecoming" to pay back something to the culture and society that have nurtured his or her talent. Talent may be God-given but it is impossible for talent to exist in isolation of the community which gives it the raw material upon which it simultaneously feeds and reflects. Thus, the "homecoming" is a summons to community service to contribute to human development in whatever way possible with the writing. Chinua Achebe's Tortoise in *Things Fall Apart* is an apt metaphor in this respect. After being enabled by feathers from birds to fly to the sky to partake in the divine banquet, it ought to allow everybody in the party communal sharing rather than be humiliated with leftovers! In other words, a sense of community should impel the writer to promote virtues in individuals that will make the society grow stronger.

Let me comment on certain trends that some may find troubling in contemporary African literature. In the works of some writers living outside Africa, there is graphic representation of physical sex. Generally in traditional African society sex is private but so much is the desire for a large foreign audience that the Ghanaian Benjamin Kwakye's *The Other Crucifix* is filled with it. Many of Cameroonian Calixthe Beyala's works also fall into this category of African literature with so much sex as if aimed at pleasing Western readers rather than Africans whose place and society are the background of the literary works. Needless to argue that there is anything artistic more than mere sexual exhibitionism in the South Sudanese Kola Boof's works, especially in her book covers. Of course, one can argue that sex is part of life and this is more so in contemporary African societies with the effects of Westernization, modernization, and globalization. Some will argue that casual non-procreative sex and incidents of incest have always been part of life in Africa but had gone underreported till recently. However, it appears that such "African" works that deal graphically with sex tend to sell very well in the West. There have been reports of African American males, who normally don't read literary works, lining up at Boof's book-signing events to buy her books to relish her nude book covers rather than experience the works for their literary merit.

Also there is a Western obsession with the child soldier, violence, and misery, which some African writers now focus on as in Uzodinma Iweala's *Beasts of No Nation*, E. C. Osondu's Caine prize-winning "Waiting," Uwem Akpan's *Say You're One of Them*, and Olufemi Terry's "Stickfighting Days," among others. No doubt some of these writers exploit the sad side of Africa to gain Western readership. They practice what Chimamanda Ngozi Adichie has described succinctly as telling the "single story," focusing on only the negative and not also on the positive side of Africans. One is not denying that there is misery in Africa or there is not so much violence around with civil wars or other conflicts. These things are there but do not need to be so emphasized to leave out any good things that we also possess and cherish. One can understand the frustration of writers about Africa's misery, the corruption, and the failure of political leadership in most countries. However, writers should be cautious so as not to give only a picture of gloom that will discourage rather than inspire. The writer should be balanced in telling the good and the bad in the African experience. Examples are copious but Sefi Atta's *Everything Good Will Come* and Chimamanda Adichie's *Purple Hibiscus* tell the good and the bad in us.

While I stress the need for relevance of content to the realities of Africa, I do not encourage writings by Africans to be seen as literary if they do not pay attention to form or craft. These writings are works of literature because they are imaginative, creative, and artistic. Literature is an art and works of poetry, drama, and fiction that deal with prevalent issues but exhibit no literary qualities should not be regarded as models of the African literature that I speak about. There are some writers who overemphasize content at the expense of form. In a few cases, the writers emphasize contentious issues that grab the attention of foreign agencies that fund local NGOs. One can therefore write on HIV/AIDS, female circumcision, child-bride, "breast ironing," environmental degradation, human rights, and other subjects as if doing a sociological rather than a literary work. The point being made is that there must be a balance of content and form for a work to be good literature. Among others, Femi Osofisan's *The Oriki of a Grasshopper*, Ahmed Yerima's *Hard Ground*, Chimalum Nwankwo's *The Womb in the Heart*, Niyi Osundare's *The Eye of the Earth*, Wale Okediran's *Tenants of the House*, and Zakes Mda's *The Heart of Redness* are very artistic works about the African experience that have balanced content and form.

African literature has to promote literacy to ensure human development. A literate people do not forget and so learn from past mistakes and failures and resort to strategies that succeeded in the past. Fortunately, we now write and should never forget. As I write, there is looming catastrophe in the Horn of Africa—the worst drought in about six decades! What mechanisms, after the last famine, will help us surmount the current challenge rather than wait helplessly for death or the international community, a code name for primarily the Western world, to save us from the imminent doom? African literature should be put at the service of Africans to promote literacy and solutions to African problems. What use is a literature based on a place and its people who do not even read it? What use is a people's literature that does not uplift, ennoble them toward higher goals of society, nationhood, and humanity? Literature should sensitize readers and people toward solving their problems and making them better human beings. In pursuit of this objective, African writers should create works that our people can read and learn from. Such literary creations should be aimed primarily at African readers rather than others, especially North Americans and other Westerners who have more money to spend on books. Special effort should be made to promote literature for children, the common people, and women because they are disadvantaged in the primarily patriarchal continent. A mind developed through book culture can be the catalyst for other forms of development.

"Homecoming" for African literature entails tapping from our roots to affirm faith in our indigenous virtues and values. With literature, writers build memory that should be a guide to the people. Here the Ghanaian Akan Sankofa is pertinent to African literature— simultaneously looking backward while facing the challenges of the future! A "homecoming" of this literature involves a return to the positive old ways that can be used to solve current problems that keep us down and backward. What can we learn from our literary archives? This could bring about a spiritual renewal different from the current spate of churches and religions that seem to be ironically fuelling corruption at all levels and increasing our materialism and underdevelopment. As we retrieve virtues of the past, literature should also critically address current problems and issues. In other words, the African writer should be aware of his or her society's problems and address them toward their solution. The writer may not always provide a solution, but by raising an issue in an artistic manner for public reflection he or she is contributing to the sensitization of his or her people. And, as in the Sankofa representation, the writer imbued with experience of the past must lead to the future by offering a vision of possibilities. In this way, the writer plays the role of a guide and a prophet constructing an imaginary nation or society of an ideal polity to which readers and the entire society are constantly riveted.

The literary pursuit of human development is made more urgent in Africa because of globalization that has swept across the world. Do we Africans go with the wind of globalization or inscribe our local humanity in the global and thus negotiate a new identity that is African but has absorbed the relevant positive features of others? There appears to be the recognition that "others" are not much different from "us" after all, and all share similar problems and a common humanity. African literature has to be involved in the advocacy of this new cosmopolitanism of making Africans aware of others and others aware of Africans. Issues of freedom, individual human rights, new identities, migration, ecological and environmental concerns, disability, and sexuality, among others, are borderless and draw attention to our oneness as human beings. African literature should assist in engineering a new sensibility, which is transnational, cross-cultural, and humanistic. African writers should not use globalization as an excuse to jettison their own culture and values into oblivion but should affirm themselves as Africans and not be imitative of Western ways masked as global features. As I have stated elsewhere, "Globalization should not be a one-way traffic but must be an integrative phenomenon in which all communities...have to contribute their special talent to advance universal literary creativity."

For African literature to contribute to human development effectively, it has to feed readers with the milk of truth. It has to avoid being used to promote jingoistic, partisan, xenophobic, fanatical, ethnic, and other partisan causes. Over time some writers' works, statements, or silence have been part of the problem rather than the solution. In the Nigerian Civil War, the Eritrean-Ethiopian War, the genocide in Rwanda, and ethnic unrests as in Kenya, writers have been involved and in some instances their involvement has been controversial at best and in some cases fueled insensitivity and destruction of lives. As Wole Soyinka has put it, "the man dies in all who keep silent in the face of tyranny." A work of African literature is no longer anonymous in its written form because it carries the identity of an author. African literature is the creation of writers and their own behaviors and actions matter as much as their literary viewpoints. There should be no separation of their lives from their literary creations in order to create an image of integrity. A respectable messenger's or ambassador's message is treated with respect. African literature should range on the side of the disadvantaged and be at the vanguard of human development toward lifting Africans from backwardness to a position of envy among other peoples of the world.

I make the following recommendations:

1. Literary creation imposes a huge responsibility on writers from countries and a region at the bottom of rankings on human development in the world. The writer who serves only himself or herself is arrogant and selfish. African writers have to use their writings to address the eradication of ignorance, superstitions, and myths that adversely affect people's health and life

expectancy. Writers should cultivate sensitivity in their writings to make all human beings really human. Writers must fight against the situation in a country where women cannot bail the accused, they cannot buy land without their husbands' or fathers' consent, deny husbands infected with STD sex, take responsibility over their own bodies, and many other denials that make them not equal to men even in the twenty-first century. Literature should lead the people to more rational decisions and sensitivity to others.

2. African literature should be geared toward African readership first before outsiders interested in the African experience and values. Africans will identify with works and learn from them if aimed at them. The choice for the writer is between advancing human development in Africa or making personal financial gains by pleasing foreign readers who seek to confirm their negative views of Africa in works written by so-called Africans about Africa without any redeeming features.

3. African literature should advance literacy in the continent. This means writers should have at the back of their minds engaging their readership from so many levels of society, especially children, women, and the common people in a language they can understand and will uplift them toward higher goals. This will diminish not only gender and socioeconomic gaps but also inequality in society. Literacy and education will advance public enlightenment and health to raise the level of human development. With literacy and education, people will get to know their human, civil, and other rights and exercise them or resist their being violated.

4. Writers should be bolder in their imaginative projections to challenge the people toward realizing higher goals and inventions. Literature should not just be reactive dealing with current corruption and class differences but also proactive in preoccupations. Literature should prepare folks to be good human beings that will affect governance and social cohesion. Literature should warn against future problems. In fact, writers should also dream in such a way as to stretch the potentials for inventions.

5. African writers should be balanced in their presentation of the African experience—the good and the bad. Literature runs the risk of undermining human development in Africa if it paints such a sordid picture of the place and people that turns people off or drives people into despair or out of the continent.

6. The life of the writer should not be separated from the literary work created so as to earn more credibility and followership. Writers should not only do the talk but also the walk! A teacher should be a mentor and a role model.

7. Inscribe our values in the global and incorporate the relevant from others into ours. Our literature should not be just imitative of American or European writings but pursue its own cultural identity toward a canon that is consonant with Africa's needs to improve drastically its human development.

8. The Association of Nigerian Authors and other national writers' organizations in Africa and their state branches as well as Departments of English/Creative Arts in universities should engage young writers in holiday camps or creative writing workshops to teach them what it takes to be a good/successful writer. By attracting talented young writers and giving them classes in creative writing, older writers will stimulate creative enthusiasm in the young and also train them professionally in mastering the writing process. Products of such programs would be at the vanguard of deploying literature toward human development in their respective societies.

9. African publishers should pursue discovering local talents and not just publish those already published in the West. If they discovered local talents and promoted them, they would gain a lot of pride and profit by receiving fees from foreign publishers for reissuing such books. If the local publishers have a philosophy of human development in the continent, the writers will help them to meet their goals. Local publishing houses should be professionalized in the areas of editorial staff, promotion of works and their authors, and distribution and marketing of literary works. They could go as far as organizing literary contests calling for works that address the theme of human development or good citizenry in their respective countries or societies and publishing the winning entries.

10. Our African literary scholars and critics should elevate their role as critics of the cultural productions that meet African aesthetic and canonical needs.

African literature surely needs "homecoming" on many fronts: physical, spiritual, and metaphorical. It must promote human development of the continent which should later be translated into industrial, social, political, and economic development. Literature should be deployed to mend the world we live in which is not even, fair, just, or balanced. Literature should sensitize the readership and African citizenry to transparency, probity and integrity in governance, environmental and ecological balance, public health, democracy, and social, economic, and political equality that will bring peace to create the enabling engine for true development.

CHAPTER 4

Defining Niger Delta Literature: Preliminary Perspective on an Emerging Literature

The terms Literature of the Niger Delta and Niger Delta Literature are used interchangeably in this study to mean works of literature that have been produced by both indigenes of the Niger Delta and outsiders about the region. These literary works are either set in the Niger Delta or take their themes from the experiences of the people of the region. This study attempts to define Niger Delta literature and examines it as a reflection of the experiences of the region's people. This literature also reflects the locale and is informed by, among others, geographical, bioregional, sociocultural, and political factors.

Niger Delta literature has received more prominence in literary discourse since the judicial murder of Ken Saro-Wiwa, the Ogoni minority rights and environmental activist in October 1995. Saro-Wiwa's activism and the worldwide abortive campaign to save him from being hanged by the brutal Sani Abacha junta in Nigeria generated a lot of interest in the Niger Delta region. The body of literary works on this oil and gas-producing region forms a corpus that can be described as Niger Delta literature because the writings attempt to reflect the worldview, sensibility, identity, and experiences of the people as well as the society and landscape that form the Niger Delta.

Without doubt, Niger Delta literature has been enhanced by worldwide interest in the related areas of climate change, the environment, and ecocriticism. This has been more so because of the highly publicized political campaign to draw attention to the excesses of multinational oil corporations working in the Niger Delta since 1958 and the subsequent environmental and ecological degradations that have adversely affected human and nonhuman lives in the area. Additionally, one can anchor Niger Delta literature on the incorporation of the folklore and shared experiences of the people in the writers' works. Among the writers of the area are J. P. Clark, Ben Okri, Ken Saro-Wiwa, Isidore Okpewho, Gabriel Okara, Tess Onwueme, Elechi Amadi, Okogbule Wonodi, Ogaga Ifowodo, Kaine Agary, Ebi Yeibo, Ebinyo Ogbowei, Onookome Okome, Nduka Otiono, Dike Okoro, and Tanure Ojaide. Two writers who are nonindigenes of the area but have written sensitively about the Niger Delta are Ahmed Yerima and Helon Habila in their respective *Hard Ground* and *Oil on Water.* This list of producers of Niger Delta literature is not meant to be definitive or finite but includes most of the best known authors of the literary tradition as will be defined and discussed in this chapter.

While this literature has received increased attention in recent times, it is important to acknowledge the older writers who have always set their works on the Niger Delta region. Writings such as Okara's *Fisherman's Invocation* (1975), Amadi's *The Concubine* (1966), J. P. Clark's *Song of a Goat* (1965), and Ojaide's *Labyrinths of the Delta* (1986) were published long before the wave of environmental awareness and distress from oil exploitation. These earlier literary productions about the area were not studied as Niger Delta literature until only recently. It is important to state then that literary works can be classified as Niger Delta literature that remain Nigerian, albeit African, literature. Writings that are studied as Niger Delta literature receive more attention in depth and breadth and are also open to interdisciplinary approaches that impinge on the people's specific experiences, especially in the areas of ecology and environment, folklore, and politics. Also while critics have tried to see postcolonial literature as antagonistic to the literature of place such as Niger Delta literature, in this particular case the literature still carries the features of Nigerian and African literatures, which are highly postcolonial.

Since the literature of the Niger Delta is set in a specific place, it is important to know what constitutes the Niger Delta. The Niger Delta in Nigeria is not synonymous with the South-South geopolitical zone, one of six of such zones that make up the Nigerian federation. Edo, Cross River, and Akwa Ibom States are in the South-South geopolitical zone but are not part of the core Niger Delta. However, Cross River and Akwa Ibom residents consider themselves as part of the Niger Delta. The exclusion of Edo State as part of the Niger Delta could be because for a long time the former Midwest Region that became Delta State always comprised of Delta or Warri Province and the Benin side. It is true that the minorities of the old Western and Eastern Regions had struggled in the 1950s to be separated from their respective Yoruba and Igbo majority groups. While the Midwest

Region came into being in the early 1960s (later split to Edo and Delta States), the Eastern minorities got separated from their dominant Igbo group during and after the Civil War and today make up Cross River, Akwa Ibom, Rivers, and Bayelsa States.

Several factors clarify this delimitation of the core Niger Delta. The old Warri/Delta Province basically became the basis for the creation of Delta State. The addition of the Anioma and Aniocha areas to the old Warri/Delta Province to form the current Delta State identifies them as part of the Niger Delta region because those areas are close enough to the River Niger. So it is not the old Midwest Region that should be seen as belonging to the Niger Delta but only the old Warri/Delta Province and its recent appendage in Delta State. Thus, to consider, for instance, such established writers as Festus Iyayi, Harry Garuba, and Funso Aiyejina, who hail from Edo State, as Niger Delta writers will be to overstretch and overstate the size of the Niger Delta. It is my contention that people of Edo State do not feel in their psyche that they are best identified as Niger Delta folks. On the other hand, the old Rivers State that has been split into Cross River, Akwa Ibom, and Bayelsa States is problematic. Doubtless this area has historically been a political unit; however while Akwa Ibom and Cross River States may not be at the core but are still politically and marginally geographically part of the Niger Delta. Joseph Ushue hails from Cross River State. In his poetry, there is a feeling that he is very attached to the Obudu Ranch and hills as well as the Niger Delta landscape.

Similarly, the Niger Delta region is also not synonymous with the oil and gas-producing states of Nigeria, which include states such as Abia and Ondo. And it will also be a further overstretch and overstatement to consider Tayo Olafioye of Ondo State or an Eastern Nigerian Igbo writer of Abia State origin as a Niger Delta writer. Those people also, like those of Edo State already mentioned, do not carry the sentiments of Niger Delta indigenes. While all three core Niger Delta states of Delta, Bayelsa, and Rivers are oil-producing, there are other oil-producing states that are not part of the region. Thus, the region is not a political creation done by administrative or political fiat of various military or civilian regimes in Nigeria. The Niger Delta is more of a geographical, bioregional, and sociocultural area that has a uniqueness of its own that sets it aside from other parts of Nigeria and imbues it with common and shared experiences of self-affirmation, resistance to majority domination and multinational exploitation and oppression, and a defense of the piece of the earth the people call their own.

The Niger Delta is a geographical and bioregional reality. It is currently inhabited by about 12 million people of over 20 ethnic groups, the majority of which are Ijo, Ikwerre, Isoko, Itsekiri, and Urhobo. The area, consisting of Nigeria's Rivers, Bayelsa, and Delta States, mainly of floodplain makes 7.5% of Nigeria's landmass. It has been described as the largest wetland in Africa with a lot of biodiversity and is also the third largest drainage area in the African continent after the Nile and the Congo deltaic areas. The Niger Delta can be divided into four ecological zones: coastal barrier islands such as Bonny, Akassa, Forcados, Escravos, and Burutu; mangrove swamp forests as in the Ogbia area of Bayelsa; freshwater swamps as in Okwagbe of Delta State; and lowland rainforest that covers the northern section of the region ranging from places such as Abraka in Delta State to Bori in Rivers State. The area provides habitation for different species of plants, reptiles, fish, mammals, birds, other creatures, and minerals. This region has helplessly witnessed its biodiversity, ecology, and environment destroyed by oil and gas exploration and exploitation for the past six decades.

The very threat to the environment and ecosystem of the Niger Delta region by the oil corporations has led to focus on the biocentric and ecocritical approaches to the literature of the region. A biocentric view involves a broadening of human conception of global community to include nonhuman forms and the physical environment. It also addresses the relationship between human culture and the environment, which has direct impact on the Niger Delta people. After all, the people are traditionally farmers and fishers, who rely on the soil and the abundant water for subsistence and the herbs, plants, and animals for their medicines and foods. The Niger Delta is surely a bioregional unit in its shared ecological and environmental experiences. Bioregionalism, according to Rob Nixon, is the "responsiveness to one's local part of the earth whose boundaries are determined by a location's natural characteristics rather than arbitrary administrative boundaries" (Olaniyan 757). Bioregionalism advocates eco awareness and the need to maintain a harmony between humans and nonhuman forms in the environment (Branch xiii). The attempt by Niger Delta writers such as Isidore Okpewho in his *Tides*, Kaine Agary in her *Yellow-Yellow*, Ogaga Ifowodo in *The Oil Lamp*, Ebinyo Ogbowei in *Song of a Dying River*, and Ojaide in *The Activist* and *The Tale of the Harmattan* to protect the environment and halt ecological damage has brought to the fore the role of activism in Niger Delta literature.

Nature and the environment have always been very important in the lives of traditional people who interact with the soil and the rivers as well as the fauna and flora with which the humans maintain a balanced relationship. The oral literature of the people, in the forms of folktales, legends, epics, myths, folksongs, and proverbs, draws on tropes and symbols of the environment. For instance, the tortoise and the iroko tree appear in Niger Delta folktales and other forms of folklore which are incorporated into the written literature. Thus, taking the cue from the oral tradition, the written works of Gabriel Okara, Okogbule Wonodi, and J. P. Clark, among many others, reflect how much Niger Delta folks appreciate nature and their environment. Okara's *Fisherman's Invocation* and Clark's *A Reed in the Tide* are illustrative of the interactive nature of humans and nonhuman forms in the Niger Delta. Okara hails from Bomoundi, a town beside the River Nun in Nigeria's Bayelsa State. Here is the poet's "The Call of the River Nun":

> I hear your call!
> I hear it far away;
> I hear it break the circle
> of these crouching hills.
>
> I want to view your face
> Again and feel your cold
> Embrace; or at your brim
> To set myself and
> Inhale your breath; or
> Like the trees, to watch
> My mirrored self unfold
> And span my days with
> Song from the lips of dawn.
>
> I hear your clapping call!
> I hear it coming through;
> Invoking the ghost of a child
> Listening, where river birds hail
> Your silver-surfaced flow.
>
> My river's calling too!
> Its ceaseless flow impels
> My found'ring canoe down
> Its inevitable course.
> And each dying year
> Brings near the sea-bird call,
> The final call that
> Stills the crested waves

And breaks it in two the curtain
Of silence of my upturned canoe.
O incomprehensible God!
Shall my pilot be
My inborn stairs to that
Final call to Thee
O my river's complex course?

To the poet, the river, water, the entire environment, as well as he and other humans, are closely related; hence the poet "hear(s) your clapping call!" The personification of the river and the passion involved in the "call" tell the close kinship the poet establishes between humans and the natural environment in the form of the river.

J. P. Clark makes copious use of nature as relates to the Niger Delta locale and environment in his poetry, especially in *A Reed in the Tide*. In "Streamside exchange," Clark writes:

Child: River bird, river bird,
Sitting all day long
On hook over grass,
River bird, river bird,
Sing to me a song
Of all that pass
And say,

Will mother come back today?
Bird: You cannot know
And should not bother;
Tide and market come and go
And so has your mother. (*A Decade of Tongues* 20)

This is a simple poem set in the Niger Delta's natural environment. In it, the speaker, imbued with wisdom, teaches and counsels a child who has lost its mother by explaining the transient nature of life. By saying "Tide and market come and go," the poet educates the child about life and death in a way it can understand. The flux of the tide and the regularity of the market day, aspects of nature and culture of the Niger Delta people, become metaphors to instill in this child the notion of the brevity of life and the harsh reality of the finality of the mother's death. In another poem, "Night Rain," J. P. Clark further reflects the Niger Delta environment with its abundant rain and the fragile habitation of the people. These two poems reflect Clark's early work in which there is passionate evocation of the Niger

Delta environment. There is often a sense of nostalgia in these early poems of Clark that will be lost with the discovery of oil and gas whose exploration and exploitation will destroy the Edenic landscape of the Niger Delta. His *All for Oil* about five decades later will tell a different tale of the Niger Delta environment.

Writers generally reflect and project the aspirations of their people, and Niger Delta writers are no exception to that phenomenon of African literature. In the literature of the Niger Delta, the writers advocate environmental justice. The Niger Delta communities are among the poorest not only in Nigeria but also in the entire world despite the huge resources of oil and gas that bring in billions of dollars to the Nigerian government yearly. And that is despite the fact that the people's traditional sources of livelihood, the soil and water for farming and fishing respectively, have been destroyed by pollution brought about by the recklessness of the multinational oil companies of which Shell is a major culprit. The example of Ogoniland is a sore reminder of the exploitation and oppression of the minorities that make up the Niger Delta. By 1993 Ogoni had benefited the Nigerian government over $30 billion and yet the place had no light, tap water, and hospitals. Also, for a long time Ughelli in Delta State produced one of the best types of crude oil in the world but it also had no light and basic amenities. There is apparent collusion between the Federal Government and the multinationals, since a Federal edict took lands from its rightful owners for oil exploiters to have a free hand across the Niger Delta, a situation that did not take into consideration the environment or well-being of the local population. It is this situation that has turned many Niger Delta youths and writers into "resource rebels," what outsiders, exploiters, and oppressors call "militants."

It is important to look at two significant environmental human rights documents from the area and which not only reflect the aspirations of the people but also the focus of literary thematic pursuits of the writers: the Ogoni Bill of Rights (1990) and the Kaiama Declaration (1998). In 1990, the Movement for the Survival of the Ogoni People (MOSOP) under the leadership of Ken Saro-Wiwa, in response to Shell's total neglect of the people and their environment, submitted the "Ogoni Bill of Rights" to the Federal Nigerian Government. The group demanded, among others, "political control of Ogoni affairs by Ogoni people; the right to the control and use of a fair proportion of Ogoni economic resources for Ogoni development; adequate representation in all Nigerian national institutions and the right to protect the Ogoni environment and ecology from further degradation" (qtd. in Gedicks 46). They lament that "it is intolerable that one of the richest areas of Nigeria should wallow in abject poverty and destitution." These environmental rights are human rights which the people had to ask for after no compensations were paid to the Ogoni people after Ogoniland had been polluted and the environment degraded without any measures taken by either the multinational oil companies or the Federal Nigerian Government to remedy the situation. "The Drilling Fields," a television documentary shot by the British Independent Television, gives a graphic picture of the wasteland that Ogoniland had become as a result of oil spillages, blowouts, and gas flares that were left unchecked. Shell often blamed the local communities for sabotage even when blowouts and spillages resulted from their shoddy maintenance and old equipment, and the Federal Government, on the side of the oil company, usually sent mobile police to terrorize the people.

The Kaiama Declaration, on the other hand, was spearheaded by Ijo youths, the Egbesu Boys and other groups, in November 1998. In the document, the "Ijaw youths drawn from over five hundred communities from over 40 clans that make the Ijaw nation and representing 25 representative organizations" at Kaiama in Bayelsa State on the eleventh day of December 1998 declare that: "all land and natural resources (including mineral resources) within the Ijaw territory belong to Ijaw communities and are the basis of our survival." They demand the immediate withdrawal from Ijawland of "all military forces of occupation and repression by the Nigerian state" (qtd. in Gedicks 50). This was after the destruction of Odi in Bayelsa State by Olusegun Obasanjo's troops and the punitive raids on Mbiama, Kaiama, and Patani, contiguous Ijo towns in Bayelsa and Delta States.

The appropriation and exploitation of the lands of Niger Delta people are blatant forms of oppression, a trend that Joni Adamson notices of governments and multinational corporations worldwide. Thus the fight "for the environment and fight for *all* forms of linked oppression" (qtd. in Branch 14) are the same. Michael Branch links the oppression of people to the despoliation of their environment and lack of political power, which is reflected in the political marginalization of the Ogoni and Ijo ethnic groups. The alliance of majority groups in Nigeria and that between the Federal Government and the multinational oil corporations form a powerful force that dominates the minority people of the Niger Delta and despoil their environment.

Okpewho's *Tides*, Clark's *All for Oil*, Ogaga Ifowodo's *The Oil Lamp*, and Ojaide's *The Activist* and *The Tale of the Harmattan* directly address the issues of oil exploration. These works highlight the pollution that has taken place and the consequences on the local communities. Other writers such as Kaine Agary, Ebinyo Ogbowei, and Ebi Yeibo also touch on the pollution of the region's environment. Niger Delta writers use their literary works as weapons in the fight to decry their marginalization, exploitation, oppression, and the devastation of their environment.

Much as the environment and the ecology of the Niger Delta have generated much interest because of the threat from pollution resulting from the oil and gas exploitation, it is the sociocultural factor that has held together the people of the region. Literature deals with the experience, worldview, sensibility, and other shared values of a people to which the writer responds in a creative manner. Writers generally project a vision out of their people's experiences, and the writers of the Niger Delta often do this in their respective writings. The different ethnic groups of the Niger Delta share in direct or indirect manner Pan-Edo sociocultural traditions. These cultural groups were at the periphery of the Old Benin Empire and were under constant domination and harassment of Old Benin warriors. The traditions of origin of most of the groups, ranging from Ijo, Epiye, and Itsekiri to Urhobo relate to Old Benin, what could be described as Pan-Edo because of the affinity to other groups outside the Niger Delta such as the Bini, Ishan, and Etsako, among others. The Epiye, a small group of people in the Yenagoa area of Bayelsa State, trace their origins to Benin; their language appears to have strong Edo resonance. Deep inside Ijoland, in such places as Brass and Nembe, there are residues of Old Benin culture in names and institutions. The traditional kingship and chieftaincy customs are very much akin to Old Benin. In fact, until the early 1950s some Urhobo kingship contesters went to Benin to seek the seal of approval from the Oba's court to validate their kingship. Thus, there is a cultural matrix of a Pan-Edo nature that covers many aspects of the traditional lives of the Niger Delta people.

The masquerade and many other artistic traditions are highly connected. Niger Deltans, such as some of the inland Urhobo, admit that the masquerade cult came from the waters, which the Ijo, Itsekiri, Ogoni, and the Urhobo perform in almost similar fashion. The drumming style and the songs are similarly close. One very important artistic tradition that cuts across the region is what the Urhobo call "Iphri," the Isoko and some Urhobo call "Ivwri," and the Ijo call "Ifri." This sculptural tradition started during the slave raiding days, when the helpless people sought assistance from their deities to protect them. They thus invoked the divine spirit of resistance so that they could resist the slave raiders and also acquire the ability to escape capture. The people invoked the god of Iphri to "roast" their foes, make them invisible to slave raiders, and give them the resources to escape capture. The spirit of Iphri involves resistance and revenge.

To a large extent, therefore, there has been a warrior spirit among the different groups of the Niger Delta. The traditional sensibility evolved into a spirit of resistance, which outsiders call militancy but which is a form of rebelliousness against subjugation and domination. By invoking the spirit of "Iphri" Niger Delta people challenge a new form of slavery—their resources being taken away from them without consideration for their well-being. This warrior spirit is evoked by the protagonist of Ojaide's *Activist* to get back what has been taken away from his people in the form of oil exploitation. Both Pere and the Activist go into bunkering to subvert the oil companies by reducing their profits. Ojaide observes a certain irony in the oil exploitation by the multinational companies as a form of slavery as the major Niger Delta slave port of old, Escravos, is today Shell's major port of shipping out Niger Delta oil to ports in Europe and North America! The "rebels" in Okpewho's *Tides* also express this spirit of resistance. Of course, in life as in his treatises, Ken Saro-Wiwa expressed the ultimate spirit of resistance against exploitation of the natural resources of his Ogoni and other minority peoples as well as a robust defense of the environment and ecology of the area.

The oral traditions of the region are similar and point to a common origin and shared experiences. Doubtless the similar terrains the people share are bound to evoke similar experiences. Folktales, legends, myths, proverbs, and other aspects of oral tradition are very similar. Somehow the Ogiso legend runs through many of the areas with differing emphases. Tortoise tales and other folktales, as of the beautiful young woman who wants to marry a spotless man, manifest in the folklore of the different groups of the Niger Delta. To a large extent, the plight of the Niger Delta minority groups is played out in trickster tales with the weak depending on their wits to survive among the strong majority groups.

Niger Delta men and women dress about the same way. Since the area was among the earliest to be penetrated by the Portuguese and then the British, the coastal habitation has brought a lot of European products, including wrappers and other "luxuries" such as plates, cutlery, shoes, and gold to the area, from where inland groups got their supplies. Across the region, the women dress in "wrappers" and blouses. Urhobo, Ijo, and Itsekiri men wear Victorian-style shirts and

orature. Tanure Ojaide has borrowed copiously from the udje songs of the Urhobo people, especially in poems directly modeled on the udje satirical form in *Delta Blues and Home Songs*. Here is an example of a poem that carries intrinsically the spirit of udje satiric poetry, which the writer has researched into and which influences many of his poetic compositions:

"Professor Kuta"

I would have kept my peace
if Professor Kuta doesn't parade himself
in a field where he doesn't belong.

A trail of hisses always follows the so-called don.
Robber don, adulterer don, don of nothing learned.
If you know Professor Kuta, you would pity him.
He is a robber masked in an academic gown—
if you don't pay five hundred naira for his three-page handout,
he will fail you even if your head is a computer.
Unless you give five thousand naira to change F to A!
. . .
He professes poverty, professes robbery of young ones,
professes nothing scholarly—no book to his credit;
of the articles he cites in his cv, three appeared
in *The Nigerian Observer* and *The Daily Times*;
the other two paid for and printed in street tabloids.
. . .
I heard from his colleagues that he has no Ph.D.
but an ABD; he thrice flunked his Ed.D. defence.
Who doesn't know some doctors are impostors?
Tell Professor Kuta to bring his transcripts for all to see.
The sort of Professor Kuta would be better for trading
than robbing students in the mantle of a don.

Kuta is not the professor he calls himself.
I would have shut my mouth to his masking,
if he doesn't parade himself as a university don. (76–77)

In the poem the writer employs the form and techniques of the udje satiric form to comment on aspects of Nigerian university life.

In poetry and drama there tends to be a stronger influence of folklore of the Niger Delta people than in fiction, which seems not to bear many of the features of the folktale. However, Elechi Amadi's *The Concubine* touches on the rare type of women said to belong to the gods and who, when married or taken by humans, cause problems for their men because of the jealousy of their supernatural lovers. Amadi uses the Ikwerre variant of the myth to tell an interesting story. The interface of orality and the written Niger Delta literature validates the rootedness of the literary works of the writers in their own culture, which gives a certain identity to these works.

Still on the cultural identity of the literature of the Niger Delta is the invocation of deities of the region. As a result of the omnipresence of water in the area, water spirits and deities are common. The most commonly invoked deity is Mami Wata. In fact, Onookome Okome has a series of Mami Wata poems in his *Pendants*. Other writers invoke or mention this water deity that is supposed to be not only beautiful but also brings fortune to those she loves. J. P. Clark invokes the Ijo Tamara in his plays and poetry and I invoke Aridon, the Urhobo god of memory and poetic inspiration, in my poetry. The invocation of and allusions to these deities affirm the cultural rootedness of the writers who employ their cultural icons and symbols to communicate their feelings and thoughts.

Rootedness in culture in Niger Delta writers is reinforced by evocation of the locale or the physical geography and ecology of the region. The entire landscape of the Niger Delta forms the backdrop of the poems such as Clark's *A Reed in the Tide* and Ojaide's *Labyrinths of the Delta*, plays such as Clark's *Song of a Goat*, *Ozidi*, the Bikoroa plays, and *All for Oil*, and Ahmed Yerima's *Hard Ground*, and fictional works such as Okpewho's *Tides*, Agary's *Yellow-Yellow*, and Ken Saro-Wiwa's *Lemona's Tale*. The poems, plays, and fictional works cited all manifest not only the physical landscape of the Niger Delta but also the sociocultural, political, and economic aspects of the region all of which give the literary works the reality of lived experiences. In each of the plays and novels the center of human activity for the characters is the Niger Delta and the characters do not only reflect Niger Delta names, lifestyles, accents, but also the spirit of the region. The language of characters, as in some of Clark's plays, seems to be a transliteration of the Ijo into English. In *The Voice* Gabriel Okara experiments linguistically in basically Anglicizing the Ijo language to reflect the unique experience of the characters.

It is significant to note the place of Pidgin English in the Niger Delta area. In fact, it is the lingua franca of the people. Originating from the coastal ports of Sapele, Warri, and Port Harcourt, where foreign sailors and Nigerians first met, Pidgin English integrated English and local languages into an effective communicative currency.

Pidgin English spread from the coastal Niger Delta inland to other Nigerian places. While writers from other parts of Nigeria also use Pidgin English, among Niger Delta writers it is mostly deployed to express the dialogue of characters as in Okpewho's *Tides* and Agary's *Yellow-Yellow*, among others. The use of Pidgin English by Niger Delta writers in fiction, poetry, and plays affirms the writers' faith in their people's means of easy communication. Since Pidgin English is mainly spoken by the common people, its use therefore reflects the Niger Delta writers ranging on the side of their people to whom the language has become a sort of lingua franca.

To the Niger Delta writers of these literary works, their region is the center of the universe and the vortex of human existence in all its ramifications. In Ben Okri's *Dangerous Love* and many of his short stories, especially *Stars of the Curfew* and *Incidents at the Shrine*, the Urhobo parts of the Niger Delta become the theater of human experience. In some cases, as in Okpewho's *Tides*, Clark's *All for Oil*, and Ojaide's *The Activist* while the center is the Niger Delta, the region is set against the Federal Nigerian side of which it is a part but a marginalized and exploited one that Niger Deltans want to subvert. One can therefore posit that a Niger Delta work places the region at the center of its literary exploration.

A literature acquires a certain volkgeist which gives it a sense of cohesion. Niger Delta literature exhibits cohesion in expressing the sensibility and mindset that make it uniquely Niger Delta literature. In addition to the cultural identity and shared experiences already discussed, this literature affords the Niger Delta people ample opportunity to share in the experiences of the characters as no other literature, be it Nigerian, African, or world literature can do to the same extent. There is a measure of shared experience between the Niger Delta reader of these works and the characters involved or the experiences and vision expressed by the writers. The recurring themes of exploitation, oppression, marginalization, and resistance, among others, are shared by the Niger Delta person who sees the region's wealth taken to the federal center at the expense of those whose means of livelihood have been negatively impacted by the oil and gas exploration and exploitation. The writers' vision tends to coincide with the sociopolitical, cultural, and economic aspirations of the people of the area and thus reflecting the evolving zeitgeist of the people. Thus, the content and form of the works have a uniqueness that makes them stand out as typically Niger Delta works because of their focus on the area and the Niger Delta perspective or viewpoint expressed in them.

One can observe a certain style and/or form emerging too from this literature. On one level, there is a plaintive and tragic sense as expressed in Clark's *Song of a Goat* and *All for Oil*, Ogbowei's *Song of a Dying River*, Ogaga Ifowodo's *Oil Lamp*, Okpewho's *Tides*, Agary's *Yellow-Yellow* and Ojaide's *Delta Blues and Home Songs* and *The Tale of the Harmattan*. On another level, there is evocation of the past which reflects a sense of nostalgia for the past pristine environment of the area. Consequently, there is lamentation for what is lost and a dirge-like lamentation of the current devastated environment. Protest too appears to be embedded in the viewpoint of the writers who lament marginalization and helplessness.

Let us briefly examine three texts by different authors and see what features make them part of the Niger Delta literary tradition. The three texts are J. P. Clark's *Song of a Goat*, Isidore Okpewho's *Tides*, and Ahmed Yerima's *Hard Ground*. Published in the 1960s *Song of a Goat* is set in the Niger Delta riverine environment with the waterways and wetlands evoked in the dramatic presentation of aquatic life. There are creeks and canoes mentioned. Water is a means not only of transportation but also of sustenance. Tonye has fishing nets and hooks to show his fishing occupation. Fishing is a major occupation of the Niger Delta people. Ebiere wants to go to the market to barter her husband's catch from fishing for other foodstuffs such as farina and starch that the more inland people of the region produce. Farina, also called tapioca, and starch are staple foods of the people. Furthermore, the names of the characters are Ijo names: Tonye, Zifa, Ebiere, and Dode. As common Ijo names, the people and Niger Delta audience of the play can better identify with the characters than those from strange lands whose names make no meaning to them. The play also reflects the folklore of the Niger Delta as in the wrestling activities and the use of sacrifice to appease the gods and cleanse the land after the taboo of a man sleeping with his brother's wife even when the man has lost his manhood. After Zifa kills himself, it is only sacrifice that can cleanse the land of the abomination. Thus, Clark's play carries the features that make it a piece of Niger Delta literature.

Okpewho's *Tides* also easily fits into the Niger Delta literary tradition. The novel is prefaced with an Ijo song. Water is very important as the title suggests. The novel is set in Seiama which is in the Beawotu nation of the Niger Delta. As a result of ethnic chauvinism, the journalists Piriye Dukamo and Tonye Brisibe of Niger Delta origin were unjustly retired. This is the fate of minorities that Niger Delta literature tends to highlight—a seeming powerlessness before the majority groups of the country. The novel focuses on oil exploration and exploitation as well as the reduction of the water going downstream that affects water dams meant to generate electricity and the impact on rural communities that rely on fishing for livelihood. Like Clark's play, the characters' names are Ijo: Piriye, Tonye Brisibe, Zuokumor, and Ebika Harrison, among others. The novel also exposes the corruption of Niger Delta community leaders who deal with the oil companies and the Federal Nigerian Government and shortchange their people in their greed. As for the warrior spirit of revenge, Harrison destroys the bridge, oil pipelines, and Kwararaga dam after his release from detention. Okpewho thus tells what is responsible for the unemployment of Niger Delta people and the reason for the restlessness in the region. It is a literary work that carries the spirit of the Niger Delta and the determination to resist majority oppression as well as exploitation by the oil companies and the Federal Government.

Ahmed Yerima is not an indigene of the Niger Delta but researched to write and produce *Hard Ground* that deals with the so-called militancy of youths in the Niger Delta. In a suspenseful work, the audience/readers wait to know the militant leader, who is an ordinary man with a family and who goes about his duties without being suspected as a militant. The setting is also the Niger Delta with a swampy forest terrain that has crocodiles. Mention is made of a sea goddess and canoe boys. Again, the names are Ijo ones. The play deals with the minority status of the people and their marginalization. The people feeling exploited are involved in the pursuit of environmental justice and mention not only the Ogoni Bill of Rights but also the Kaiama Declaration. Mimi is a "resource rebel" and draws the audience's attention to the relationship between the Federal capital of Lagos and the exploited Niger Delta. The spirit of revenge is expressed in the desire to blow up oil pipelines. The foods, masquerade traditions, traditional medicines, and other sociocultural aspects of the Ijo people are also evoked.

All three texts are illustrative of Niger Delta literature. They all show a Niger Delta setting and context with the characters reflecting the worldview, sensibility, and experiences of the people. The works all have relevance to Niger Delta problems and issues and reflect the historical as well as the sociocultural, political, and economic lives of the people of the region. The fauna and flora of the place are evoked as well as the oral traditions of the people. As minorities, the people struggle for rights that the majority groups in Nigeria take for granted. There is a cultural identity established in these literary works with place names and characters that bear names of Niger Delta ethnicities. The characters speak their indigenous languages or Pidgin

English, which has spread from the Niger Delta into the hinterland of Nigeria. In some specific cases, the writers translate expressions from Niger Delta languages into English as when a man in *The Activist* is asked to "try another leg," meaning he should marry another woman to prove his fertility. In the same work, it is known that the "keeper" of a man's keys is his wife. Okara and Clark have abundance of terms translated from the Ijo language in their respective *The Voice* and plays. Many of the major characters also carry traits of Iphri in their efforts to revenge against or subvert the capacities of their outside oppressors and exploiters.

It is also significant to note a growing intertextuality in Niger Delta literature. As already noted, Yerima's *Hard Ground* refers to Ken Saro-Wiwa's struggle as well as both the Ogoni Bill of Rights and the Kaiama Declaration. Okpewho's *Tides* displays awareness of J. P. Clark's poetry and plays that deal so much with tides. And the intertextuality has come full cycle in Clark's *Full Tide: Collected Poems*, which came out in 2010. Tanure Ojaide alludes to Clark's borrowing of the concept of a goat-song from the Greeks to convey a sense of lamentation or tragedy in "The goat-song," the opening poem of *The Tale of the Harmattan*. Also in the same poem there is reference to Ozidi that Clark exposed to non-Ijo readers of his works. As more textual studies of literary works are carried out, more intertextual connections in Niger Delta literature are bound to be found, especially of younger writers acknowledging or echoing the works of their elders.

There is no doubt that Niger Delta literature is a localized literary tradition, an attribute which can limit its appeal or be a source of strength depending upon the use the writers make of this region. If the writers focus exclusively on the Niger Delta region without extending their vision to all humanity and others suffering the same plight such as marginalization, exploitation, and environmental degradation, then the literature will not gain traction with time. However, if the writers use that piece of the earth to explore the complexities of life and humanity, then the literature will be extolled for its universality and humanity despite the specific setting. The local should be able to reflect the global, universal, and human to endure in literature as works of classic writers do worldwide. Niger Delta literature has the opportunities to make the global local as its local global. This is a literature that has been galvanized by globalization and its media forces especially in the environmental and minority rights campaign of Ken Saro-Wiwa and the growing worldwide interest in climate change and eco awareness. In the Niger Delta literary tradition, therefore, one can see the globalization of Niger Delta issues as well as the glocalization of world issues. These two opposite directions have the potential to create tension that could be the source of literary strength.

In conclusion, there is no doubt that there is a Niger Delta literature that is produced mainly by the indigenes of the area touched by their land and by outsiders who sympathize with the Niger Delta cause; all the writers attempt to interrogate the Niger Delta experience and, in differing degrees of passion and commitment, each brings out what he or she considers uppermost in the literary exploration of this Niger Delta experience. One should not be accused of essentialism in this preliminary definition because there are features in other literatures which make them unique. The Niger Delta literature is steeped in the oral traditions and folklore of the people and has acquired more intensity with sociocultural connections and the newly picked up theme of environmental and ecological degradation that globalization and the world climate change have helped to promote. It is a literature that though unique is part not only of Nigerian but also of African literatures and by being part of those literatures is postcolonial. As a new literature, one cannot easily foretell its future as a Niger Delta indigene, Goodluck Ebele Jonathan, has assumed political leadership of Nigeria and thus reducing the political marginalization of the region. While a lot of damage has been done to the environment, some of the oil companies have admitted their culpability and promised to be more efficient in controlling their exploration and exploitation to avoid damage to the environment and ecology. Another decade will show in fuller light what has now acquired certain aggregates of a unique literature that can be described as Niger Delta literature.

CHAPTER 5

Chinua Achebe's *Things Fall Apart* in World Literature

Very few authors enter into the canon of World Literature and Chinua Achebe is one of the very few African authors in that category. His debut novel, *Things Fall Apart*, is in that privileged position of being acknowledged as a world classic. Doubtless so much has been written on Achebe's classic whose fiftieth year anniversary (published 1958) was celebrated all over the world some years ago. After the renowned Nigerian author's death on March 21, 2013, most of the tributes to the author mentioned his first and best known novel, *Things Fall Apart*. There is much in that novel that elicits a multiplicity of critical responses but despite the wealth of controversies, debates, praises, and other forms of critical discourse relating to the work, it is still very much open to more critical responses. *Things Fall Apart* is not just taught in World Literature classes but also published in Norton's Anthology of World Literature and also in the Norton Series of World Literature texts. The novel has been translated into more than 50 languages. The focus of this chapter is to examine *Things Fall Apart* as a World Literature text. Why is it often used in a course on World Literature and what does its inclusion in that canon mean? Chinua Achebe has, in writing *Things Fall Apart*, inscribed African culture through its Igbo variant into the canvas of world culture.

The concept of world literature has been evolving for about a century. Westerners used to see world literature as the assembly of their literatures across nations and times. However, European colonial adventures at the beginning of the twentieth century expanded literature in the creative works produced in the colonies. Also a growing desire to know about others led to awareness of other literatures as of China and Japan. Frank N. Magill sees world literature as "representative of the places and the times" from which they spring (v). In this concept, by the middle of the twentieth century, world literature had grown to involve the literatures of the countries and times one did not know. In fact, what used to be *Literature Abroad* published by the University of Oklahoma, Norman, became *World Literaure Today*. It is this concept of world literature that is extended to refer to literary works now accessible outside their nations of origin into a wider world of readership. What used to be North American and Western European masterpieces now incorporates literary masterpieces from other parts of the world. Achebe's *Things Fall Apart* thus falls into literature of another "country" outside the West.

However, there are other aspects to the concept of world literature. Steven R. Serafin in *Encyclopedia of World Literature in the 20ᵗʰ Century* notes that it is the works of writers that make "significant literary contribution" and "work of popular interest and critical importance" (xxix) that are described as world literature. These attributes are embedded in the high artistic value of a work and the influence of such a work on the human mind. A literary work makes its mark in time and place before its being translated and made accessible beyond its cultural or national borders. While world literature used to be mainly Greek and Roman classics and the literatures of major Western powers, it has opened up to literatures of other lands. Factors that have led to the opening up of world literature include the globalization of the world economy and increased migration in the world from the 1980s through the 1990s. *The Norton Anthology of World Masterpieces* (1956) that featured only Western European and North American works expanded and changed in 1995 to *The Norton Anthology of World Literature* that includes many non-Western writings. Longman, Bedford, and other major publishers now have their own editions of world literature.

As a result of the multiplicity of cultures involved in world literature, there have also arisen a variety of ways to define what constitutes world literature. For instance, traditional African literature tends to be functional, quite unlike Western literature which is more of art for art's sake. Many theories have thus been brought to bear on the definition of world literature. David Damrosch, in *What Is World Literature?* (2003), uses translatability to define world literature. To him, works that when translated gain in meaning and other ways, constitute world literature. From his argument, it is not a canonical connection but the more a literary work is circulated and received outside its cultural context, the more it meets the requirements of world literature. The French critic, Pascale Casanova, in *La République mondiale des lettres* (1999) defines world literature as works of "peripheral writers" coming to circulate in metropolitan centers. In that case, Third World literary works that are well received in metropolitan places like the United Kingdon, France, and the United States become world literature. Of course, *Things Fall Apart*, the work of a writer from a formerly colonized country (Nigeria) that circulates in metropolitan countries, is world literature.

Since many World Literature texts are translations, Gayatri Chakravorty Spivak argues that a literary work suffers in the effort to be part of world literature in the sense of its translation and its being removed from the place where it is set or for which the work is written. With varying types of translators, a world literature text loses its linguisitic richness and compexity when translated into another language. She also feels that the political force of a work could be lost in its being read or studied outside the political space in which and for which it is written. However, a good literary work has the power to overcome these limitations. World literature that was once studied in Europe and North America is now studied all over the world and has become a means not only of peering into serious issues of other cultures but also of affirming universality and common humanity.

Chinua Achebe's novel is in English which is informed by a subtext of Igbo language and folklore. As already noted, it has been translated into so many foreign languages. It has done well in circulation and is a work from the periphery of the world brought into the limelight of metropolitan cultures. It no doubt has "exemplary artistic value" and its influence on the "development of humankind" and of literature(s) of the world is acknowledged. It represents the African region on the world stage. According to Amy Sickels in "The Critical Reception of *Things Fall Apart*," the "language of the novel has not only intrigued critics but has also been a major factor in the emergence of the modern African novel" (6). *Things Fall Apart* deserves its World Literature status.

One can say that metaphorically *Things Fall Apart* is a literary coin; one side reflecting indigenous African ways and the other side reflecting European colonialist/imperialist mentality. There is that tension in the novel with these two contrary but connected discourses of colonialism and indigeneity of a historical experience. One is not complete without the other and each stands in bold relief against the other in the author's historicist approach. One can deduce that Chinua Achebe wrote *Things Fall Apart* with two audiences and for two main reasons in mind: the African and the European. He has openly written about these issues in his essays and interviews. On the one hand, he writes that "Africans did not hear of culture for the first

time from Europeans…Their cultures were not mindless but frequently had a philosophy of great depth and value and beauty…they
had poetry and, above all, they had dignity" (qtd. in Killam 8).
In the interview with Bill Moyers, he talks about "much that was
thrown overboard that should not have been" with Africans abandoning their ways and accepting the European ways sold to them as
superior to theirs. Furthermore, he told Bill Moyers that Europeans
did not bring democracy to the African countries they colonized
but in fact brought colonial dictatorship and that there was democracy among the Igbo and other African peoples before the coming
of Europeans to the African continent. In his seminal essay, "The
Novelist As Teacher," he writes that his major mission as a writer is
"to help my society regain belief in itself and put away the complexes
of the years of denigration and self-abasement" (Achebe 44). He thus
wants to make his African people regain confidence in themselves
after colonialism made people doubt themselves psychologically and
emotionally. Seeing the novelist as a teacher, Achebe wants his fellow
Africans to know "that their past—with all its imperfections—was
not one long night of savagery from which the first Europeans acting on God's behalf delivered them" (45). These various comments
speak to two major things: exhorting his African people to have self-
confidence and condemning the European colonization of Africa. He
basically debunked the Western rationale for colonialism of attempting to civilize Africa instead of the economic and political reality of
colonialism. One is thus not surprised about the white man's so-called
burden being self-inflicted because of the inevitable consequences of
a selfish economic and political enterprise that still reverberates across
independent African countries till today.

Things Fall Apart is thus written as a counter discourse to the imperial literature of the likes of Joseph Conrad in *Heart of Darkness,* Joyce
Cary in *Mister Johnson,* and the works and ideas of their kind. Achebe
admits to writing "applied art" to make a point. To him, any African
writer who writes art for art's sake will become irrelevant to his people.
He thus uses art to fight on his people's behalf. Since, for instance,
Conrad's and Cary's works portray Africans as one-dimensional characters and not realistic, Achebe deploys his narrative talents to portray
Africans as he experienced them as kinsmen and women in his work.
According to him, "the story we [Africans] had to tell would not be
told for us by anyone else, no matter how gifted or well-intentioned"
(*Morning Yet On Creationd Day*123). Bearing in mind his home audi-
ence, the Nigerian author wants his African readers to identify with the

characters that he creates and are like them and share the same culture and society that are continually changing from within and from outside pressures. He uses the Igbo language with its wealth of proverbs and other tropes to show the importance of orality in this nonliterate culture. When he says that proverbs are the palm oil with which words are eaten, he is saying the obvious among the Igbo people.

At the same time, in this work, Achebe is telling the foreign writers about their being blinded by European imperialism and racism from seeing other people for what they really are: neither devils nor angels but just human beings with virtues and foibles. Achebe is in fact condemning the Hegelian principles that Conrad, Cary, and other imperialists adopted despite their so-called agenda of enlightenment. To Achebe, these European writers having their works set in Africa are not better than Trevor-Roper and Hegel who saw Africa as mere gyrations of history, a tabula rasa having no history and no culture. By casting Africans as "the Other," the Europeans are attempting to justify their negative practices of racism and exploitation of the weak, in this case colonizing Africa under the pretext of civilizing and Christianizing its people. Achebe, more than any other African writer, has been able to excoriate the conscience of Europeans who window-dress their economic and materialistic greed with false moral justifications.

According to Abiola Irele, "The work [*Things Fall Apart*] has acquired the status of a classic, then, by reason of its character as a counterfiction of Africa, in specific relation to the discourse of Western colonial domination, and its creative deployment of the language of the imperium; it has on this account been celebrated as the prototype of what Barbara Harlow has called 'resistance literature.'" *Things Fall Apart* is a damning critique of European colonization of Africa. Achebe portrays the arrogance of those who feel that their way is the only way. Two contrasting issues are involved in the European arrogance. The Europeans whose civilization is based on Judeo-Christian culture want others to abandon their ways of life to emulate theirs in colonial policies. They believe that their way is the only right way to do things; hence "the other" ascribed to the non-European. Achebe also tells Bill Moyers of Christianity talking of one way to salvation, which he disputes with an Igbo proverb that says that where one thing stands there is bound to be another! Ironically, the Igbo people believe that there are more than one way to things, a belief which castigates the unipolar vision of the European as not based on human experience that the proverb affirms.

The European characters in *Things Fall Apart* are meant to bring out what the European *is* to the African. There is a disconnection between the self-promoting image of a Christian and civilized race that is attempting to civilize a savage race and the actions and thoughts of that person. Incidents of treachery, dishonesty of the whites and the humiliation the colonialists inflicted on Africans as those invited to meet the district officer being arrested do not show them as Christians and civilized. The table is turned upside down when one thinks of what obtained in both *Heart of Darkness* and *Mister Johnson*. The callous and insensitive district officer could care less about the death of a great Igbo man, Okonkwo. Obierika and others may consider him great and driven to take his own life by the activities of the colonialists but the cold-blooded and calculating district officer is only thinking of the book he is planning to write on the pacification of the people of the Lower Niger and the space he would devote to it! Achebe thus questions the humanity of the white man in his dealings with others which did not stop with enslaving Africans but also colonizing them for his personal economic profit. This counter discourse of the Hegelian and colonialist ideas portrays the Europeans as being Africa's burden.

Achebe insists that Africans would have developed in their own ways if left alone by the Europeans who used the might of their firepower as a right to subdue and subjugate others. Europeans disrupted Africa's development since change was taking place within African culture before the Western intrusion. As represented in *Things Fall Apart*, many harsh aspects of the Igbo culture were changing even before the arrival of the foreigners. For instance, the punishment for breaking the Week of Peace was no longer dragging the culprit on the ground till he died but a seven-year exile that Okonkwo would survive. There were already grumblings or unease with the throwing away of twin babies by such people as Obierika, Nwoye, and Uchendu before the Europeans came. Such questioning of negative practices would eventually lead to their being changed or abandoned totally. By implication, Achebe is blaming the Europeans for Africa's woes because of their interrupting the way of life of the people which would have continued in its inevitable path of sociocultural transformation.

Achebe uses the plight of the Igbo under colonial rule to represent European disruption of areas across Africa. European colonial policies stagnated and underdeveloped Africa. *Things Fall Apart* is only a slice of European atrocities in Africa. The punitive expedition to wipe out Abame is similar to the historical sacking of Benin in 1897 because one or two British soldiers were killed when they resisted the Oba's order that he would not receive any foreign visitors. The Belgians, under King Leopold, devastated Congo in their greed for rubber and ivory. That one person bought a whole African country bigger than his own country shows the nature of European greed. The Portuguese had their own exploits in their African colonies and Wiriyamu in Mozambique is known for its massacre too.

As Achebe has said of the Igbo way of looking at things, where there is one thing there is bound to be another. For long, World Literature was taught as Western Literature from the Ancient to the Modern. However, the inclusion of works from Africa and other cultural areas outside of Europe shows a readiness to see a common humanity enriched by difference. Europeans in their unadmitted guilt about colonialism, after their anthropologists have exacerbated the concept of the "Other," wanted to know more about other peoples to validate their own humanity. After Africans have helped liberate France and the British to fight Fascists, they knew that people facing danger were the same. All humans thirsted for freedom and dignity and that there was a common humanity on earth. *Things Fall Apart* came out after Britain had boasted that the sun would never set on its empire! But that was the time that also fanned the winds of change. The novel can thus be seen as a window through which one knows Africa and Africans; this window was constructed by an African who provided the outsider the lenses with which to see the people and the part of the world he knew so well. It is the work of an African affirming African humanity. In postcolonial discourse, *Things Fall Apart* can be seen not only as a critique of European inhumanity but a defense of African humanity through the Igbo way of life before and at the beginning of European disruption of African life.

Achebe presents the normal happenings in society before the coming of Europeans. The hardworking Igbo people went about their farming and practicing their social and religious ways. They had their annual calendar with a time for work and a time for relaxation. They had their festivals and had their prohibitions as against the use of violence during the Week of Peace. Long before modern nations started to designate a particular day or week for something such as Earth Day and so forth, the Igbo in their thoughtfulness centuries earlier had set aside a Week of Peace! Any infraction by anyone irrespective of his social rank was met with punishment; hence a great farmer and person as Okonkwo was still subjected to the punishment of breaking a communal edict. The ideas of nobody being above the law, the sense of communality of helping one in need, one rising to greatness despite parenthood, the representation of the old, women, and youths in the ruling of Umuofia, and other virtues of the community indicate a social stage in human evolution and development that Europeans, despite their craft in firearms, had not attained at that time. Then and now one's birth in Britain mattered as the hullaballoo in Prince Andrew's marriage and having a child! Who is he other than the grandson of Queen Elizabeth II and the second in the line of succession? The Queen is the Head of the Anglican Church and one asks what spirituality does she possess to head a church when compared to Chielo, the priestess of the Umuofia people? What democracy is there in the House of Lords other than a gathering of the thoroughbred of English society? Again, to repeat Achebe's words, there was genuine democracy before the coming of Europeans to Africa. Thus, the Europeans had and still have a lot to learn from Africa through its presentation by a knowledgeable African.

Things Fall Apart exhibits the complexity of Igbo culture through its cosmology, ontology, and epistemology. The Igbo are a people who are balanced and not fanatical. They do not appropriate to themselves the total wisdom of humanity as the Europeans presume for themselves. Like the Ashanti, the Igbo people believe that each human being or group has a good share of human wisdom from the pot of wisdom that broke and scattered! So, where there is one thing, there is bound to be another! The Igbo acknowledge the knowledge of others but believe in theirs. Achebe thus provides another image of Africa from the colonial one. Abiola Irele in his seminal essay, "The Crisis of Cultural Memory in Chinua Achebe's *Things Fall Apart*," cites the sophistication of Igbo thought in the destruction of Okonkwo's house following the accidental killing of the young man. Even Obierika, his best friend, took part. According to Achebe, "They had no hatred in their hearts against Okonkwo. They were merely cleansing the land which Okonkwo had polluted with the blood of a clansman" (*Things Fall Apart* 88).

The belief in the androgynous nature of human beings and things indicates another aspect of the sophistication of the Igbo culture. Though still staunchly patriarchal in sociocultural practice, there seems embedded in the same culture a sense of androgyny. The Igbo people see the male complementing the female and vice versa. As shown in the characters of Ezinma in *Things Fall Apart* and Beatrice in *Anthills of the Savannah*, the girl should have some masculinity to be a successful being. The same holds for a man who should have some female qualities. Where there is too much of one in the other, it becomes a problem as with Okonkwo who is too masculine in being a man of action and not of thought. Similarly, his father,

Unoka, though a man has too much of the female principle in him. Okonkwo's anxiety about his son Nwoye is because of his perception of the boy being too "weak" for a man. His sorrow of fire begetting cold ash is his interpretation of his fate of having what he considers an unworthy son. The novelist wants outsiders to know the type of complex society that the Igbo one is.

A close reading of the novel shows the importance of the female principle since too much manliness in Okonkwo is destructive. In fact, the female principle is nurturing unlike the male one that is destructive. Chielo, Ezinma, and Uchendu's speaking of "Nneka" (Mother is supreme) all tell the importance of the female principle. Okonkwo's life is ironically spared after killing the young man because it is a "female offense." As put succinctly by Irele: "The male–female dialectic thus serves to maintain effective and ideological balance of the group; in this, it corresponds to a certain primary perception of a felt duality of the cosmic order as a principle of the universal imaginary" (8). There is the nuance in naming the setting of the novel *Umuofia*, bush place. It is ironical that the so-called bush people of Africa in the Hegelian reasoning could be so sophisticated in their thoughts and ways!

Things Fall Apart is not only an African classic but an integral part of World Literature because of its comparative discourse. A few examples will suffice here. The concept of tragedy is amplified as not just the Aristotelian, Shakespearean, or modern but also African. Okonkwo rose by dint of hard work and circumstances to be one of the greatest men in Umuofia. However, he was a man of action and not of thought! After being acknowledged by the community as a great man in his wrestling prowess, his large household, and farming, he began to question his own "chi." He believed, against Igbo reasoning, that he was the one destined to do what others would not do; hence his taking part in the killing of Ikemefuna who called him "father." In this African tragedy, the killing of this young man who called him father and whom he loved more than his biological son haunted him the rest of his life. His life took a downturn for the worse immediately after because he would break the Week of Peace and be exiled from where his greatness used to be acknowledged. His eventual suicide after things had so changed that he was no longer in agreement with the new thinking of his people made him take precipitate action to kill the court messenger rather than wait for the communal decision. Rather than be humiliated, as he surely realized after the act, he went to take his own life. Suicide is often seen as a form of cowardice, an inability to face the consequences of one's actions. But suicide could be a way of avoiding humiliation and asserting one's own dignity. When Japanese soldiers killed themselves rather than be captured by the enemy, the action is praised as an act of fortitude. I think Achebe wanted Okonkwo to remain with some sense of dignity rather than be further humiliated by being executed by the foreign occupiers of his land.

Things Fall Apart does well in World Literature because of the resonance of certain episodes in other cultures. Achebe was the son of a pastor and was named Albert not just for the British Empire but more importantly to signify his conversion to Christianity. In fact, Irele sees Chinua Achebe as a "Westernized African" in the way he writes as if distancing himself from his own people on certain occasions. That is the "disjunction" Irele sees in Achebe "between condemning colonialists and the ambiguous presentation of the African culture." As he puts it, "one cannot fail to discern a thematic undercurrent, which produces a disjunction in the novel between its overt ideological statement, its contradiction of the discourse of the colonial ideology, on one hand, and on the other, its dispassionate and even uncompromising focus on an African community in its moment of historical crisis" (456). The novelist appears as an external observer when he writes that "Fortunately among these people a man was judged according to his worth and not to the worth of his father" (6). In any case, Achebe was a highly Western educated African. He was very knowledgeable as far as the Bible was concerned. One can see the comparison between Abraham's sacrifice of his son to Okonkwo's sacrifice of who called him father. In the Bible, Abraham submits his son without any hesitation but Okonkwo is advised by both Obierika and the oldest man in the community not to take part in the killing of Ikemefuna. Ikemefuna's sacrifice is demanded to consecrate the truce after an Umuofia man killed a lady from another town and the peace reached demanded the guilty side surrender a virgin to be wife of the man whose wife was killed and Ikemefuna to be given to Umuofia folks for eventual sacrifice to their god. Okonkwo could accept his "son" being sacrificed without his personally taking part in the act. It is the arrogance that if he did not take part, who else would do it that doomed him. And when the young man ran to him for protection, crying out to him "They kill me, father," the dazed Okonkwo gave the killing blow! To the Igbo, horrendous as the death of Ikemefuna is after being used to the Okonkwo family and loved, it was meant to solidify the peace agreement already reached.

The controversy over sacrificing Ikemefuna is comparable to the practice in Old Oyo of the Elesin willing himself to death, a form of suicide, for communal peace. Though Elesin does not do so in Wole Soyinka's *Death and the King's Horseman*, it was meant for the stability of the state so that the powerful Elesin did not usurp power after the death of Aalafin. Sacrifice or self-sacrifice in both Achebe's *Things Fall Apart* and Soyinka's *Death and the King's Horseman* involves sacrificing the individual for the community's good. In the West, there are numerous examples from bombing to other horrendous actions done in a sanitized way and made to look clinical so as to avoid the guilt involved. In any case, the sacrifice of Ikemefuna, as of Elesin Oba, brings into perspective the comparative cultural understanding of concepts present in various cultures in the world.

Chinua Achebe's genius is responsible for his debut novel being appropriated into the canon of World Literature. The subtlety in fictional characters expressing themselves in Igbo language in a traditional Igbo society is done with such finesse that in diction *Things Fall Apart* stands out in creating a different type of English from the British or other types of English in the world. Achebe's is English with Igbo linguistic particularities in semantics, syntax, and other qualities. There is linguistic mediation in writing in English what the Igbo characters are saying. This diversification of the English language is done with such success that calls for the novel's world literature status. One can say that Achebe has used proverbs the most of world writers. With the proverbs, he is able to infuse into the text the wisdom of the Igbo people and the orthodoxy of the spoken word in a nonliterate society.

Also *Things Fall Apart* establishes brilliantly the interface between orality and literacy. With the use of proverbs, folktales, songs, and myths, Achebe converts what had hitherto been the preserve of writing into a smooth interface. The work shows that the oral and the written are not mutually exclusive of each other and each can advance the literary aims of the other. *Things Fall Apart* is a unique novel because of the dexterous way that Achebe has deployed Igbo folklore into English expressions. His use of images is remarkable, especially calling the white people locusts, Okonkwo a kind of tortoise who benefited from the community but does not want to obey its dictates, and so forth.

In this Achebe's novel the concept of the glocal is affirmed as the local is made global in its being translated into over 50 languages and studied in schools and universities worldwide from South Africa to Russia, Australia, the United States, and Canada, and so many other places. It is a text that is used in anthropology, sociology, literature, history, political science, religious studies, cultural studies, Africana

Studies, and so many departments in the Western academy. The use of cultural tropes of kola nut, palm wine, yam, and others establishes the cultural norms of the Igbo people; hence, according to Irele, the work provides "an image of a coherent social structure forming the institutional fabric of a universe of meanings and values" (1). A younger Igbo author, Chris Abani, would model his *GraceLand* almost a half century after the publication on these Igbo cultural icons that Achebe displayed in *Things Fall Apart*. And Chimamanda Ngozi Adichie would also a half century later in her *Purple Hibiscus* tell through Pa Nnukwu another variant of the tortoise story.

Above all, *Things Fall Apart* addresses the relativity of social norms worldwide. There is a common humanity expressed in different places. Life becomes a type of masquerade dance and one observes it from one's vantage point. Achebe has made it from the Igbo space and one has to move from one vantage point to another in discourse to get a full view of life expressed in *Things Fall Apart*. Achebe has done the representation of the African experience of life in traditional times and in a period of transition in a very memorable manner for the world to marvel at.

SECTION II

CHAPTER 6

After the Nobel Prize: Wole Soyinka's Poetic Output

It has become a truism many literary scholars believe that nobody writes better after winning the Nobel Prize for Literature. While this could be true of most writers who won the prize at the zenith of their writing careers or had peaked in their writings, there are exceptions whose writings, at least in one of the genres they practice, surpass in creative strength their pre-Nobel achievements in that particular genre. Doubtless, some writers win the Nobel Prize toward the end of their lives or careers and might have gone into creative menopause. However, in recent times, Derek Walcott's *White Egrets* has won the T. S. Eliot Prize, Britain's most prestigious award for poetry, long after he won the Nobel Prize. Walcott's collection of poems on ageing and dying is described as "a moving, risk-taking and technically flawless book by a great poet" (*The Independent on Sunday*, January 25, 2011).

Wole Soyinka may not have had the same output overall as before he won the Nobel Prize because his dramatic and fiction output is slim and not with the same prolific rate and creative energy as before. There is nothing Soyinka has published in drama since 1986 that compares to the dramatic success of *Death and the King's Horseman*, a play whose poetic drama of existence the Nobel Committee specifically cited for the award. Nor has he produced plays of the stature of *A Dance of the Forests*, *The Road*, or *Kongi's Harvest* since 1986 when he won the Nobel Prize for Literature. *A Play of Giants*, *From Zia with Love*, and *King Babu* have not had the success of the earlier plays. The dearth of output since the Nobel award is far more acute in fiction. Soyinka has brought out no fictional work since receiving the Nobel award and so his fictional works remain *The Interpreters* (1965) and *Season of Anomie* (1973). He has come out with a nonfictional work, *You Must Set Forth at Dawn*, a prose work that compares with *Ake: Years of Childhood* and *Isara* even though one might argue that it does not possess the former's poetic lyricism.

It is in poetry, however, that Soyinka has produced two major works that appear to be not only the culmination of his poetic writing career but also offer new vistas in vision and techniques to his poetic writing. These two post-Nobel poetry collections are: *Mandela's Earth and Other Poems* (1988) and *Sarmakand and Other Markets I Have Known* (2002). These two literary works represent Soyinka not only covering what he has been for so long associated with as a poet but also at his peak and shedding many of the "euromodernitst" features that clutter such earlier works as *Idanre and Other Poems* and *A Shuttle in the Crypt*. This chapter aims to discuss these two poetic works in comparison to Soyinka's earlier works and situate them in the poet's overall literary achievements. The chapter also opines that a writer can do more in a chosen genre even after winning the Nobel Prize for Literature.

Both *Mandela's Earth and Other Poems* and *Sarmakand and Other Markets I Have Known* are powerful poetic works that place Wole Soyinka on a very high pedestal in contemporary African poetry. It is not that Soyinka was not recognized as a poet before their publications, even though his poetry has always been in the shadow of his plays. However, his pre-Nobel poetry has been a source of controversy, especially since Chinweizu and others launched a vitriolic attack on his poetry in their *Toward the Decolonization of Modern African Literature* in 1983. Many critics have continued to harp on his "obscurantist" tendencies in those pre-Nobel poems. But Soyinka is an artist who is very aware that culture is not static, and, since literature is a cultural production, his writing is not static. The post-Nobel writings of Soyinka, especially his poetry, are the result of a dynamic artistic evolution that represents the poet's continued development, maturity, experience, and ability to relate vision or content to form or craft. These new poems generally do not suffer from the "euromodernist disease" that Chinweizu and others accuse Soyinka of. These later poems are generally elevated but not bombastic and combine a sharp vision of humanity and society with a refined artistic craft that make the poetry appealing in what Mazisi Kunene, in an interview with Dike Okoro, calls "heavy stuff" instead of the padded "light stuff" of many contemporary Western and African poets. These poems seem to be a strengthening of the poetic gains of *A Shuttle in the Crypt*, his prison poems, and *Ogun Abibiman* in which he presents his revolutionary vision anchored on Ogun, the Yoruba god of war as well as of creation and destruction, and Shaka, the Zulu leader who built a state through military exploits.

Of course, *Mandela's Earth and Other Poems* follows *Ogun Abibiman* rather naturally as in that volume Soyinka moves from the antiapartheid struggle in South Africa and the Mozambican President Samora Machel's declaration of war against apartheid to celebrating the strong will and heroism of Nelson Mandela, who has become the icon of the antiapartheid movement. There, too, he condemns acts of inhumanity done by apartheid and such an African leader as Sergeant Samuel Doe of Liberia. *Sarmakand and Other Markets I Have Known* builds on the struggle for justice and humanity as well as a sharper sensitivity to social issues. These later poems do not celebrate individuality the way poems in *Idanre and Other Poems* have done, especially in the "lone figure" section of that collection. The focus is no longer just the individual personality, whether it is of abiku (the wanderer-child), the archetypes, or others but more of the entire society/community and humanity. The sagely poet of the last two collections is not so much interested in individuality but the freedom of a people and the entire humanity, which he seeks through the condemnation of all oppressive regimes and the flaunting of a red flag on the menace of religious fanaticism.

The post-Nobel poems draw from the experience of the prison poems of *A Shuttle in the Crypt* to express solidarity with the oppressed of the world, fellow writers, and a general sensitivity unparalleled in the earlier poems. In *Sarmakand and Other Markets I Have Known*, Soyinka writes about his country and shows patriotic concerns about the direction of his Nigerian state. These poems interrogate the Nigerian sociopolitical situation as done in the crisis poems of *Idanre* and many of the poems of *A Shuttle in the Crypt.* Here in the latest collection, there is a strong sense of patriotism even as the poet reaches out to the rest of the world and humanity. As will be covered in the discussion, Soyinka also hones his craft to a higher level in these later poems and they embody a style that is assured, experienced, and flowing smoothly as the poet communicates his feelings and ideas. He uses oral traditional techniques and Yoruba folklore to explore his chosen themes. There seems to be a more artful and effortless use of oral traditions blended with Western allusions and references, which make the poet rooted in his Yoruba/African environment while retaining the option, when necessary, of drawing allusions from wherever possible to express his feelings and thought. These new poems thus embody and stretch further the strengths of the earlier poems while eliminating or diminishing such weaknesses of his early poetic career such as contrived rhymes and alliterations, conscious poeticism, obscure and difficult allusions and references, and, of course, the "euromodernist disease."

Mandela's Earth and Other Poems came out in 1988 as Soyinka enjoyed the copious afterglow of the Nobel award. It is significant to note that the collection came out before the release of Nelson Mandela from Robben Island, where he had been incarcerated for his antiapartheid activities in the African National Congress (ANC) for some 26 years. It was thoughtful, prophetic, and timely that Soyinka's collection came out a year before his release and his becoming the first African president of a democratic South Africa in 1994. The collection drew attention to the African National Congress's icon and helped to embarrass the wielders of apartheid in South Africa. Poems such as "Your Logic Frightens Me" and "'No!' He Said" extol Mandela's stoic resistance of apartheid and the efforts being used to sway him from his stubborn resistance of injustice. The poet says, "Your logic frightens me, Mandela, your logic / Humbles me" (4). In "'No!' He Said" the poet also praises Mandela's indomitable will despite the harsh and lonely environment of Robben Island and the promise of material comfort outside prison. Furthermore, Samora Machel's rapprochement with South Africa and the rise of a Black elite class in the Bantustans are conditions that would in an ordinary person weaken the ANC leader's resolve to accept conditional freedom. However, Mandela stubbornly resists because he sees such concessions as diversionary tactics meant to frustrate his struggle for black freedom (Ojaide 112). Mandela's steadfastness is daunting:

> Through every turbulence, spectator of our Brave New World.
> Come, Ancient Mariner, but—no, he said—
>
> *No!* I am no prisoner of this rock, this island,
> No ash spew on Milky Ways to conquests old or new.
> . . .
> In and out of time warp, I am that rock
> In the black hole of the sky. (23)

Many people will argue that literature does not matter, but, to others, literature matters a lot and Soyinka's *Mandela's Earth*, in its own way, contributed to the psychological warfare against the wielders of white minority rule in South Africa at the time in much the same way that Dennis Brutus's poems did. When *Mandela's Earth* came out,

Tanure Ojaide had written: "*Mandela's Earth and Other Poems* may not be Soyinka's last poems, but they will remain a fitting culmination of his poetic work so far. It combines the light-hearted playfulness of observations of individuals and society abroad and the highly critical condemnation of negative sociopolitical practices of tyranny, injustice, oppression, and exploitation" (Ojaide 123).

In the earlier poems, except the very early ones written while in England as a student or worker, Soyinka focuses on sociopolitical happenings in Nigeria. In the "October '66" section of *Idanre*, the poet deals with the political crisis in Nigeria in 1966, the political violence in his own Western Region and the killings of Nigerians of Igbo extraction in the predominantly Muslim Northern part of Nigeria. Both "Harvest of Hate" and "Massacre October '66" are representative of these poems in which the poet is very much involved and concerned about the events that led to the civil war that resulted in the deaths of so many Nigerians, especially of Igbo people. In the early poems, Soyinka continues to be steeped in his Yoruba folklore; hence the title poem of the collection, "Idanre," deals with Ogun that Soyinka describes as "God of Iron and metallurgy, Explorer, Artisan, Hunter, God of war, Guardian of the Road, the Creative Essence. His season is harvest and the rains" (*Collected Poems*, 89). Ogun is thus the god of war and destruction as well as of creativity. In *A Shuttle in the Crypt* the poet reflects on his own incarceration during the Nigerian Civil War and how he survived the inhumanity meted on him in solitary confinement. From his personal experience of tyrannical rule of a military dictator, he is impressed and inspired by Samora Machel's symbolic declaration of war against apartheid, which inspired *Ogun Abibiman*, a quasi-epic poem in which the poet summons the spirit of Ogun and the heroism of Shaka Zulu to inspire victims of apartheid to fight for their liberation. Soyinka here uses Yoruba folklore to deal with a problem outside of Nigeria, and this time the South African apartheid problem. In his last collection before the Nobel, Soyinka had stretched his field of imagination from the Nigerian political scene to the African sociopolitical landscape to involve the apartheid then in South Africa as his subject of poetic inquiry. He has raised the stakes of his revolutionary ethos, quest for justice, and political freedom by calling on Africans to rise against the inhuman practice of apartheid perpetrated by the white minority regime in South Africa.

Mandela's Earth in a way is Soyinka's poetic window to the outside world, which he will intensify in *Sarmakand and Other Markets I Have Known*. It is a broadening and deepening of the humanity and quest for justice that had occupied him in the Nigerian political scene in the crisis poems. It is not surprising that in addition to poems on Nelson Mandela, there are poems on Liberia whose dictator then, Samuel Doe, would himself face a savage death. The poem condemning Doe's tyranny, "The Apotheosis of Master Sergeant Doe," is an extension of the poet's condemnation of the Nigerian military leader during the Civil War, Yakubu Gowon. "New York, USA" is part of Soyinka's widening trajectory of humanity; a playful poem in which the poet pokes fun at the shallowness of American culture. As written elsewhere, "New York, USA" "affirms the poet's response to his immediate environment, even if it is an alien one…the poet does not approve of the social behavior and values of the American society. He is against its artificiality, glibness and trivializing of serious things" (Ojaide 118).

Since the Nobel award confers authority on its recipient, by the time a writer wins the literary award his or her vision and craft are validated and the writer assumes the status of a master and sage in the field. With *Mandela's Earth*, Wole Soyinka assumes the role of a sage, which he continues to intensify in *Sarmakand*, especially in "Elegy for a Nation," dedicated to his fellow Nigerian writer, Chinua Achebe at 70 years of age. The poetic voice is no longer of the brass young poet of *Idanre and Other Poems* who wants to impress with his poeticisms in a very euro-modernist fashion nor the whining victim of dictatorship in *A Shuttle in the Crypt* or even the activist poet calling for a revolutionary war to gain freedom in *Ogun Abibiman*. He is rather a cynical sagely figure trying to expose artificialities in behaviors, falsity of lifestyles, and singing praise-chants of those who embody his vision of heroism. There is a growing effort in the post-Nobel poetry for Soyinka to minimize individuality, which has been at the core of many early poems, and maximize a sense of communality. After all, by this time, the poet had realized that "the man dies in all who keep silent in the face of tyranny" (*The Man Died*, 6). While there remains focus on individuals which he does positively on Mandela and negatively on Samuel Doe, individuals have a strong impact on communities and societies in a way the "archetypes" of *A Shuttle in the Crypt* do not. The persona of Ogun that the poet appropriates directly in *Idanre* and indirectly in both *A Shuttle in the Crypt* and *Ogun Abibiman* is more rightly the "orphans' shield" in *Mandela's Earth* than ever before in his condemnation of apartheid and tyranny.

In *Mandela's Earth* there is use of traditional African oral literary techniques as in the praise-chants for Nelson Mandela and

Muhammad Ali. Much as the reader knows Soyinka's indebtedness to Yoruba folklore, especially in his plays, it is in the later poetry that his use of oriki rhythms assumes a mesmerizing incantatory cadence. In "Muhammad Ali at the Ringside, 1985" he describes the black American iconic boxer thus:

> Black tarantula whose antics hypnotize the foe!
> Butterfly sideslipping death from rocket probes.
> Bee whose sting, unsheathed, picks the teeth
> Of the raging hippopotamus, then fans
> The jaw's converge with its flighty wings.
> Needle that threads the snapping fangs
> Of crocodiles, knots the tusks of elephants
> On rampage. Cricket that claps and chirrups
> Round the flailing horn of the rhinoceros,
> Then shuffles, does a bugalloo, tap-dances on its tip.
> Space that yields, then drowns the intruder
> In showers of sparks—oh Ali! Ali!
> *Esu* with faces turned to all four compass points
> Astride a weather vane; they sought to trap him,
> Slapped the wind each time. (*Mandela's Earth*, 48)

This is incantatory poetry at its most sublime, a far higher level of poetry in its communicative and aesthetic fulfillment than Soyinka has written before now. Here the poet is able to fuse in a very harmonious manner the traditional and modern in techniques to achieve his poetic goal. One cannot read these lines and others such as "Do you call that / Pounding?... / Pound, dope, pound!" and "Cassius Marcellus, Warrior, Muhammad Prophet, / Flesh is clay...(49) without noticing that the poet once accused of the "euromodernist disease" is highly versatile in African-derived poetic tropes.

However, "Soyinka's new poems are still occasionally intellectual and academic. The new poetry of the Nobel laureate may not be as obscure and difficult as in *Idanre*, but the diction is very Soyinkan, a correlation of distorted clichés, literary terms, double-barrelled words, and a nature and science-suffused vocabulary" (Ojaide 123). In Soyinka's later poetry, he increasingly sheds those negative poetic aspects and becomes more accessible with time.

Sarmakand and Other Markets I Have Known (2002) came out 14 years after *Mandela's Earth* and 16 years after Soyinka received the Nobel award. Many of the poems in this collection might have been written while Wole Soyinka was in exile, which he had fled to after falling foul of Sani Abacha's dictatorial and tyrannical government in

Nigeria. Soyinka was very much involved in the pro-democracy move-ments that sprang up in Nigeria after General Ibrahim Babanginda annulled what most Nigerians then considered to be the fairest dem-ocratic election ever conducted in the country. Moshood Abiola won the elections but was denied victory by a dictator's pronouncement. Opposition against the military dictatorship of Babangida coalesced under National Democratic Coalition (NADECO) of which Soyinka was a prominent and vocal member. In the pro-democracy protests that followed the annulment of the June 12 Presidential Election, Soyinka, Chief Anthony Enahoro, and Mrs. Kudirat Abiola, among many others, worked unsuccessfully toward the rescinding of the annulment. Moshood Abiola, the presumed winner of the elections, later died in mysterious circumstances in Abuja. General Babangida stepped aside for an interim administration that was overthrown by a Babangida ally, his former Defense Minister, General Sani Abacha, who perpetrated an unprecedented rule of terror in Nigeria. It was during this period that Wole Soyinka fled into exile. He spent many of the years in academic institutions in the United States, includ-ing Harvard, Emory, and the University of Las Vegas, where he brought refugee writers such as Syl Cheney-Coker of Sierra Leone to be employed for several years. It is in this context of Soyinka the exile traversing the world but concerned about the affairs of his country that *Sarmakand and Other Markets I Have Known* should be seen.

Soyinka wrote most of these poems outside Nigeria as an exile tra-versing the world as a refugee. The titles of some of the sections of the collection such as "Outsiders," "Of Exits," "Fugitive Phases," and "The Sign of the Zealots" tell the physical exile of the poet. This traversing of the universe is an indication of the poet's attempt to universalize his experiences to express a common humanity, a pro-cess started in the poems on Mandela of South Africa, Sergeant Doe of Liberia, and the American poems in *Mandela's Earth and Other Poems*. The other poems of *Sarmakand*, especially those relating to Nigeria, appear based on memory. "Low Cost Housing" is based on the housing program initiated in the Shehu Shagari administration that was infested with corruption that led to abandoned or shabbily built houses that were substandard during the early 1980s in Nigeria.

This collection synthesizes old and new concerns as the poet ranges from national issues such as the assassination of Kudirat, a Nigerian pro-democracy activist and wife of Moshood Abiola the presumed winner of the June 12, 1992 elections in Nigeria, and sociopolitical issues as in the poem for Chinua Achebe, a fellow Nigerian veteran writer, and to observations in foreign cities as Sarmakand, the capital of Samarkand region in Uzbekistan, and is said to be one of the oldest cities in the world and the oldest of Central Asia. One can say that Soyinka's poetic writing has come full cycle because all aspects of earlier works as in "Telephone Conversation," *Idanre and Other Poems, A Shuttle in the Crypt, Ogun Abibiman* to the post-Nobel *Mandela's Earth and Other Poems* are reflected in *Sarmakand and Other Markets I Have Known.* Yet the earlier poems are a preparation for this collection which appears more refined in vision and craft, especially in the social awareness and attitude to women. This collection is vintage Wole Soyinka poetry but also a little more than we have seen in his poetry before the twenty-first century.

As stated earlier, Soyinka was very much involved in the pro-democracy movement after Ibrahim Babangida annulled the June 12, 1992 elections as was Kudirat, the presumed winner of that election's wife. "Some Deaths Are World Apart" is dedicated to Kudirat. The poet acknowledges that "The death of one, we know, is one death / One too many" (19) during a tyrannical rule. However, the poet pays tribute to Kudirat for her special courage and heroism which put her in the class of the memorable heroines of old and of the contemporary world:

> Courage is its own crown, sometimes
> Of thorns, always luminous as martyrdom.
> Her pedigree was one with Moremi,
> Queen Amina, Aung Sung Kyi, with
> The Maid of Orleans and all who mother
> Pain as offspring, offer blood as others, milk. (20)

To the poet, Kudirat is a political martyr in an exceptional class of female heroines who die in the process of attempting to save their societies. Moremi is a mythical Yoruba princess while Amina was queen in the patriarchal Hausa kingdom of Zazzau (now called Zaria). Burma's Aung Sung Kyi won the Nobel Prize for Peace and has been jailed for over a decade to deter her from her pro-democracy activities in Burma. The poet also compares the Nigerian political activist assassinated for her struggle to Joan d'Arc of France for her heroism and martyrdom. It is significant that the poet highlights Kudirat, a woman in the patriarchal Nigerian society, for this special praise. The poem concludes with:

> She seeks no coronet of hearts, who reigns
> Queen of a people's will.

> Oh let us praise the lineage
> That turns the hearth to ramparts and,
> Self surrendered, dons a mantle that becomes
> The rare-born Master of Fate. (*Sarmakand*, 20)

While Soyinka has presented female characters in his plays and fictional works, his treatment of women in poetry seems to have been confined to the "For Women" section of *Idanre and Other Poems*. The poetic characters, as in "Black singer" and "To One, in Labour," deal with women in the sense of their mere womanhood. In the plays the older women, such as Iyaloja in *Death and the King's Horseman*, are positively portrayed. It is noticeable that the women do not seem to have the depth of character that the writer has used to represent male characters. However, in the poem for Kudirat, the poet pays tribute to "the lineage / That turns the hearth to ramparts," warrior and activist women who are dedicated to the transformation of their societies into better places whether politically or socially. This, no doubt, is a welcome development in the Nobel laureate's recent collection.

In *Sarmakand* the poet expresses solidarity with other writers in a shared humanity. There are poems dedicated to or dealing with the lives of Russian Josef Brodsky, Nigerian Ken Saro-Wiwa, Egyptian Naguib Mafouz, and Nigerian Chinua Achebe. In "Calling Josef Brodsky for Ken Saro-Wiwa," the poet reminds one of Joseph, one of the "archetypes" in *A Shuttle in the Crypt*, whom he calls a "dreamer" to describe Josef Brodsky, the former's "namesake." In "Joseph," the poet exposes the hypocrisy and lies of Mrs. Potiphar who attempts to seduce Joseph but failing lies against him:

> O Mrs Potiphar, your principles
> Which I would not embrace you swore
> I tried to violate; I see you wave a trophy
> Tattered pieces of your masquerade
> Of virtue, and call them mine. (*Collected Poems*, 119)

The poet reflects on the fate of the writer under tyrannical rule as life in labor camps and in exile, as he was also, to relate to Ken Saro-Wiwa's struggle for minority and environmental rights in Nigeria's Niger Delta. The poet describes Saro-Wiwa as being in a kind of exile even though at home in Nigeria because of the collusion of the multinational oil companies and the military dictatorship of his country. Like the Biblical Joseph lied against by Mrs. Potiphar, all dissidents, according to the poet, "must learn the comedy of law" (27). Saro-Wiwa had his day in court but was not given a fair hearing and was hanged by the Sani Abacha junta. The activist/dissident or "dreamer" must not be deterred by the political manipulations of the judicial system of his or her government from the dream of defeating injustice and inhumanity. The poet, Josef Brodsky, Saro-Wiwa and others suffer the same fate, the sacrifice they have to make to fight for a better world.

There is much social awareness in these poems of "Low Cost Housing." The poet is aware of contemporary issues, and warns against religious fanaticism whether it is the "Born-Agains," "Christian Talibans," or others. The poet asks, "We who neither curse their gods nor desecrate / Their texts, their prayer mats or altars— / What shall we do, Chinua, with these hate clerics?" (75). Religious fanaticism is seen as a viral contagion that must be stopped because it often causes wars and civil strife. The urgency of stopping religious fanaticism is to ensure a more peaceful world of human coexistence. These later poems also present a poetic patriotic voice that is concerned with the sociopolitical happenings in the poet's native country as in "Elegy for a Nation." There is a feeling of nostalgia for the state of things in Nigeria before now. The poet asks whether contemporary Nigerians have leisure to love, as the elders did.

In form and technique, Soyinka brings in some old techniques. The allusions to Demosthenes, Joan d'Arc, Biblical Joseph, Circe, and Icarus in *Sarmakand* are similar to those in the poet's pre-Nobel poems. Similarly, there are images from Yoruba folklore as of "Ajapa" (the tortoise), Orunmila (the Yoruba goddess of fertility), and Ogun the god of iron that is capable of creativity in the forging of iron as well as destruction in accidents he is supposed to cause on roads. The poet employs references from wherever he finds them, be they Yoruba or Western, to express his feelings and ideas because he is representing humanity as a whole. It is in the area of diction that Soyinka continues to use words that are very learned and intellectual. Words such as "senescence" (7), "regurgitated" (8), "obsequiousness", "obsequies" (9), "crustacean" and "liposuctions" (12)), "bagiomanic" (19), "palimpsests" (23), diaphane (35), "marsupial" (36), "mucilage" (37), and many others show that Soyinka's diction has not changed much since the poems of the 1960s. He still uses copious alliterations, repetitions, as well as humor and irony as in his pre-1986 poems. The self-mockery in "Doctored Vision" shows the poet's wit and sharp sense of humor, which goes back to "Telephone Conversation" through the prison poems of *A Shuttle in the Crypt,* and now honed to a higher state.

In *Sarmakand*, Soyinka is very much aware of his old age, for "In our now autumn days, behold our leaden feet / Fast upheld to the starting block" (70). The poet persona speaks from the position of experience, aware of the difference between the past and the present and projecting a sense of nostalgia about the past whose potentials have not passed to the present. There is a philosophical edge to the title poem in which the poet brings together the Yoruba concept of life as a market and universal notions of the market. The poet uses the market space to bring the world together as humans whether in Sarmakand, Johannesburg, or anywhere else in the world. Also showing a streak of nationalism and patriotism as never expressed in his poetry, the poet is now more focused on a sense of community rather than exercising individuality, which used to be a major preoccupation in many of his early poems in *Idanre and Other Poems*.

Soyinka's post-Nobel poems, *Mandela's Earth and Other Poems* and *Sarmakand and Other Markets I Have Known*, point to a mature, self-assured sage who expresses his vision in an effortless manner that does not make the reader forget the past idiosyncrasies of his craft. He basically remains a product of his generation of African poets and still stuck with his style which he elevates to a new height. He does not write in the manner of the next generation of Nigerian poets in the "Alter/Native tradition" of simple language or concerned with issues of the environment as Niyi Osundare or Tanure Ojaide. There is no doubt that Soyinka might have peaked in drama with *Death and the King's Horseman* in 1975 but in poetry it is after his Nobel award that he has brought out his best, perhaps aware of criticisms of his earlier poetry, but of course developing and communicating more naturally and growing to embrace the entire humanity even as he gets more rooted in his Yoruba culture and more concerned about his native Nigeria.

CHAPTER 7

An Unusual Growth: The Development of Tijan M. Sallah's Poetry

INTRODUCTION

Tijan M. Sallah is not the conventional African poet like Kofi Anyidoho, Frank Chipasula, Jack Mapanje, Chimalum Nwankwo, Niyi Osundare, and Tanure Ojaide, among so many others, who studied literature and teach literature in universities in Africa or in the West. He studied economics at both Berea College and Virginia Polytechnic Institute and State University and is an economist by profession. After a short period of university teaching in the United States, he joined the World Bank and has been working there till now. For over a decade, as part of his professional assignment working on rural development in the World Bank, he traveled extensively in Africa and the Middle East.

While on this busy work schedule, he has continued to cultivate and nurture his poetic passion. He is a voracious reader of poetry and a writer of poetry and fiction. He has written scholarly essays on African literature and has consistently shown perspicacity for scholarly interpretation and analysis of literary works. Among his many scholarly essays on literature is the well-researched "Phillis Wheatley: A brief survey of the life and works of a Gambian slave/poet in New England America" which appeared in *Wasafiri*, a literary journal of postcolonial literature, based in England. Thus, he is not the typical contemporary African poet who has one leg in the academy and the other in poetry. In this light, his growth as a seasoned African poet becomes phenomenal and unusual, since he devotes only his sparsely free time to poetry. He is very much like his senior compatriot and veteran African poet of the First Generation, Lenrie Peters, who was a medical doctor. As Peters brought something fresh to modern

African poetry, so does Tijan M. Sallah bring a kind of freshness to contemporary African poetry because his poetry is mostly unencumbered by the baggage of literary traditions that other poets who studied literature often bring to their works. Sallah's poetry is natural, spontaneous, and carries his personal and public experiences as a stream's current runs effortlessly to the sea. Sallah is the natural heir to Lenrie Peters in many ways, especially in being outside the academy and pursuing the literary genre of poetry that best suits his temperament.

A Wolof (also spelled Wollof), from Sere Kunda, born 1958, Tijan M. Sallah has devoted time to studying and publishing on the Wolof people of The Gambia. He authored *Wolof* published by the Rosen Publishing Group in The Heritage of African Peoples series (New York, 1996). Writing a book on the Wolof indicates a commitment to the culture and history of his ethnic group. In addition to editing *New Poets of West Africa* (1995), he has with Tanure Ojaide also edited *The New African Poetry: An Anthology* (1999). He and Okonjo Iweala have also written *Chinua Achebe: Teacher of Light, A Biography* (2004). From his academic accomplishments, he belongs to the scholar-poet tradition rather than simply a poet. Though relatively young compared to other members of the Second Generation of modern African poets, he is very much in the "alter/Native" tradition that Funso Aiyejina (Ogunbiyi 128) identified in modern African literature because he is very knowledgeable about the folklore of his people and pays much attention to the content of his poetry. This is in the manner of Jack Mapanje and his Chewa people, Kofi Anyidoho and his Ewe, and Tanure Ojaide and his Urhobo culture. Proud of the griot tradition and the music of his Wolof people, Sallah's innate experience encompasses the Wolof experience. He deploys aspects of Wolof folklore into his writing to give a cultural identity to his work.

To appreciate the unusual growth of Tijan Sallah's poetic career and the development of his poetry over decades in the four volumes that I intend to study, it is important to know the zeitgeist and the poet's personal circumstances that have conditioned his poetic themes and style. A Muslim, he had gone to St. Augustine's High School, a Catholic institution, in the mainly Muslim Gambia before leaving for the United States, a mainly Christian nation. In an interview with Sandra M. Grayson, Tijan Sallah says, "We were fed with a heavy dose of the British classics—Shakespeare's plays, Coleridge, Joyce, Yeats, Orwell, Robert Stevenson, etc. We had to memorize passages and regurgitate them word for word" (1). Sallah admits to Sandra M. Grayson:

> My first start at writing poetry was linked to my early influences under the tutelage of an Irish priest/English teacher called Reverend John (sic) Gough...I thought it was purely and simply rhyming, so I tried my hand first time on a rhyme—"The African Redeemer"—a poem written as a tribute to the continentally admired, Pan-African nationalist leader and first head of state of Ghana, Dr. Osagyfo Kwame Nkrumah." (1)*

The poet's openness to other cultures and religions from an early age and his observations of new societies while looking back to his African homeland will help to formulate his poetic themes. For some years he has been working on a novel that deals with what he describes as "the three Abrahamic religions" of Judaism, Christianity, and Islam, all of which originated in the same place—the Middle East. Also an admirer and friend of not only Chinua Achebe and Wole Soyinka of the first generation but a buddy to many of the second generation poets, Tijan Sallah is familiar with African literature in general and poetry in particular. He has a strong sense of history in his work and uses his socio-politico-economic as well as spiritual perspectives to enrich his poetic mission.

EARLY POETIC CAREER

Though he started writing poetry in his third year at St. Augustine's in The Gambia, Tijan M. Sallah took his poetry-writing more seriously as an undergraduate and had his first collection, *When Africa Was a Young Woman*, published in 1980 by the legendary Writers Workshop in Calcutta (now Kolkata), India. It is remarkable that this work was not published in The Gambia or anywhere else in Africa, nor was it published in the United States where the poet was studying and would later work, but in faraway India. The Writers Workshop has consistently introduced young Indian and some foreign poets to the world and Sallah is one of their very many published "budding" poets. It is significant that Sallah titled his collection *When Africa Was A Young Woman*. There is the inference of the collection's title

---

*In a personal correspondence, Tijan Sallah says he told the interviewer the Reverend Father was Joseph Gough and not John Gough in the published interview.

about the pure and vibrant condition of Africa before colonialism or before Europeans would "take over" the continent. Africa's "young" age could also mean the early years of independence with so much euphoria and hope for the socioeconomic advancement of the continent that future leaders will betray with corruption and poor political leadership.

It is significant also to know the context of Sallah's early poems and their content. He took writing seriously when he arrived in the United States in the later 1970s. He thus had two sociocultural spaces to contend with: Africa and the United States. He must have fantasized about the United States with Hollywood movies and not knowing much of the reality of American life. On the other hand, he knew more of Britain, the colonial master of The Gambia, before leaving the Mother Continent. Thus, Sallah's knowledge of the West was based on his experience of the aftermath of British colonialism and what he read about or saw in old movies about the United States of America. He would ever since his initial coming to the United States be visiting his native country now and then, thus carrying the "nation" in his head and heart.

When Africa Was a Young Woman is in two sections: "On Africa" and "On People, Places and Things." The collection poetically explores the condition of his native Africa and the rest of the world, here represented by his early American experience. In "Writing from the Third World," *World Literature Toady*, the veteran American critic, Charles R. Larson, describes the poems as "somewhat uneven" but that "there is little question about Sallah's talent" (58). Larson cites Sallah's major preoccupation at this time as the "rapidity of cultural change still continuing in Africa" and highlights "We Let Tourists" where the poet is very critical of tourism in The Gambia, which relies almost exclusively on tourism for its foreign revenue. This overdependence on tourism means that tourists are given freedom to do as they like because the nation needs their contribution to the national economy. Thus there is the abuse of tourism which the poet strongly condemns in very moving lines:

> Our economy is flourishing
> Like a flower
> But my niece is now a prostitute
> (tourists pin her on the bed for 10 kronor)
> My little brother
> Has dropped out of high school
> (he guides tourists for few dalasis)
> And my family does not have meat to eat

(hotels consume all)
But the government says tourism
Makes the country rich. (*Dream Kingdom*, 120)

The poet exposes the irony of the benefits of tourism to The Gambian people: it has adversely affected the morality and ethics, education, and health of the common people. This subtle criticism of the Government makes the poem not just a moral outrage but a political statement of a young poet who is concerned about the direction of his native country that is dependent on foreigners and not diversifying its economy to include internal generation of revenue from agriculture or other sources. It is true, as Larson points out, that there is an "overly moralistic" trend in many of these early poems. The example of "Dialogue on Poverty" in which the pet owner feeds his cat salmon while his next-door neighbor suffers from kwashiorkor also shows moralizing. However, even at this early stage, we can see the economist having an ideological position of the haves and have-nots, a Socialist view that many of his fellow contemporary poets (Jared Angira, Syl Cheney-Coker, and Niyi Osundare, among others) carry in their poems of the 1980s. What appears to be moral outrage is based on ideological Marxist principles of the large gap between the rich and the poor and not necessarily religious moralizing.

Most of the early poems derive from the poet's observation of the new American environment and life he had just come to as a student. Poems such as "Tarzan Is Everywhere" and "Snowflakes" are the poetic testimony of the young poet's fresh experience of America. Of course, Sallah, as an international student from Africa, would have been exasperated or irritated, like other African students, by the ludicrous image of Tarzan in the United States. In a way, the poet is trying to assert his African identity and defend his African people from the onslaught of many Americans whose seemingly only image of Africa is of Tarzan. The creator of Tarzan never set foot on African soil. It is thus very understandable that the poet writes that "If all the media teaches is ignorance / Then (what) the whole world learns is ignorance" (*Dream Kingdom*, 113). It is in the context of American history of slavery and poor race relations that this poem should be read. With the general distorted image of Africa filled with negative things that the various forms of the American media promote, the poet exhorts Americans:

We need to see the flower and the angel
In Africa.
And, of course, the gravestones. (114)

This is because Africans are like other peoples the world over: "Africans kill / Just like the Germans, Just like the saffron Indians" (114). The anguished poet pleads for a more realistic and balanced picture of Africa rather than only the negative.

"Tonight" and "Snowflakes" tell the physical environment the poet has come to. In highly imagistic language, he personifies nature in the forms of the moon and snowflakes. To him, "the moon / a huge white cookie" "Feeds us with light / And we graze / Our way like cattle" (128). On the other hand,

> At midnight,
> Snowflakes
> Whisper
> On my roof
> Like witchdoctors
> Muttering incantations. (129)

The two short but profoundly beautiful poems register the emotional disposition of the young Gambian poet in the United States. He conflates his American and African experiences into a unified persona of one excited by a new environment with all its novelty and convenience but whose enthusiasm is dampened by prevailing racism and nostalgia for his African home.

There is always nostalgia for his native African home, a condition which builds tension, as many African immigrants or exiles are familiar with, in the relationship between the adopted foreign home and the abandoned home. "I Dream of Africa" best illustrates this tension in the poet:

> Under the perilous snow,
> I dream of Africa;
> This ancient garden where spiders mate with butterflies,
> Where hopes rise daily
> With the nurturing efforts of determined women,
> Where women stand tall like giraffes
> And want to rebuild the moon. (*Moon Dreams*, 115)

It is still in this vein of living the life of double consciousness of being black in a racist white America that some other poems reflect. "If You Ask Me Why My Teeth Are Ivory White" (112) brings Africa and America together in contrast. It is as if the poet is defensive because of constant assaults by Americans on his Africanity; hence "Now if you ask me why my teeth are ivory white / I will tell you I come from grandma's Africa" (112). To the poet, "grandma's Africa" signifies a life of natural ways, love, and unspoiled by unhealthy habits that are promoted in the West. He also talks of the experience gained from his grandma and teacher, so that he should not be seen as someone ignorant but one who has learned a lot though young. He tells his American audience:

> But I went to St. Augustine's High School
> And studied health science and my Irish teacher
> Would say, "Sweets are baard for yaar teeth"
> (he was talking from experience).
> His rust-colored teeth radiated with plaque. (112)

It is interesting that his white teacher has "rust-colored teeth" that "radiated with plaque," while his African teeth are "ivory white" and healthy looking.

In his first collection Sallah already displays enough talent and craft that he will in the next three decades hone to poetic finesse in his later poetry. As will be expatiated upon later, there is some indebtedness to Negritude in the portrayal of traditional Africa in a rather romantic manner to underscore the difference between life in his home continent and the American society. The poems are simple and making meaning appears to be important to the poet who wants to communicate his poetic ideas and feelings in a clear but figurative manner.

THE SECOND PHASE

It is interesting that Tijan Sallah's next collection of poems, *Kora Land*, that came out in 1988 seems to be almost totally focused on his homeland and its culture. Only the poems on the fall and spring seasons seem to show the American environment. In the progress of his poetic career, it is significant that the poet, while still living in the United States, brought out a collection that is totally devoted to his homeland, a signification that the poet has acclimatized himself to the American environment and feels confident enough to do his own thing. He is no longer responding to American social pressures and racism but asserting his Africanness. Nostalgia has possessed him to relish the culture, society, and people of his African homeland. The Gambian nation, home of the Wolof and other Sahelian ethnic groups (Mandingo, Serer, Fula, etc.), is the "Kora Land" based on that artistic musical instrument for which the people of the Senegambian region are known and which the griot plays to entertain and educate his people. Leopold Sedar Senghor, a Serer from neighboring Senegal that also has Wolof people, made popular the kora instrument that he asked to accompany some of his poems when performed. In this collection, Tijan Sallah plays the sociocultural role of the griot, since he is a modern griot writing poetry rather than doing oral poetic performances. Titles such as "The Elders Are Gods," "Dialogue With My Dead Grandfather," "You Must Come to Kamby," "Grandmother Weaving," and "Mr. Agama," among other poems, tell this poetic tale of the Gambian people and the poet's own cultural experience.

A rather introspective poetic stance that makes the poet explore the world of his own people differs from one in which he invites his American readers and neighbors to "look" at the way he finds the United States, as he exhorts in the earlier collection. But at the same time there is the intention, conscious or unconscious, that the poet is now confident enough that he is inviting his readers, Africans and foreigners, to share his experience of where he left for America. Emotionally, it is more engaging to him than the new environment in which he finds himself. It is this comfortable stance of "I am Gambian" or rather "I am African" though in America that gives these poems not only their identity but their beauty. The poet is thus educating Americans and "others" about his origin, which has so many good things to recommend it and quite different from a Tarzanic image.

Much as the poet focuses on his homeland, he is not going to sing its praises blindly. Rather, he uses a playful and subtly satiric tone to tell the tale of his home experience. He plants his feet deep in his homeland, embracing his native culture and its ways, while being open to the rest of the world as he lives it in the United States. "The Elders Are Gods" is typical of these poems. He writes:

> The old folks say that
> If you eat fish-heads, or
> Drink coconut juice, you would
> Turn stupid. But the elders
> Eat everything and get wiser every day. (*Dream Kingdom*, 68)

The same old folks who warn children against sex indulge in it. The same holds for palm wine they ask children not to drink. The poet attempts to poke fun at the explanations the elders give to young ones about denying them what are privileges of only the elders. Their explanations are simply not rational if they indulge in what they warn others against. Thus, what seems to be the wisdom of elders is irrational and only a ruse to protect their privileges and fill their greed. It is both witty and ironical that the elders say if you drink coconut juice, "you would / Turn stupid. But the elders / Eat everything and get wiser every day" (*Dream Kingdom*, 68). Sallah uses the indigenous culture, represented by his grandfather and grandmother, to interrogate the changes which have been brought by the so-called civilization of the West. In "Dialogue with My Dead Grandfather," there is mockery of the new things that represent modernity or the so-called gains of civilization. He writes:

> He will send me
> A marrow-telegram
> To watch out for all
> The evils of modernity
> Which are disguised as civilization. (70)

The intuitive knowledge of the poet's grandfather of nature and life appears lost in modernity. So the poet proudly invites the African or foreign reader to Kamby, the Mandingo name that the British colonialists changed to The Gambia: "You must come to my land / And meet the emerald of our smiles" (82) and again:

> You must come to my land
> And meet the pure-gaze of our faces.
> Never lonesome, our faces;
> Never like stone-walls, our eyes. (83)

The poet living abroad is indirectly criticizing the inadequacies of the United States: loneliness and unhappiness despite material comfort. Both "Banjul Afternoon" and "Dance of Passion" reinforce the life in Africa that though technologically lagging behind and with its inconveniences is a happier one than the American. It is ironical that Africans are happier than Americans, a point made about Banjul's Wolof women, who "spat at every corner, / Trading happiness for hygiene" (87). "Grandmother Weaving" pays tribute to the devotion of the poet's grandmother to her trade. Other poems such as "The Faith of Mourides" and "Pilgrims to the Magal" tell the religious and mystical life of the poet's homeland, perhaps meant to draw a contrast with materialistic Americans who seem to care more for the body than the soul.

These are definitely well-crafted poems with a consistent formal structure. The poems are in stanzas which vary according to what the poet is talking about. The figurative language is expressed in metaphors, similes, irony, and personification. The poet is often musical as he uses repetition and alliteration and assonance in an effortless manner. The poet's tone is confident and assured, his themes meant to draw a sharp contrast between his so-called uncivilized homeland of The Gambia/Africa and the civilized America. He succeeds in giving the reader a poetic narrative of the Wolof/Gambian experience, thereby proffering an alternative humanity to the American one. No doubt, by *Kora Land*, a tribute to The Gambia and the people, Tijan Sallah has fully established a unique voice in contemporary African poetry.

Building on the Early Stage

Dreams of Dusty Roads builds on Tijan Sallah's early poetic experience. As I wrote in the review of the collection when it first came out in 1993, "*Dreams of Dusty Roads* expresses personal experiences which, though individual, are reflective of the contemporary African intellectual abroad, who has to grapple with the realities of a new environment while always mindful of the indigenous African heritage" (*WLT*, 1993). Tijan Sallah is drawing on his experiences from two earlier collections of poetry and his confidence of having adapted to the American society in this collection. It is not surprising that Sallah names the first of the three sections of the collection "Roots," after Alex Haley in his narrative, later adapted to television, which promoted The Gambia as the origin of Kunta Kinte from his capture to his appearance under slavery in the United States. The poet has become more conscious of craft; hence his three sections are fused. It is for this craftsmanship that

> the collection is divided into three sections: "Roots (Africa)," "Branches (America)," and "Dream-Clouds (In the Mind)." There is movement which starts outwardly from Africa to America and continues in an inward return to the poet's inner self and virtues associated with traditional Africa. The three sections are also connected by recurring images and a passionate poetic personality. (Ojaide, rev., *WLT*, 1993)

The first section deals with Africa—it looks at the African experience in a balanced manner. In "Prayer for Roots," echoing Wole Soyinka's prison poem, "O, Roots!" in *A Shuttle in the Crypt*, Tijan Sallah exhorts the tenacity, endurance, and memory of Africa. At the same time, in other poems of this section, he decries corrupt politicians and women who sell their bodies. He finds it ironical in "Mothers of the Empire" that older Africans should still be talking nostalgically of colonial days. Of the second section comprising of the poet's American experience, two poems stand out for my attention: "Television as a God" and "Pope Johnny Carson." In these poems he uses sarcasm, puns, wit, and humor to portray American culture.

The third section, "Dream-Clouds," reinforces a theme he introduced in *Kora Land* about the spiritual nature of his people. He explores the Sahelian environment of The Gambia with its baobab, tamarind, and other flora and fauna. Furthermore, he delves into Islam, which is also touched in the earlier collection but much more here. In "Before the Breaking of the Fast," the poet advocates spirituality in the midst of crass materialism. In "Share," he asks for communion for a closer humanity.

As written in the review,

> In *Dreams of Dusty Roads* Tijan Sallah has matured into a master word magician. His lines are strong, varied, and interesting. The voice is confident in its movement, with appropriate and recurring images, repetitions, and other techniques employed to talk about his homeland, his sojourn abroad, and his faith that a spiritual/mystical preoccupation would make life meaningful in the contemporary oppressive materialism
> …Sallah imposes on the mind a powerful message that will live with the reader, and he does so with freshness that only a passionate and sensitive observer can bring to poetry. (Ojaide, rev. *WLT*, 1993)

Recent Poetry

I consider both the "Harrow" and "New Poems" sections of *Dream Kingdom* Tijan Sallah's recent poetry. In these poems the poet is surer of his craft and his figurative language and techniques come to him effortlessly. In this mature phase of his writing, the poet experiments with rhyme in the "Harrow" poems. In a pun that the careful reader is not meant to ignore, with knowledge of Ezra Pound's Pisan Cantos, the poet writes "Persian Cantos." Reading these poems and others that I quote from in this section, there is no doubt that the writer has fully mastered his craft and, added to his talent and inspiration, produces exhilarating poetry that is intellectual delight of the first order.

In 2000 Tijan Sallah was passing through London on a World Bank rural development assignment to Yemen and took a rest stop.

The weather was bad that night and, as he stepped out of his hotel to get a bite, was knocked down by a "maniacally" speeding car. The incident is recorded in "I Must Not Look Down": "The driver stopped to cover me with his jacket. / Sour hospitality, at least, he was not a hit-and-run. / Conscience sometimes polices evil with a bracket" (*Dream Kingdom*, 143). An ambulance took him to a hospital in the Harrow district where he was told he suffered a spiral femur fracture and remained in the hospital for several weeks. It is this hospital experience that gave rise to these poems.

It is interestingly ironical that it was at Harrow, known for the highbrow high school where many British elites are trained, where he was hospitalized that the poet suffered such a harrowing experience. The ironical pun on Harrow is thus clear. In these poems the poet uses rhyming quatrains and ends some with a rhyming couplet. He often alternates the rhymes. It appears the hospital experience offered the poet the opportunity with time to rhyme and philosophize about the fragility of life.

"Here I Lie Now" opens the series in a philosophical tone:

> Life has a way of coming to a bump,
> When I am speeding aimlessly on the bump
> Of the quest for coins and fame. (136)

The pursuit of money and fame led to the accident that threatened to maim him. This philosophical trend is continued in the following poem, "The Nights Can Be Long." The repeated "The nights can be long when in pain" tells what every patient in a similar situation experiences. The poet is often witty and makes fun of himself or his situation, as when he asks "But why should my pains and time be mating?" The poet uses repetition perhaps to stylistically represent the boring period and is musical in the axiomatic "The nights can be long when in pain."

"Tribute to the Body-Carpenter" is an extended metaphor in the form of a metaphysical conceit—the sick body is described as "broken furniture" and the doctor a "body-carpenter" (138). Rhetorically, the poet asks: "But who knows a carpenter who does not leave marks?" (138). There is humor and sober reflection in these poems of convalescence. "Next to God, the Doctor" illustrates the poetic maturity of Tijan Sallah:

> When in pain, next to God is the doctor.
> The universe collapses when pain soars in the nerves and bones,

And all one could do is to summon the nurse as the proctor.
The doctor's words ring like God's trombones,
Every syllable must be weighed with an ounce of good measure.
And the prescription must be held with the sacredness of treasure.

When in pain, next to God is the doctor.
And one is reminded of Epicurus's dictum:
That Nature bestowed on humanity
Two sovereign principles—pain and pleasure.
It is in our nature to seek money, fame, wine and good posture,
And to avoid snakes, scorpions and pinches on the rectum. (141)

Though short of 14 lines, this is a classic sonnet style in the use of rhymes and balancing of ideas in a concise and carefully crafted poem. This poem showcases Sallah at his best when he entertains as he philosophizes. It is fascinating that in a period of sickness and recovery in hospital when the poet is immobile that the poetry of his experience moves with so much vitality. There is the added irony of a night storm that not only "fracture(s) tree limbs to block roads and rails" (142) but also made the poet to forget his pain. Fear of death makes a seriously injured person to forget pain!

The period of being stuck in a hospital bed gave the poet the opportunity to reflect about life and also comment on the British society and environment. He talks of Harrow high school and the weather. In "Enlightenment," "Today, the sun is out and bright, / and it feels like the Enlightenment" (149). The poet, oppressed by the British weather, aptly ends the series with "Nostalgia for Sun":

When shall I see the sun again?
When shall I see the sun?
Autumnal leaves break into a rainbow train.
When shall I see the sun?

North London is blustery cold;
Even the feathery pigeons lust for the sun.
I must look out and appear bold,
For sunlight is rare here as a unicorn. (151)

Again, this is poetry at its most intense expression of thought and feeling.

New Poems were written between 1995 and the *present* (2006). Though of different themes and inspired by diverse circumstances, the poems are daring, experimental, and mature in thematic exploration and technical deployment of tropes. The poems deal with travel, topical issues of the time, Gambian politics, and spiritual reflection. In these poems there is sensitivity to humanity as the poet is concerned with justice, fairness, and marginalization of women. These are ambitious poems whose style is elevated almost to a Soyinkan manner in diction, tropes, and techniques, especially in the opening poem of the section, "Bosnia Hercegovina" and the two following poems ("Melodies in the Crypt" and "Hallucinations") with their respective refrains, incantatory rhythm, and rhetorical questions. One goes back to Wole Soyinka's *A Shuttle in the Crypt* and *Mandela's Earth* to draw comparisons with these Sallah poems. In "Hallucinations" the various forms of metamorphoses are highly metaphorical.

One of the most daring poems in this section is "Persian Cantos" in four parts. In "Persepolis," the poet, again in a near-Soyinkan voice, uses an extended metaphor, a conceit, to describe how he marveled at the Persian civilization:

> My mind became a backhoe excavator,
> A primitive search-engine, a jack-root searching,
> Embracing the sublime groundwater.
> It moved, detoured, but kept the focus;
> A groundhog drilling through runnels of time,
> To lick the dross of history. (163)

While aware of the "blows and counterblows" between Persia and Greece, the poet pays tribute to the slaves/serfs that built the monuments but who are now forgotten: "How many little folks get sacrificed / On the altar of royal power and expediency?" This concern for the small ones is carried into the next poem, "Farrokhzad and Khayyam" in which the poet pays tribute to a talented female poet who died tragically but who appears erased from the national Persian memory. In a rare feminist streak, the poet asks, "how many women stories are / Between a camel rider and a camel? / How many Farrokhzad to an Omar Khayyam?" (166). The Socialist-cum-feminist temperament is continued in "Bamboo Freedom" in which the poet condemns peasants working very hard but making no profit because of capitalist market manipulation. As for the African rural farmer, "the more he works, the more he realizes / It is a cruel lie" for him to prosper. In the last two parts of "Persian Cantos" the poet recalls the Persian folklore of love as between Leyla and Majnoon. The last segment tells how Iraqi scud missiles destroyed some Persian villages and towns and wreaked fear in the citizens of the fabled city of Shiraz, the city and tomb of the poet, and the holy city of Hafiz, reminding the reader of the memory of history and evil.

In other poems the poet focuses on politics of The Gambia. Both "Let It Not Happen Again" and "The Second Republic" deal with the military coup and the corrupt civilians overthrown. Still related to national Gambian politics, but representative of African and developing countries worldwide, "The Foreign Expert Game" condemns the practice of developed countries of the West using so-called experts to enrich themselves and impoverish more the poor developing countries. It is a satirical poem filled with irony and sarcasm, and humor. The collection aptly ends with spiritual explorations which reinforce the mystical side of Tijan Sallah in both "Field of Wheat" and "Death." The poet writes:

> I want to think of life as a field of wheat.
> And the Almighty as the Big Farmer.
> And some wheat plants as neuralgic agnostics,
> Defying the green hopes that the Big Farmer
> Intends for them. Short-circuiting their dreams,
> Ruining their destiny, they curl back; bend
> In rebellion towards the dry earth. (180)

CONCLUSION

Asked by Grayson, "In what ways is your recent poetry different from your earlier work?" Tijan Sallah responds thus:

> I think my earlier work was much inspired by the poetry of the Negritude Movement—the works of David Diop, Leopold Senghor, Aime Cesaire, etc. As you may know, Senghor was in Senegal just across the border from the Gambia. He was head of state, and his literary influences often slipped into the airwaves of the state media—Radio Senegal in particular. As a young emerging poet then, I admired (and incidentally still admire) his work. My earlier poetry was simpler, message oriented—the use of poetry as "talking and fighting words." There is...."Tarzan Never Lived in MY Africa," which is a defense against the negative stereotyping of Africa, the so-called "Tarzan myth," the jungle Africa of social Darwinian struggles, where you have continuous war, famine and death, where life is "nasty, brutish and short"—to borrow from Hobbesian categories. This image of Africa is, of course, common in the US print and visual media—the Africa the untutored West wants to see versus the real Africa I know. (3–4)

Sallah continues: "My recent poetry is more deliberative, perhaps more complex in its use of symbolism and imagery, more preoccupied with enduring themes: 'roots,' 'memory,' 'family,' relationships with elders and ancestors,' perhaps a movement more towards the personal. I think the era of grandstanding in poetry is over; I now write about the essences of my particularities. If you take my poem, "Banjul Afternoon" in my collection *Kora Land*, it captures a particular mood of Banjul, the capital city of The Gambia—of course, viewed from the vantage point of the poet" (4).

Tijan M. Sallah's poetry has grown considerably from the 1980s to now, from an apprentice stage to mastery of the poetic art and craft. The themes have changed from the poetic persona of a young African immigrant in the United States responding to the new environment's social observations and excitement with snow and Western accouterments and affirming his Africanness in a racist society. At the early stage the poet's persona looks back to Africa with nostalgia and contrasting its nature, cultural norms, upbringing, and communal happy life with the individualistic American life. What Americans took as pleasure were unhealthy habits. The materialism of the West is also contrasted with the spirituality of Africans. There is a shift to primarily African themes, a representation of the poet's nostalgia while abroad. What is significant is that the mature poet moves away from the American-African contrast to address universal themes and the human condition in the "Harrow" and "recent poems." The frailty of the human body, human mortality, and the supremacy of God are preoccupations in the more recent poems. Also there is a shift to issues that could be related to Socialist ideology in the concern for the underprivileged, the poor farmer, and serfs/slaves, among others. In the same vein, the erasure of women from celebration even when they achieve as much as men is condemned in "Persian Cantos." The poetic themes have grown from mere observation of the environment and society to concern for the exploitation of the developing countries by the developed countries through so-called technical assistance. There is a certain mystical tenor in the latter poetry which has been foreshadowed by earlier spiritual and religious concerns.

The development in style of Sallah's poetry from the early collection to the recent poetic work is even more revealing. The widening of the poetic field from the United States and The Gambia is matched by a more learned style with allusions from other cultures the poet has traveled to. While the early poetry uses figurative language that is simple in the "Alter/Native" style of the second generation of modern African poetry, the more recent poetry displays a poet comfortable enough with his craft to experiment with rhyme and a form as the canto. The techniques of repetition, irony, sarcasm, humor, and other tropes flow effortlessly. The poet's style appears more elevated in many poems and he sounds Soyinkan without the Nigerian poet's early but later abandoned "euro-modernist" excesses. In other words, Sallah's poetry avoids the difficulty, obscurity, disjointedness, and extreme learning that Chinweizu and others associated with modern African poets' "euro-modernist" tendencies in their indebtedness to Western modernist poets like T. S. Eliot and Ezra Pound. In Sallah's "recent" poetry, the metaphors are more extended and look more like metaphysical conceits.

In the more than three decades in which Tijan Sallah has been writing, his poetry has matured both in themes and style and his poetry has become robust and at the same time flowing musically. The poet is anchored on his Gambian, Wolof, Islamic, Western education, and personal experience to produce poetry whose voice admonishes the reader to be less materialistic and more humane as well as care for fairness and justice. One can say that Tijan Sallah's poetry has moved from observations of a foreign society and environment with nostalgic feelings toward his African homeland to poetry that exposes the experience of a humanist who happens to be a Gambian/African with foreign experience. He is no longer concerned with individual societies and cultures per se but the human condition.

CHAPTER 8

An Insider Testimony: Odia Ofeimun and His Generation of Nigerian Poets

I cannot despair

—*Odia Ofeimun*

INTRODUCTION

Odia Ofeimun's early life experiences, the sociopolitical condition and intellectual climate of his youth and adult life, and national and other historical circumstances appear to have not only prepared him for but also goaded him into an activist poet's career. He ranges on the side of the common people and is at the vanguard of forces struggling against tyranny, dictatorship, oppression, injustice, and other sociopolitical vices so as to establish humane and democratic values. Because of this historicist approach, the specific contexts of historical period, geographical place, and local society and culture will be used to locate and interrogate Ofeimun's work among his peers' literary contributions since he shares similar public but often different individual experiences with members of his generation. The evolution of democracy must begin with its antecedents of dictatorship, tyranny, and undemocratic governance and vices, which are gradually eroded through struggle for more humane and democratic values.

At the same time, Ofeimun's individual life experiences, especially as a young man, would have helped to shape his poetic activist philosophy. Thus, there is no contradiction between the historicist and individualist theoretical approaches adopted. Rather, they reinforce each other in foregrounding Ofeimun's life and literary work in the effort to make the world better than he and members of his generation met it. This unified historicist–individualist approach to Ofeimun the man and the poet will elicit the high degree of his achievement not only in print but also in the real world. Consequently, the poet's persona, like most in the postcolonial literary tradition, takes an activist role in the politics of his society and resists the literary influences of the West, especially the modernist features, and chooses the style of the indigenous poetic tradition to express his feelings and ideas.

Odia Ofeimun has been understudied, bearing in mind that he has produced a large body of work that is beautifully crafted and whose vision is articulated in highly poetical language. With five collections of poetry, comprising *The Poet Lied* (1980), *A Handle for the Flutist* (1986), *A Feast of Return/Under African Skies* (2000), *London Letter and Other Poems* (2000), and *Dreams at Work* (2000), Ofeimun deserves serious scholarly investigation. It is with this aim of exposing the poet's opus to a wider readership and rigorous scholarly inquiry that wherever I have had the opportunity, I have included either the showcasing or the study of his work as in my respective *The New African Poetry: An Anthology* (2004) and *The Dictionary of Literary Biography, Vol. 360: Contemporary African Writers* (2011). Focusing on Odia Ofeimun in a conference on "The Writer and the Evolving Democracies" therefore is a deserved recognition of not only the high quality of his poetic oeuvre but also of his steadfast commitment and action to merge art and the man, poet and poetry, into one. In a colloquial parlance, Ofeimun does not only talk the talk but also does the walk. Ofeimun is a quintessential literary artist who occupies a special place in the generation of Nigerian poets after the Wole Soyinka–Christopher Okigbo–J. P. Clark group that in this chapter will be called the "second generation." This periodization is mindful of the much earlier group of poets called the "pioneer poets." A literary generation may break from its predecessor gradually until it establishes its own unique voice. In Nigerian/African literature, most of those in the second generation in their early writing careers might have modeled their works on their literary elders until they established themselves as a different literary group. In fact, there is much echoing of Wole Soyinka in some of Ofeimun's early poetry and there is much intertextuality in the two generations. Ofeimun's "Never ask me why" is a good example.

If Odia Ofeimun is today being celebrated as a poet who has deployed his artistic talent into the struggle to transform the Nigerian society from dictatorship to democracy and from corruption to good governance, it is because of the trajectory his poetic work and activism have taken from about the mid-1970s to the present. I intend to situate him in the second generation of Nigerian/African poets described by our colleague, Funso Aiyejina, as starting the "alter/

native" tradition. I am revisiting an area which I first discussed in 1988 (see "The Changing Voice of History: Contemporary African Poetry," 1989, pp. 108–122) and also in *Poetic Imagination in Black Africa*). Other scholars of African literature have also written on this (see Funso Aiyejina, Harry Garuba, etc.). However, this discussion focuses on Odia Ofeimun as a peculiar member of the generation, his contribution to the poetry of sociopolitical commitment and activism, and his legacy as a poet with solid democratic credentials.

Ofeimun belongs to the generation of Nigerian/African poets/ writers who believe in the transformative role of the literary art and deploying it as a weapon toward regaining the lost ideals of nationhood; in Nigeria's case, the vision of a model independent African state. The art this generation advocates is utilitarian and meant to advance the goals of humanity, especially in the areas of good governance, equality, justice, and human development. A generation's philosophy or artistic viewpoint is not formulated in a vacuum. It is always reactive to societal, national, and human needs and demands. The second generation of Nigerian poets' ideas and literary manifesto are no exceptions to this phenomenon. Their ideas were formulated intuitively to address and solve contemporary problems. Concomitant with the issues of the time, these "new" poets started to project a vision for the future of stability, peaceful coexistence, freedom and equality, and economic well-being of the common people. There was no meeting to form a literary school but these poets were all products of the zeitgeist, which inevitably affected their writings.

Sociopolitical Background

Odia Ofeimun was born on March 16, 1950 at Iruekpen-Ekuma in the current Edo State that used to be part of Midwest Region, which was created out of Western Region after a successful plebiscite in 1963. After completing his elementary school education, he entered secondary school but, because of financial difficulties, could not complete the program. He would read on his own to pass the General Certificate of Education (Advance Level) examination to ensure admission into the university. He belongs to the Ishan ethnic group but, since leaving for Lagos in 1969 to work before going to study at the University of Ibadan, he has spent his life, apart from four years in the United Kingdom, in the Yoruba-speaking region in whose politics he was deeply involved, once as private secretary to Chief Obafemi Awolowo, national leader of the Action Group. It is worthy of note that his colleagues in the generational group include

Chimalum Nwankwo (born 1945), Niyi Osundare (born 1947), Femi Osofisan (born 1947), the writer Tanure Ojaide (born 1948), Funso Aiyejina (born 1950), and Harry Garuba (born in 1958). All of these, except Nwankwo from the Eastern Region, attended Awolowo-established free elementary schools.

Financial difficulty might have made Ofeimun drop out of secondary school, but there is no doubt that he and the other writers went to school in the same sociopolitical climate. They were youths during the nationalist struggle for Nigerian independence and Ofeimun, by the nature of his origin and early upbringing, would have heard of his fellow Ishan, Chief Anthony Enahoro, a major nationalist figure whose political struggle and commitment to democracy and human rights would continue for decades. He would write a poem later to pay tribute to "Uncle" Chief Enahoro on his fiftieth birthday anniversary for the "so much fire" still "left in him" (*The Poet Lied*, p. 53). The members of the generation witnessed the euphoria of Nigeria's political independence evaporate and the new nation slide into political violence in both the Western Region and the Middle Belt in particular. Soon there would be a military coup, which some parts of the country felt was tribally motivated and that led to the ethnic cleansing of Igbo people primarily in the North. One coup followed another until it culminated in both the Ibrahim Babangida and the Sani Abacha juntas whose dictatorship violated in absolute terms human rights and other democratic principles. The short civilian regimes were rife with corruption, ineptitude, misrule, tribalism, and electoral fraud. Both the Tafawa Balewa and Shehu Shagari administrations manifested these sociopolitical maladies that threatened the corporate existence of the nation. It is in this type of sinister climate that members of Odia Ofeimun's generation grew up and matured. It is not surprising therefore to see their poetic works used to criticize the failings of the various military and civilian governments.

Ofeimun's poem "The new brooms" in his first collection of poems, *The Poet Lied*, was written in the context of the state of the country in 1974. The poem reads thus:

> The streets were clogged with garbage
> the rank smell of swollen gutters
> claimed the peace of our lives
>
> The streets were blessed with molehills
> of unwanted odds and bits

Then, they brought in the bayonets
to define the horizons of our days
to keep the streets clear
they brought in the new brooms

To keep the streets clear
they brought in the world-changers
with corrective swagger-sticks
they brought in the new brooms
to sweep away public scores away.

But today listen today
if you ask why the waste bins are empty
why refuse gluts the public places unswept
they will enjoin you to HOLD IT:
to have new brooms, that's something.

And if you want to know why
the streets grunt now
under rank garbage
under the weight of decay, of nightsoil
more than ever before
they will point triumphantly, very triumphantly
at their well-made timetable:

"We shall get there soonest;
nightsoil clearance is next on the list." (5)

This poem describes the state of things during successive military juntas from the 1960s through the 1980s in Nigeria, a situation which
also inspired my "The owl wakes us." Any criticism of dictatorship,
as of Ofeimun's "The new brooms," as in his "The Messiahs," is an
effort at restoring democracy.

INTELLECTUAL CLIMATE OF THE TIME

Of significance in the formative years of the Nigerian second generation
poets is the intellectual climate of the time. Two significant intellectual
currents of the time, political and literary, impacted on the poets in
their formative years: the University of Ibadan experience of political
awareness and radicalism and Chinweizu's criticism of modern African
poets, particularly Wole Soyinka, for embracing the Western modernist poetic tradition instead of the African indigenous poetic tradition.
The University of Ibadan then, touted as Africa's premier university,
had among the teaching staff the likes of Professor Essien-Udom and

Dr. Omafume Onoge fresh from Harvard University and bristling with Marxist ideas and rhetoric. Essien-Udom had written *Black Nationalism* after experiencing the Civil Rights movement in the American South. These and many other African academics at the institution inspired students with their radical ideology. This period was also at the peak of the Cold War between the Soviet Bloc and the West. To the radicals and most African intellectuals of the time, the West was supporting African military dictators and corrupt civilian regimes such as Mobutu Sese Seko of Congo Kinshasa, Felix Houphuet-Boigny of The Ivory Coast, Daniel Arap Moi of Kenya, and Dr. Hastings Kamuzu Banda of Malawi, among others. The academics and their students thus showed appreciation for Marxist ideology and the fact that the Soviet Union was supportive of liberation movements in Africa as in Angola and Mozambique. Ofeimun's poems for Che Guevara and Ortega in *Dreams at Work* show his radical orientation.

Student politics was very lively at the time. In 1969 the Gbolade Osinowo cry for revolution apparently won him the student union presidency because students craved for revolution even at the national level because of the dashed hopes of the nationalist struggle. Many times students were bused to Lagos, the national capital then, to protest Western interference in African affairs as the abortive coup in Guinea Bissau. By 1970 Boye Agunbiade won the student union presidency with his alias of "Chairman Mao." Whenever called "Chairman Mao," he responded "For the people." Odia Ofeimun tried unsuccessfully to win a position in the student union office by the mid-1970s. The point being made is that there was a pervasive radical temperament in the universities in which most of the poets of the second generation studied. This university conditioning will place these poets on the side of the masses—whether Marxist Socialist ideologues or not—as well as the poor and the underprivileged. "Demolition Day" in *London Letter* exemplifies Ofeimun's pro-people humanist viewpoint. The poor lady who is victim of the demolition "knelt, dry leaf against iron hoofs / among the forgotten of Lagos, / the homeless of Maroko, wishing / the Lord would nod at her withered hands" (6).

For better or worse, Chinweizu, Madubuike, and Jemie's *Towards the Decolonization of African Literature* and the debate it stirred among students, academics, and the literati was a major factor in the formulation of the second generation's literary ideology. Chinweizu's *bolekaja* brand of literary criticism rebuked modern African poets for not following an African indigenous tradition of their chosen genres but aping Western poets, especially the modernists such as T. S. Eliot and Ezra Pound. J. P. Clark even modeled poems on Gerard Manley Hopkins's "sprung rhythm." The University of Ibadan's English Department's graduating class of 1971, for instance, was the first to take courses in African literature. These and subsequent graduates read the poetry of Wole Soyinka, Christopher Okigbo, M. J. C. Echeruo, and J. P. Clark. While the students saw their poetry, especially the early Soyinka's and Okigbo's, as being too imitative of the Western modernists, they still respected them. However, the student writers did not want to follow the modernist trail of their predecessors' poetry that involves obscurity, difficulty, and intellectual allusions. The second generation makes an about-turn to write poetry that is simple, whose content can be understood, and yet remain highly poetic. Niyi Osundare refers to this new phenomenon of rejecting the poetry of the earlier generation for a more communicative one in his poetry manifesto, "Poetry is…" in *Songs of the Marketplace*. Similarly, the writer in his "Naked Words" in *The Eagle's Vision* and Ofeimun in "Prologue" in *The Poet Lied* advocate their poetic philosophy. Ofeimun writes:

> I have come down
> to tell my story
> by the fireside
> around which
> my people are gathered…
>
> And I must tell my story
> to nudge and awaken them
> that sleep
> among my people. (Ojaide and Sallah191)

The poem is simple and addressed to "my people" in the language that they will understand; a poetic practice different from that of the preceding generation of poets whose poems were often very intellectual and fragmented. Many of Ofeimun's poems follow the syntax of prose and communicate in simple language. Like many of Ofeimun's poems, "Borana Dance: A Drunkard's Sermon" shows the wit and irony that the poet weaves with simple language:

> I said to the redcap chiefs
> as they swilled anecdotes under the nim trees
> it is your history that is drunk. Not I.

It is your worship that is drunk
Not the empty kegs hanging
their narrow necks from my shoulder. (*A Feast of Return*, p.18)

Members of the second generation of Nigerian poets generally had a "homecoming" to traditional oral literature for inspiration for its emphasis on content and simple language. Many of the poets of the same generation across Africa had to study their oral poetic traditions for stylistic direction. Kofi Anyidoho studied Ewe poetry, Jack Mapanje Chewa poetry, and the writer udje dance songs of his Urhobo people. Niyi Osundare has grounding in Yoruba poetic traditions as Chimalum Nwankwo in Igbo folklore. One can list examples from these poets of their works influenced by their respective oral poetic traditions. Chinweizu's relentless attack on the euro-modernist influence on modern African poetry appears to have worked with the second generation of poets by making them reorient their poetic language and pay more attention to content than form.

Odia Ofeimun did not go through the conventional route of Nigerian poets through the English Department, and that makes even more significant his poetic achievements. He studied Political Science whose radicalism surely rubbed off on him. The closest he came to the English Department was the submission of his now famous poem, "The Poet Lied," for a literary contest which won the first prize. He is also peculiar because he does not display copiously as others the "alter/native" interest in the oral tradition of his Ishan/ Pan Edo culture. While there are references to Edo history in some of his poems, it is the Yoruba folklore of his adopted home that comes out in his poetry. There are references to Ogun, Sango, and abiku in *Dreams at Work*. He evokes warm memories of his father who was a mechanic in Ogunian terms:

I meet my father's eyes now
-a steady gaze that melted nuts,
Bolts and screws into a healer's art
-a faith, washed in petrol and engine oil
In praise of Ogun, god of iron and roads,
In praise of the first *mekaniki* of the turf
Who woke dying Opels and Austins
Chevrolets, Zephyrs and Bedfords. (23)

However, it is in *A Feast of Return/Under African Skies* that he draws copiously from African folklore across the continent, especially

Yoruba and the various groups of southern Africa. He admonishes in "Bata":

> Lest rulers fatten into a snore
> O kings who forget their people
> Bata drums compel the day
> when they must eat up their own heads. (15)

One needs to understand Yoruba folklore which relates how the Oba has to commit suicide if he fails to listen to the wishes of his people, a veiled warning to contemporary African leaders.

OTHER FEATURES OF THE SECOND GENERATION'S POETRY

It is in the aspect of commitment, deploying poetry to sociopolitical and economic struggle, that Ofeimun stands even taller among his second generation peers. He has garnered enough experience from work in organizing protest at an early age. It was trendy for young writers of the generation to be politically conscious and ideologically aligned to the Left even if not Marxist ideologues and to range on the side of the masses. Ofeimun's ideological commitment resulted from life experiences, ranging from dropping out of school for financial reasons, early work experience in the print media and factories, and self-teaching to pass exams that others take from school. In place of the cultural and racial conflict expressed by the earlier generation that experienced colonialism and nationalist struggle, Ofeimun's generation in the 1970s and 1980s believed in class conflict. This conflict is expressed in works of Syl Cheney-Coker as in "Peasants," Niyi Osundare's as in "Sule Chase," and many others. Ranging on the side of the common people by itself is an effort at making everybody in the nation matter rather than only the rich or educated in a country of primarily farmers and traders. The criticism of the military and political leadership of the country was intense. Ofeimun's poetry has a plethora of such acerbic criticism of the corrupt and dictatorial leadership of the country. The sarcastic tone of "The new brooms," "The Messiahs," and "Wait for the Roadblocks" tells the poet's scorn for the military no matter their rationalization for coming to power.

Ofeimun's poetry deals with sociopolitical issues of the time as that of his colleagues. In "the unsayable to be done," he finds contemporary Nigerian leaders as "now the vagabonds in power" who "go crawling / to off-shore Bankers" (*Dreams at Work*, p.10). In "wait for the roadblocks!" the poet represents the pervasive corruption and violence of police and army at checkpoints on Nigerian roads. To the poet,

> this whole country, man, is one swarming roadblock
> *for wetin you carry an' wetin you no carry*, you pay
> while princes of loot pass overhead in private jets…
> ....
> And not for them the butt-end of the corked Mark Four
> the accidental discharge that flattens the breadwinner
> they wait for the roadblocks and acquit the roadblocks. (*Dreams at Work*, p. 11)

The police and soldiers inflict "lusty horsewhip" on road travelers (12). Ofeimun shows awareness of his sociopolitical environment and sensitivity to its helpless victims.

A major preoccupation of the second generation of Nigerian poets is self-criticism. Instead of blaming "others," as the earlier generation did of Westerners for colonialism and economic exploitation that impoverished Africans, this group of poets blamed "ourselves," African leaders and populace. They believed that Africans had to take responsibility for their fate and not continue to blame outsiders for their economic and political woes. This phenomenon has to do with historical realities as writers respond to their times. The preceding generation at first responded to the colonial condition and then responded to the years following Nigeria's independence. Soyinka's *Idanre and Other Poems*, *A Shuttle in the Crypt*, and *Mandela's Earth* as well as Okigbo's *Poems Prophesying War*, and Clark's *State of the Union* are works that deal with Nigerian realities. The main difference with their predecessors is that the second generation poets focus almost entirely on internal criticism. There are many poems attacking the corrupt political leadership and societal ills in works of the generation.

Odia Ofeimun went further in self-criticism to question the role of the writer in a crisis-ridden country as Nigeria was during the Civil War (1967–1970). The writer, to Ofeimun, must be true to his vocation by being responsible and should attack negative forces in the society. In other words, literary artists should not just criticize others for societal ills and feel they owe no responsibility to their profession not to live above board. It is in this context that "The Poet Lied," the title poem of Ofeimun's first collection gained its literary traction. As Harry Garuba writes:

> "The Poet Lied" began a tradition of…the 'manifesto poem' in Nigerian writing (See "Lightness of Being"). In this type of writing,

the poem becomes a political and literary manifesto, contesting antecedent political positions and also outlining a new aesthetic in contra-
distinction to previous literary practice. In specific relation to Nigerian
poetry, "The Poet Lied" initiated a new practice by contesting the
ground of the mimetic adequacy on which earlier writers had positioned themselves in their bid to challenge colonialist writing about
Africa. The notion of "writing back" to the colonial library had been
the basis on which modern African literature written in European
languages established itself, claiming to be more accurate representa-
tions of African societies and cultures than the literature of Empire. By
directly challenging this claim of representational truth and authen-
ticity, this poem helped to establish an alternative ground for literary
expression, moving away from the culturalist poetics of anti-colonial
nationalism to a more robust contestation of the largely ontological and
essentialist positions that had held sway. (qtd. in Ojaide, *DLB*:2011)

This poem from its animal imagery and sarcastic tone was read by
many, when it was first published, to be a response to J. P. Clark, a
poet of the earlier generation, whose *Casualties*, poems about the
civil war, positioned the writer as a rather indifferent observer of war,
violence, and ethnic atrocities rather than one condemning such hei-
nous acts or taking the side of humanity. The speaker of Ofeimun's
poem says:

> Sometimes if he felt like it
> he would come away from his corner
> to take a closer look at things:
> fishermen in their canoes, hounded by tides,
> swimmers drowning, hounded by tides.
> And he would take snapshots –
> No need to caption them –
> He would not mind at all
> if he was called the poet of snapshots
> a quack of visions, a quack of visions. (26)

One can place the attitude of this poet beside Wole Soyinka's view
that "the man dies in all who keep silent in the face of tyranny" and
lobbied to form The Third Force to bring the feuding parties together
toward national reconciliation and peace. Ofeimun's activism is an
extension of Soyinka's deeds to prove that writing is a responsibility
to be on the side of truth and humanity.

One of the stylistic features of the second generation, which
Ofeimun uses to poetic advantage, is the device of repetition. While
employed primarily for emphasis and rhythmic flow of the poem,

it is also a strategic device to control the "free" verse. Unlike Wole Soyinka who uses rhymes in some of his poems in *Idanre*, poets of the second generation often use repetition in the refrain style of African oral tradition. In all of his poetry, Ofeimun varies his use of repetition and gives the poems a rhythmic movement whose cadences reflect the meaning he envisages. *Dreams at Work* and *London Letter* are illustrative of Ofeimun's use of repetition to advantage in his poetry. In *Dreams at Work*, poems such as "We must take leaves of iron from Ogun," "Your words touched us," "Wait for the roadblocks," "Ortega," and "Mafagejo's Story (1)," among many others, exhibit the poet's dexterous use of repetition. In his poem paying tribute to his father, "Giagbone," in *London Letter*, the poet repeats "I scour with my father's eyes" (25), a refrain which not only provides an organizing principle but also aesthetic beauty to the poem. Repetition has the same effects in both "The Ogbeni of Stroud Green Road" (34) and "Mara" (52–53). In Ofeimun and members of his generation, lack of rhymes and regular stanzas does not mean lack of form; they use a poetic strategy of such devices as repetition to impose some discipline on their verses.

Partisan Politician and Activist

Odia Ofeimun has a long history in different capacities of outside involvement that promotes democratic values. His involvement in journalism and partisan politics has provided him avenues to struggle for democratic values. As a young man, according to Harry Garuba, he worked briefly in 1968 as a reporter for *The Midwest Echo* (*DLB*, vol. 360). As an undergraduate, he edited not only *The Campus Defender* but also *The Kutite* (*DLB*, vol. 360). Later Ofeimun would work for *The Guardian*, *A. M News*, *The News*, and *Tempo* writing articles criticizing the military or societal vices toward democratic rule that ensures equality and justice for the general populace.

Ofeimun has been an avowed Awoist in Nigerian politics, irrespective of the evolution or transformation of the original Action Group that Chief Awolowo founded. He has been close to fellow Awoists such as Bola Ige and Asiwaju Bola Ahmed Tinubu in the Action Congress of Nigeria. He has undoubtedly been a partisan in political affiliation but that has not diminished his democratic values. He was on the side of the National Democratic Coalition (NADECO), after General Ibrahim Babangida annulled the election of Moshood Abiola on June 12, 1993. This shows that when it comes to justice, fair play, and democratic concerns, Ofeimun affirms his support irrespective of his political affiliation. He has consistently been on the side of the underprivileged, the common folks, and the voiceless. He has gone as far as widening representation even in the literary profession when he was president of the Association of Nigerian Authors by not only publishing an anthology of young writers, *Voices from the Fringe*, but also raising funds to publish some six poets. He has an unfinished business—his promise to do an anthology of Nigerian women's poetry—to realize his goal of empowering and giving voice to female literary artists. As Harry Garuba puts it, "Though many Nigerian writers, like their counterparts in other Third World countries, are often cast by circumstances in the role of public intellectuals of one sort or the other...., Odia Ofeimun's direct political engagement at a party political level and his social activism at an institutional, organizational level is not a very common practice among Nigerian writers" (*DLB* vol. 360).

Conclusion

Each era or generation provides the special talent, tools, voice, and the necessary wherewithal to cope with its problems. The writer who evinces commitment and responsibility goes a long way to meeting the demands of the time and fulfilling a sense of history. Odia Ofeimun has deployed his talent and resources to cope with the postcolonial society of the postindependence Nigerian nation and done so with singular dedication that is unparalleled in his generation of writers. He has used his poetic works and sociopolitical activism to sustain attention and struggle to build true democratic governance with justice, fairness, propriety, and other virtues to its credit. We have not arrived there yet but literature in the form of Ofeimun's poetry jumps from the printed page to force awareness of democratic values. His type of writer puts art to the service of society and not just to make money and win prizes. Literature thus matters in Nigeria, thanks to the likes of Odia Ofeimun, in shaping the democratic direction. In the narrative of the gradual and persistent march toward true democracy in Nigeria, Ofeimun's poetic output and practice together with his activism outside the book have facilitated the process that will make Nigeria a nation of humane and democratic values.

CHAPTER 9

Traditional Izon Court and Modern Poetry: Christian Otobotekere's Contribution

Introduction

Few rulers in traditional African societies practice poetry or can be called poets. Rather, they surround themselves with poets by whatever designations they call them. One can say that the kingship or chieftaincy institution in Africa is steeped in poetic traditions. The Asantehene of the Ashanti people in Kumasi, Ghana, has his "linguists" who are poets. Similarly, Hausa, Fulani, and Kanuri rulers in Northern Nigeria have their musicians and praise-singers. The Yoruba obas by their respective titles also have those who chant their orikis. In the Senegambian and Mali parts of West Africa, rulers have their griots who are not only poets but advisers and chroniclers of their people's history. Zulu and Tswana kings in Southern Africa have their imbongi who sing their praises through the established medium of *izibongo*. It is thus a surprising and pleasant change to see the Okun of Tombia, Christian Otobotekere, a modern poet, heading a traditional institution in which poets are supposed to serve him rather than be the poet himself. The surprise does not end with his being a poet. He is a modern man through his education at Fourah Bay University College, Sierra Leone, and the University of Durham in the United Kingdom. As a result of the nature of British education in the mid-1950s, though his major was Economic Studies, he still took courses in Latin and Literature. Cultures and societies are forever changing at paces that depend upon the forces driving them. It is therefore part of the postcolonial condition of Tombia to have a Western-educated traditional Izon ruler pursuing the reflective adventure of poetry as he presides over his court and other responsibilities that the office and his humanity have thrust upon him.

In African societies, the traditional ruler is expected to be the custodian of his people's culture, mores, and history, among other responsibilities. In doing so, he is at the center of many poetic traditions. There is poetry in the rites, rituals, festivals, royal and chiefly greetings, songs and chants, and even in the court deliberations in which the spokesperson for the ruler deploys proverbs to navigate serious issues at hand. In Benin and Ughelli traditions, there are specialized poetic chants and songs, music, and dance such as the *ema* that are limited to royal or court programs. Thus, being a traditional ruler in Africa means being at the center of the community's poetic experience. Of course, the traditional ruler and the priest/priestess are very much involved in yearly festivals which have a lot of poetry in their rituals.

Thus, the Okun of Tombia was not just born into a poetic society but presides over poetic functions. It is not as is put in the pop culture as "going to Sokoto to look for what is in your *sokoto!*" What has occurred in the Okun's poetic output is using his Western education to move with the times to write poetry in English and not just sing or chant in Izon.

POETRY, GOVERNANCE, AND SUCCESS IN LIFE

Being poet and also ruler, king, or emperor brings negative antecedents from many cultures. Remember Nero fiddling while Rome burned! There is the case of the British king (I think Richard IV) whose burial site was recently discovered—he was portrayed by William Shakespeare as a poet of sorts but a very weak and ineffective ruler. In traditional African societies, as portrayed by Chinua Achebe and Kofi Awoonor, among others, the traditional poet is seen as weak. Achebe's Unoka, Okonkwo's father, is one of such as Akpalu who mocks himself as seen as weak. Among the Urhobo people, the *ororile* (the poet/composer of songs) is generally viewed in the *udje* tradition as weak and bound to be poor. The question is: what is in poetry that its pursuit raises the ghost of failed kings and rulers and of traditional African poets as weaklings and failed men and women?

Is the poet too absorbed with reflection to be hesitant and to lack decisiveness and so fail in governance or other mundane pursuits? Poetry brings out the humane and the ennobling in us. The poet has a warm heart that is concerned more with others than his or her personal self. The poet sensitizes readers/audience and society to be more humane to folks suffering from poverty, hardship, handicaps, sickness, and other conditions and disadvantages in society. The poet tends to be preoccupied with pursuing policies to elevate folks not just materially but spiritually through human understanding, sensitivity, peace, and harmony. The poet as ruler may thus be filled with mercy and forgiveness and will not be strict or stringent enough and that condition could pose problems among a people who do not have their own self-control but have to be forced to exercise it. Poetry humanizes the ruler and that can be said of the Okun of Tombia. His love of aquatic sports in his membership of the Shell BP Boat Club and the Rivers State Sailing Association and other activities at one time or the other make him more human in his seeking the beauty of fulfillment in his personal and traditional pursuits. Thus, rather than make a ruler a failure, the qualities of a poet can enhance the modern traditional ruler to be humane and sensitive to the aspirations of his people. I thus believe that Christian Otobotekere faces the challenge of making a big difference among his people than other community rulers who are not poets.

The Ruler Poet and His Grassroots Subjects

Tombia Community is part of Ekpetiama Kingdom in Tombia-Yenagoa LGA of Bayelsa State. A poet writing from the Okun's position as the traditional ruler of a community in this rural area is faced by the daily mundane problems of his people. A fishing and farming community as Tombia's has to contend with the environment conducive to these occupations. While I take on nature and the environment later on, it is important to see what use the poet has made of the community's experience at the grassroots level. What issues of farming/agriculture, fishing/aquaculture, and sociocultural issues does the poet interrogate in his poetic writings? Does the poet accept the patriarchal customs without questioning? And what changes does he propose through his poetry to transform his community into a modern society that engages in sustainable agriculture and fishing and development for the well-being of the people?

The Nature Poet of Tombia

Christian Otobotekere impresses the reader of his first collection, *Playful Notes and Keys*, as a master nature poet. He celebrates birds for their beauty and wonder. He is highly imagistic as he brings to play all the senses in his descriptions. There is much of spectacle as he engages the reader's sense of sight such as

> Look, right in front
> Blink your eyes to see

Diving, vanishing, springing
Vanishing, springing, winging
Splash, splash, splash
Springing, winging, diving. (4)

Poems such as "Rainbow" (41) and "Sunflowers" (41), among so many poems, reinforce this preoccupation with the spectacle of nature. There is much about hearing in the music of the birds as in "Song" (28) and touch, smell, and taste. He writes, "Your first touch, dear water / Chilly and tingling" (8). He also describes the "bush aroma" (8) he comes across.

One can summarize the poet's use of nature in his first collection into four aspects. There is the nature of fauna and flora with birds, squirrel, iroko, and others. Second, there is nature as landscape in the land, rivers, sea, and tableland. Third is the cosmic nature of the sun, moon, stars, clouds, rainbow, and others. And finally is nature as "Nature" or "nature" which tends to indicate what in African parlance could be termed "bush." Nature is vibrant and sensual in the poems. Nature is described as a wetland in "Lake Garden" (26–8).

Otobotekere establishes himself as a highly descriptive poet from his first collection in a poem as "Farewell":

Soon we were brushing smoke clouds
In our onward glide
Soon through a white misty wall,
Suddenly bursting
Into Nature's harmonious colours
Of cerulean blue
Blue above, blue below
And at the horizon
A vista of terraced clouds,
Irridiscent and a-fire
With colours of a different world. (38)

Otobotekere is a fine poet of nature and he brings all aspects of nature alive in his poetic musings through descriptive details that touch all human senses.

The Poet and His Environment

Christian Otobotekere is a product of his riverine environment. Born in Tombia by the River Nun, which Gabriel Okara has made famous with "The Call of the River Nun," the poet has internalized his environment in his musings. He expresses not just himself but also the environment and life of his community in the nature issues he addresses in the fauna and flora. For a ruler whose traditional title is "Okun" (which bears relationship with Olokun, the sea goddess) and whose family name is Otobotekere (with Otobo being the hippo), he is very much at home in his water environment and familiarity with riverine and aquatic images which recur in his writings.

My River typifies the Okun's obsession with, or rather passion for, his riverine environment with poems addressing the River Niger and its tributary River Nun and the life around them. The wetlands are filled with kingfisher, kites, "Anambra waxbill," "koo-koo," weaver, monkey, egrets, "Osuma-opopo," crocs, eagle, hawk as well as the iroko and other plants. The collection is an ode to nature as it manifests itself in the region in which the poet was born, grew up, and lived. The river (apparently the Nun) is addressed as "Darling river" (25). Some of the most effective lines of the poet are descriptions of aquatic life as of kites in "Morning Kites":

> See the ace glider,
> Now swooping down
> With buoyant body
> Even so low, and,
> On suspended wings,
> Smoothly draws an arc
> As she drops out two orange feet
> Gently, with timed grace:
>> Shrewd picking device
>> For a neat catch, off the river. (27)

The poet presents the river and the environment as aesthetically pleasing and good for the community and the individual. Of course, it is the catalyst for his reflections on nature which results in words of wisdom. Though he finds the river beautiful, he does not fail to remind the reader of its destructiveness in the accidental loss of lives by drowning and also the floods that ravage the area.

The poet observes nature and is very passionate and nostalgic about the Rivers Niger and Nun and the environment. He describes the biodiversity of the wetland basin whose aquatic life is very vibrant. However, he does not go beyond listing and celebrating these nonhuman beings of the environment. Yes, he mentions "changing climate" in *Playful Notes and Keys* (16) but does not dwell on it. Similarly, in

My River, he talks about "The forest I knew" (19) but remains too subtle and indirect to lead the reader to imagine the current state of things. In "I am One with You," the speaker of the poem asks: "Is this the same river / Of my birth / Unknown years ago?" The speaker goes on to describe nostalgically the bygone experience, which we do not know still prevails:

> This sibilant water
> In lullaby floods
> Best known to me and to
> Those jump-and-dive kids
> And the river-bent
> Sizzling reeds:
> The same sizzling
> And whistling river,
> Stirring the welcome of
> Migrant fishes and perched canals:
> And of yellow-stricken leaves of trees
> Standing at attention. (35)

The poet brings alive the environment and the reader can feel and experience it in its totality of a vibrant biodiverse wetland area. There is no interrogation of the riverine ecology; there is no mentioning of issues of pollution, poaching, and human degradation of the riverine ecology he contemplates. From personal observation in the Amassoma and other areas of Izonland, folks use the river as the place to not only bathe and use water for house chores but also as a toilet. Why does the lover of the environment not question these things? I suppose when the Okun was young, twins were thrown into the rivers to die. What does he say of the river also as a burial place?

Life appears to stand still and the downward spiral of environmental degradation of flora and fauna not fashioned into an ecocritical discourse in the areas of ecological justice, the community's health and economy, or other environmental issues. There appears to be no problems. Questions are raised in the nostalgic yearning but no answers are proffered. In short, Otobotekere remains a nature poet in the old fashion sense of the British Romantic poets such as Wordsworth and Coleridge, simply contemplative but not politically engaged to question changes taking place around. However, he has succeeded in celebrating a life that has been there and is fast disappearing. He may not be postmodern enough but appears to see the close relationship between nature and human beings. The health of the environment is also the health of the people who share the same environment.

A Poet of Many Parts

The Okun of Tombia should not be confined to the straightjacket of nature and the environment. He is rather a poet of many parts. In his first collection, he administers the interface of orality and modern poetic tradition in the folkloric "Fabled Tortoise" (17). In the poem, he contemplates on an African folklore from his vantage point of a nature poet:

> They say,
> When at the same time
> You have sunshine
> On the one hand
> And showers of rain
> On the other,
> And the one slanting into the other,
> It is a sure token
> Of some rare event.
> It may be
> In his lair
> A leopard is giving birth
> Or other rare deed
> Is in the offing. (17)

This is a collection in which he uses folksongs to reinforce his poetry. In this collection too, he writes about "Esther" (56), a dirge-like poem.

The poet's *Next To Reality* shows a multidimensional poet even when we acknowledge that he writes about birds, animals, and rivers. In this collection, he is a poet of memory not only like John Keats, William Wordsworth but also like W. B. Yeats who writes about the "beauty" he has seen. His poetic philosophy, encapsulated in "next to reality," tells of poetry in which he displays in descriptive metaphors memories of the past. In "End of Drama," he writes:

> The drama is ended.
> But let me carry with me
> All I had seen
> Of the stunning drama along this river,
> And skyward beauty,
> Of Nature's sleight-of-hand
> And portraits live. (Otobotekere152)

And in consonance with this philosophy he describes a plane descend in "Descent," one of his most successful poems:

> We are dipping down
> With pointed nose, dipping down,
> Dipping down with
> Stomach-upsetting heave.
> Yet through the port hole, one could see
> The beauty of evening spread
> Of stranded whitish clouds.
> A fascination
> Not in any way diminished
> By speed. (21)

Appropriately, the poet likens the airplane to a bird. There is thus a relationship between nature and art/craft.

There are other poems in the collection which have philosophical, religious, and spiritual preoccupations as in "Ancestral Life" and the poem on the poet's pilgrimage. On the other hand, "One Flag" exhibits patriotism. Otobotekere thus either uses nature as a metaphor for deeper meaning or takes on themes which indicate a more expansive poetic personality.

The Poet's Lyricism

It is important to look at Otobotekere's poetry beyond the presence of nature, the riverine environment, and memories of past personal experiences. What strikes the reader in his work is the sheer lyricism of the poetry. From the first collection to the latest the poetry is filled with lyrical qualities. The poems are musical, sometimes direct addresses to the subjects in an ode-like fashion, some elements of the elegy in "Esther," and the outpouring of thoughts and feelings. Nature and the environment are the setting for the poet to let out his passion and description of the vibrant aspects of nature he has experienced in his Niger Delta area. He loves the environment as one loves a partner and the language is that of longing for the environment as it used to be.

On the other hand, the lyrical qualities of the poems help the reader to understand the nature of the poet's commitment to his environment. His use of exclamation, repetition, personification, and, above all, images that touch all the senses makes his poetry tactile and concrete. One can always imagine in the mind's eye, hear, feel, smell, touch, and taste aspects of the environment he reflects on poetically. Thus, one cannot discuss Otobotekere as a poet of nature and the environment, and I will say as a multidimensional poet, without underscoring the lyrical nature of the poetry itself that helps one to grasp the complexities of his feelings and thoughts. He is a poet of passion and deep reflections and makes his observations of nature more perceptive to experience and share with him.

The Poet and His Sociopolitical Ideology

Inevitably, critics will ask the Okun about the nature of his relationship to Shell BP and other multinational oil companies working in his area or in the Niger Delta. Are the people adequately compensated for the resources taken from their soil and the environmental damage that affects their farming and fishing? Tombia is not far from gas flares on the Amassoma-Yenagoa Road. Does the company flaring the gas deal with the health hazards of the flaring with the local community? A poet maintains silence over some things, while speaking loud about other things. What philosophy of nature and environment does Christian Otobotekere present in his poetry? Is he dynamic enough to fight for his people before their political leaders in Yenagoa and their exploiters? As far as the poems are concerned, the Okun's persona in the poems is of a tempered man who is not an activist to the extent of rousing his people to take up arms against the oil corporations. He is in a good position to know what the oil companies offer Tombia's folks as the local community.

After reading Otobotekere's poetic works, I can only come to the conclusion that he has his poetic choices that make him gravitate to nature and the environment. However, he is not a fighter but a nature poet in a Romantic sense in his contemplation about aspects, especially the soothing beauty that his Tombia environment is made of. He seeks communion with nature on a very personal/individualistic manner and contemplates the blessings of a pristine rather primordial antediluvian environment. He seems mute about the changes which have taken place over the years but which undermine the beauty he seeks. He elevates nature to a spiritual state and one can feel how fulfilled he is with the other living creatures and plants with whom he shares the same earth. His awareness of the harmony between humans and other living things is based on intuitive experience and not on eco-critical or political activism about the green gas effects. It appears the poet wants to uplift humanity spiritually in a rather tranquil mode. His poetic sensibility is sharp and simple and it is effective enough to engage the reader. With his poetic proposition, the environment will continue to give humans a kind of fulfillment that can only be said to be spiritual and aesthetic.

CHRISTIAN OTOBOTEKERE AND NIGER DELTA LITERATURE

Tombia is in the heart of the Niger Delta and the terrain, occupations of the people, and sociocultural preoccupations tally well with what happens elsewhere in the region. Can we say that Otobotekere's poems fall into the categorization of Niger Delta literature? He may have been influenced by Wordsworth and other nature poets, but over the years he has shifted to look at the environment with more critical lenses. His work may not be the poetry of Ebinwo, Ikoriko, Ebi Yeibo, and Ojaide, but one has to look at his position as the Ruler of the Tombia Community. One should not forget his age too. He is a little younger than Gabriel Okara with whom he shares the same Bayelsa State and lives by the very River Nun that Okara addressed his memorable poem, "The Call of the River Nun." His collections may not have the reputation of *The Fisherman's Invocation* but he articulates the main spirit of the Niger Delta in the proximity of nature, the importance of the environment, and the constant dedication to the humanity of all. He is surely a Niger Delta writer who has used the resources at his disposal to articulate the spirit and experience of his place from an individual perspective. In *My River* he successfully inscribes the Niger Delta ecology into the contemporary poetic landscape and it is a measure of his consistence, passion, and artistic skill that we can picture in our minds' eyes what the Niger Delta wetlands looked like at a time before oil conglomerates came to degrade the pristine environment.

THE OLD MAN AS A LIBRARY

Fortunately for us, we are celebrating a human library because of the wealth of knowledge packed into one man, the Okun of Tombia. In his eighties, it is appropriate to beat the gong for a man who could have settled down with a harem of wives and engage in a hedonistic lifestyle but instead chose the intellectual and contemplative life of a poet. There is no doubt that he must have made sacrifices to write these many books. As a poet myself, I can imagine the times spent alone and the labor to hone the poems to a beauty he affirms as his projection of the artistic quality of poetry. He presents his themes in a simple manner to convey his message. He does not contrive to be sophisticated in artistic form but the beauty of the poems lies in their being stripped of artifice. After all, he sees nature as art and beautiful.

Christian Otobotekere has had a distinguished career as a poet. He may not be well- known by students and scholars in the academy but the body of work he has done deserves critical scrutiny. He has chosen what to write on and we need to read him for his wise and experienced observations about nature and the piece of the earth he is fortunate enough to live in and express with passion and a strong sense of nostalgia. There are certain things that only age can achieve. For the Okun of Tombia, his steadfast dedication to poetry has brought us to this gathering of minds. Whether we are critical of his poetry or transported by it, we have found the work worthy of our attention.

Conclusion

My role is to challenge my fellow poet and member of ANA, the Okun of Tombia, to look at other ways his poetic imagination can lead him to. He has to engage the environment in a dynamic way and reflect on the political, sociocultural, economic, and other aspects of the environment to reflect the presence of multinational oil and gas corporations as well as how local communities through their practices help to degrade their own environment. At the same time I challenge scholars to interrogate the work of Christian Otobotekere. Is he a poet of nature like Wordsworth? Do you deploy eco-criticism to study his work? Is he a lyrical poet? What is the relevance to his community and himself of his poetic preoccupations?

From my discussion so far, there is no doubt that Otobotekere is a fine poet of nature who uses all the human senses to appreciate his environment. He is highly descriptive. He is more than a nature poet in his use of Izon folklore to reinforce his poetic discourse. He is interested in nature as well as humans and society. He loves birds, he loves flying. At his best in poetic flight, he is an accomplished poet and we would wish him to soar further and further.

CHAPTER 10

Reviving Modern African Poetry: An Argument

Introduction

It is an understatement to say that contemporary African poetry lacks vibrancy or popular appeal, compared to modern African poetry in the 1960s through the 1980s. African contemporary poetry appears to be suffering from generic exhaustion that has thrown avid readers and literary critics out of balance for what to embrace with passion. It is not that modern African poetry, by nature of being written, especially in European languages, in a society that has primarily been nonliterate and illiterate generally, has not always reached the general populace as the writers would have liked for their works to be read and studied. Also there has always been something in modern African poetry for readers and literary scholars to complain about. If it was not the naïve imitativeness of the "pioneer poets" of the 1930s to the 1950s, whose poetry was highly imitative of Western Christian hymns or Victorian writings, there was the obscurity, disjointedness, and difficulty of the African "euro-modernists" of the 1960s to the 1970s. And following that generation, there was the lack of form of the "alter/native" group of poets who paid much attention to revolutionary messages in the 1980s and 1990s. Now there is everything to complain about in contemporary African poetry from lack of a discernible African voice in the age of globalization to a palpable lightness that makes poetry seem irrelevant to the needs of the society and age.

Despite the limitations and complaints, modern African poetry in the past appears to have thrived well in comparison to the genres of fiction and drama. There was a time when the poets were aristocrats with a certain type of mystique around them. Where are the Christopher Okigbo, Wole Soyinka, John Pepper Clark, Kofi Awoonor,

Lenrie Peters, and Dennis Brutus of today? The poetry readers of the 1960s and 1970s knew the vagabond minstrel of Okigbo who would join the secessionist side of the Nigerian civil war and die fighting. Soyinka seized a radio station to make a broadcast; Brutus escaped the apartheid forces after being shot at; Kofi Awoonor was hunted by the Ghanaian military regime of the day for being associated with a coup plotter; and so on with the poet acquiring legendary status in his time.

Also in the past, one knew or heard of poems and their writers. Most writers, teachers, and students of African poetry in the 1960s, 1970s, and early 1980s knew David Rubadiri's "An African Thunderstorm," Gabriel Okara's "Piano and Drums," Dennis Brutus's "The sounds begin again," J. P. Clark's "Night Rain," Wole Soyinka's "Death in the Dawn," Christopher Okigbo's "Before you, mother Idoto / naked I stand," Lenrie Peters' "We have come home," and Kofi Awoonor's "Songs of Sorrow." In the 1980s and 1990s, perhaps one would have read or heard of Odia Ofeimun's "The Poet Lied," Niyi Osundare's "Poetry is," and Tanure Ojaide's "The fate of vultures." How far back from now over the past 20 years can we remember poems and their writers? Has contemporary African poetry become so unimpressive that it is no longer memorable or quotable? Have poems become too many that none strikes the reader's attention? Or is the problem with the reader and literary scholar that there appears to be not enough effort in generating interest in poetry in Africa today? These questions will hopefully be answered in the course of this "argument."

Factors Marginalizing Modern African Poetry

There are multifarious factors today contributing to the demise of African poetry that appear to be beyond the control of poets and readers. Literature in general is suffering from inattention as literate people in Africa would prefer to spend their money on what they consider critical areas of existence such as paying house rents, school fees for children, and their subsistence than in buying poetry collections, novels, or plays. It is only in schools that literature is mostly consumed because such literary works are required textbooks that have to be studied to pass examinations. Thus, the poor or mismanaged state of African economies has contributed to the erosion of the special place of literature in contemporary African lives. Poetry appears to suffer the most when it comes to the genres, with fiction doing relatively well as a result of promotion by foreign publishers and literary agents. Poetry from the beginning has always lagged behind fiction in readership and it is no surprise that when literature is suffering, poetry appears to bear the brunt of neglect.

In addition, today literature is competing with mass media and social media for the leisure that literature once almost monopolized. There were times in the late 1940s, 1950s, and the very early 1960s, for instance, when traders in Onitsha Market in Eastern Nigeria used to read books that became generically known as "Onitsha Market Literature." There appears to be no room for traders in that market or any others today to indulge in reading anymore. Their break time may be for prayers like some other African markets that shut down to pray at certain times of the day as the Igbudu Market in Warri, Nigeria. Now, if the Onitsha traders were not haggling with buyers, they would likely have cable televisions before them tuned to either "Africa Magic" or European football to which they appear addicted!

Of course, there are more avenues for publishing now than before in the sense of self-publishing and online publishing both of which are fairly recent phenomena or have increased astronomically in the past several decades. While the publication process has been democratized with every writer having wider options, including self-publication and online posting to get out his or her work, there are negative effects that do not favor the growth of literature in general and poetry in particular. The self-publishing is often abused with poetry manuscripts getting printed without going through the process of editorial boards in publishing. Almost anyone can now post poems or manuscripts online and there is no formal organ to review the works or assess their quality before being posted. This lack of gatekeeping in self-publishing and the online posting of works has adversely affected the quality of poetry works compared to the past when several publishing houses, especially Heinemann, Longman, and the East African Publishing House had monopoly in publishing African poetic works in their respective African Writers Series. Then, the works went through a sort of publishing filter before getting to the public. Not anymore. Now the crowded space of new works available in different media instead of generating interest is rather frustrating the interest of readers who encounter a wide range of works whose quality has not had the imprimatur of reputable publishing houses. In addition, poetry has been marginalized in Africa, since its space has shrunk considerably because of new media that have caught the attention of the literate populace. People watch cable television, music videos, "home videos," and get absorbed by other media such as Facebook that diminish the spare or leisure time for poetry.

The Vacuum in Contemporary African Poetry

A vacuum exists in contemporary African poetry that needs to be addressed and filled lest poetry will lose out totally to fiction. Currently, poetry in Africa is anemic and needs to be revived to prevent it from falling into irreversible coma. The lusterless condition of African poetry today has to be addressed to seek ways to revitalize it to stop further degeneration of the critical condition. The vacuum is a problem which appears more pronounced among black African poets and not with all poets across the continent. Many young black African poets do not look up to or see themselves as part of the same tradition as their predecessors. Rather, they want to identify with Western writers to be international. Of course, there is American poetry that no American poet disagrees with. There is Western literature with its established canon that is robustly guarded by Western literary critics. It will help African literature if writers are conscious of their oral and written literatures. It will do much good to the tradition if younger writers look to their predecessors rather than only to outsiders because they have to be aware of the African poetic tradition and aesthetics in their literary creativity. If literature is a cultural production, how will the literary production not be an aggregate of that culture?

At the same time there are many African writers/poets who embrace African culture and look to their roots and environment for models of literary creativity to express their individual responses to Africa's current reality. The African poets who incorporate African oral traditions into their works have an African cultural identity. Those ones are primarily older poets but there are also many younger ones that maintain an African identity. These ones explore the rich African folklore for materials for poetic form and techniques. Their poetry absorbs performance techniques, especially of repetition, humor, sarcasm, irony, and often the poems, when performed, are accompanied with musical instruments to be dramatically moving.

Another exception to those who want to latch themselves to the Western poetry tradition is the North African poets. These poets generally identify themselves with the Arab tradition of poetry which is very old. Many go as far as using old poetic forms of the Arab tradition to write innovatively about new realities. Since these poets do not see themselves as African and look to Arab/Muslim Rumi, Adonis, Mahmoud Darwish, and others, they are not part of the group killing African poetry slowly!

The Problematic of Originality

Modern African poetry started with the problematic of originality which still haunts it up to this day. It is not just the postcolonial problem of Africans writing in foreign, albeit European, languages alone which led African literature at the beginning to be seen as part of English or French, or Portuguese literature. There were other problems which relate to originality. The Pioneer Poets have been the least original of all the generations of modern African poets. They imitated the diction of Victorian poetry and Christian hymns to express their reaction to the Western incursion into Africa, which coincides with the arrival of modernity in much of Africa. Some went to praise colonialism and Christianity overtly and a few talked about Western racism. Their poetry was not that of deep thematic exploration even of their times: the exploitation of African economies, the suppression of political and human rights, and other aspects of colonialism that was basically an exploitative phenomenon. Some of the poems rise above the general naïve poetic discourse and Dennis Osadebay's "Young Africa's Plea" is an example of that remarkable exception:

Don't preserve my customs
As some fine curios
To suit some white historian's tastes.
There's nothing artificial
That beats the natural way
In culture and ideals of life.
Let me play with the white man's ways
Let me work with the black man's brains
Let my affairs themselves sort out.
Then in sweet rebirth
I'll rise a better man
Not ashamed to face the world.
Those who doubt my talents
In secret fear my strength

They know I am no less a man.
But let them bury their prejudice,
Let them show their noble sides,
Let me have untrammeled growth,
My friends will never know regret
And I, I never once forget.

Other poets of the colonial times were less assertive of their African culture and expressed gratitude for the colonization; an acceptance of a subject position in Africa's relationship with the West. If they are described as writing "apprentice poetry," that only confirms their lack of originality.

Much as the next era of African poetry turned out to be canonical in the sense of providing a credible poetic tradition, the second generation of poets was also not original. The generation boasts of Christopher Okigbo, Wole Soyinka, J. P. Clark, Kofi Awoonor, Lenrie Peters, Kwesi Brew, and Dennis Brutus, among others. Described as obscurantist euro-modernists who wrote poetry like the Western modernists (T. S. Eliot, Ezra Pound, W. B. Yeats, etc.), their poetry, as of Okigbo's *Heavensgate* and *Labyrinths* and Soyinka's *Idanre and Other Poems*, was obscure, difficult, fragmented and emphasized form at the expense of meaning. Okigbo was quoted on separate occasions as not only saying that he did not write with any meaning in mind and also that he did not write for non-poets. Soyinka's poetry, as in his 1967 collection *Idanre and Other Poems*, is very difficult with occasional use of rhymes and formal stanzas in the English poetic convention. But despite the influence of modernist poetry, there were poets who wrote poems that stand firmly in an African categorization. If one were to take J. P. Clark's poems as an example, one can sense the "sprung rhythm" of John Manley Hopkins in "Ibadan" and a few poems. However, "Night Rain," "A Reed in the Tide," and "Streamside Exchange," among others, show a charming innocence that enthralls the reader. Here is "Streamside Exchange":

> Child: River bird, river bird,
>   Sitting all day long
>   On hook over grass
>   River bird, river bird,
>   Sing to me a song
>   Of all that pass
>   And say,
>   Will mother come back today?
> Bird: You cannot know
>   And should not bother;
>   Tide and market come and go
>   And so has your mother. [*A Reed in the Tide*, 16]

With the general perception of poetry that was obscure and difficult, soon started the efforts to decolonize modern African poetry with Chinweizu's seminal work with Jemie and Madubuike, *Towards the Decolonization of Modern African Literature*, leading the way. These efforts by the *bolekaja* group of activist critics influenced a new generation of poets, the "alter/native" group of poets that include Niyi Osundare, Odia Ofeimun, Frank Chipasula, Jack Mapanje, Kofi Anyidoho, and Tanure Ojaide. This third generation of modern African poets went back to their indigenous African oral literature to borrow techniques for their writings and focusing on meaning in their poems since they wanted to change their society. Talking of originality, these poets have gone back to fuse tradition and modernity and cannot be said to be purely original in doing something that has not been done before. They took forms and techniques from the oral tradition and fused them into what their preceding modern poets have done.

Much of what has followed the third generation has not yet gelled into a generation but can be termed the fourth generation, which is a mixture of the features of the third generation and idiosyncratic ideas about a global African literature. Again, there is nothing original as such as their works appear to follow earlier techniques and the themes interrogate the same issues of environment, freedom and human rights, and individual experiences also covered earlier.

History, Zeitgeit, and Modern African Poetry

Modern African poetry has reacted to history since its inception in the early 20th century. As already stated, modern African poets reacted to the colonial condition before the political independence of most African countries in the late 1950s and early 1960s. Then the postindependence period had its early stage of euphoria and then the disappointment that followed soon after the governments started to fail their people. The zeitgeist impacts on individual and societal experiences that the poets express. Sometimes the experiences derive from within the nation or society and at other times from the world outside or the human condition. The military dictatorships and political corruption within Africa were reinforced by internal and foreign demands for democratic rule and representation. At the same time the feminist movement had its waves in Africa where most societies are patriarchal. Works of many female poets tapped into the feminist or womanist discourse for their poems. Molara Ogundipe and many other female poets wrote feminist poems in the late 1970s and early 1980s. One can say that female poets have become more radical over the years and Naana Banyinwa Horne's *Sunkwa Revisited* is far more brazen in diction, ideology, and thematic openness than anything earlier poets such as Ama Ata Aidoo, Mabel Segun, or Molara Ogundipe did.

Another major global movement that has its African expression is the environmental and ecological movement. Niyi Osundare in *The Eye of the Earth* blazed the trail in that direction. To him, "The earth will not die!" Tanure Ojaide has as the focus of many poems that include *The Tale of the Harmattan* the Niger Delta environment degraded by multinational oil corporations. Many other poets, especially of Nigeria's Niger Delta, have followed suit with so many poems that have to do with their despoiled environment. Such poets include Ogaga Ifowodo in *The Oil Lamp*, Ebinyo Ogbowei's *Song of a Dying River*, and Ebi Yeibo's *The Forbidden Tongue*.These poets are propelled by the prevailing realities of their societies and times.

POSTCOLONIALISM AND ORIGINALITY

While African poets have reacted to happenings around them in their individual ways, these poems carry formal and technical traits of either foreign European or indigenous African poetic traditions. The question to be asked is: can a postcolonial poet be original? Modern African poetry is postcolonial and that complicates the issue of originality. Using writing and a foreign language the African poet is saddled with by the accident of history, he or she has been forced to be a hybrid trying to blend indigenous and foreign poetic traditions. I am not saying a postcolonial poet cannot be original but it is difficult to be original with a foreign language as most Africans do with English, French, or Portuguese. Maybe the poet can only be relatively original; that is original to a certain extent.

Many have gone as far as saying that Christopher Okigbo has been Africa's greatest modern poet. And yet even his most passionate devotees will agree that he was a pickpocket as far as his poetry is concerned. If he is influenced by French composers and Mesopotamian myths and he strongly echoes some American poets and others to the point of sometimes being accused of plagiarism, how original is his poetry? However, the way one assembles materials from others into a unique form or architecture could result in a kind of, if not a semblance of, originality.

Writing in defense of Christopher Okigbo, Obi Nwakanma writes:

In his interview with Robert Serumaga at the Transcription Center in London in 1963, Okigbo acknowledged that he took from other poets and integrated these into the texture of his poetry in answer to the question about "Limits." Okigbo absorbed a variety of poetic airs from the classical to the modern; he restates the same fact clearly in the introduction to his collection *Labyrinths* acknowledging the poets from whom he had taken to integrate into his poetic expression. There is a great echo of Tchicaya U'Tami's *Brushfire* published by the Mbari books in 1965 in "Path of Thunder," and in fact in rejecting the Langston Hughes Prize in Dakar in 1966 of which Derek Walcott was 2nd runner-up and which was later awarded the African American Poet Robert Hayden, Okigbo wrote, suggesting that it be given to U'Tamsi, "a better poet than I." He was clear about himself and had not the impiety of self-regard as a poet.

From a critical point, and having studied Okigbo's work quite closely, I'm generally amused by those who keep talking about Okigbo's "plagiarism." Plagiarism occurs when you do not acknowledge your sources. What Okigbo does is radical *misprision*, to sometimes upturn, decontextualize and recontextualize an extant poetic line or imagery, and in refashioning it gives a newer more authentic feel to sometimes flat or obscure lines. Okigbo was a bold experimentalist, far ahead of his time in his form of intertextual integration. It was a poetic practice and method based on the notion later noted by postmodernist theorists which Okigbo put into practice by a system of collages, revisions, reproductions, and re-interpretations, of the boundedness of language; or as Derrida would put it: "Il n'y a pas de hors-texte." Okigbo, I think, is to modern poetry, what Picasso is to the Arts. The genius of Okigbo is that you might hear or sense say Carl Sandburg, say in "Silences" and yet be confounded at its purity and novelty in Okigbo. A prolix line of poetry recovered from their langor becomes better, fresher, more categorical in Okigbo, because Okigbo gives it a new order of movement and a force which only the most powerful poetic imagination is capable. Meanwhile, he does it better than Eliot, who can also be accused of serial poetic "imitation" and "plagiarism" for indeed we see in the body of his modernist work, lines, words, and echoes that are stolen and borrowed. Poets know, that all poetry has been written. Sometimes, to renew poetry true poets must act as carnivores of language and be piratical in their search for it. Okigbo was a master of the intertext. His poetry is a testimony, even in its leanness, of a highly scribal agency of which only few are capable at any moment in history. (posted in the Internet)

Thus, the postcolonial poet can be original in form despite his or her hybridity. This can be seen in the wider culture in which a people can talk about their traditional way of dressing with all the materials imported from other parts of the world. Many ethnic groups in Nigeria's Niger Delta, including the Efik-Ibibio, Ijo, Itsekiri, and Urhobo, have materials for their traditional dresses for men and women not made by them. The same holds for groups in South Sudan, Senegal, Mali, Ghana, and others. It is only with the style or form that they can lay claim to the dress as theirs! One can argue that the bird builds its nest by gathering materials from different sources and the end product of the nest is always unique.

Even if a poet can be original in language, in what language can the postcolonial poet be original? This has to be in language use. For the African raised in or informed by an indigenous language and sometimes many languages, there is a close association between the indigenous language and the adopted foreign one. This close relationship that involves code switching and others manifests in the poetry of the second and third generations whose poets went as far as studying and using their ethnic languages and folklores to inform their English, French, or Portuguese. Examples of J. P. Clark studying Ijo epic drama and Urhobo udje songs, Wole Soyinka studying Yoruba traditional drama with a Ford Foundation grant, Kofi Awoonor's study of Ewe "songs of sorrow" as practiced by Akpalu and others, Kofi Anyidoho's study too of Ewe poetry, Jack Mapanje's study of Chewa orature, and Tanure Ojaide's research into udje songs are known. There is always a subtext to the English many of these poets use and that gives their work a particularity that is individual and unique. When Kofi Awoonor talks of "When I clean, it cannot go" in a poem, he is transliterating from Ewe into English. That gives his English a special Ewe-ness that other Englishes do not possess.

I believe in this area of the use of indigenous language and folklore to resist the imperialness of British English that African poets can establish their own originality. Many African poets have modeled their poetic writings on the techniques of repetition, musicality, proverbs, and other features derived from the oral literature tradition.

INTERTEXTUALITY AND MODERN AFRICAN POETRY

One way that originality can be gained in the postcolonial tradition of the modern African poetry may be through intertextuality. Since the tradition of modern African poetry is established, one can be original within it by questioning and renewing the tradition. It is in the dialogic discourse as each generation confronts what has preceded it and making daring moves or taking novel risks that some form of originality can be established or introduced into the modern African poetry tradition. In its "anxiety of influence" each generation tries to respond to prevailing conditions by questioning, defying, radically renewing or even changing the direction in form, techniques, and themes of the poetry. This has happened in the Okigbo–Soyinka–Clark as the Ofeimun–Osundare–Ojaide–Chimalum Nwankwo; as of the Aderemi Raji–Oyelade–Ademola Dasylva–Akeem Lasisi–Ogaga Ifowodo groups in Nigeria. While this literary generational lineage is Nigerian, the same is roughly true of Egyptian, Ghanaian, Malawian, Senegalese, and South African modern poets. New issues may not be well expressed in old idioms but have to seek new means of articulation.

What this "anxiety of influence" means is that each generation of modern African poets tries to distance itself from the preceding one by reacting in a manner it deems new or revolutionary. The case of the "alter/native" Nigerian poets reacting against the earlier "euro-modernist" group of poets is a good example. Each generation influences what comes after it. While this is an attempt to revive the tradition, there are always residues of the preceding generation in the new one however hard the group wants to be different. So, in a way, each generation is aware of what comes before it and either wants to stretch its own peculiarities or defy or reject the antecedents. In some cases, the new generation tries to "kill" the earlier one by mouth or pen!

Despite the often conflicting relationship between generations, there is so much of acknowledgment and, by implication, of intertextuality and reverence for the past. Literary scholars or the younger poets have accepted indebtedness to the older poets: Tijan M. Sallah to Lenrie Peters, Kofi Anyidoho to Kofi Awoonor; Odia Ofeimun to Wole Soyinka; Chimalum Nwankwo to Okigbo; Tanure Ojaide to both Okigbo and J. P. Clark; Amadou Lamine Sall to Leopold Sedar Senghor; Akeem Lasisi to Niyi Osundare; and so forth. The intertextuality in these poets' works establishes a strong link between contiguous generations and helps to solidify the tradition of modern African poetry. Each generation thus builds on the earlier one in expanding the tradition in whatever direction the intellectual climate of the time leads them. The exposure of writers to those older than them in age or writing inevitably leads to an understanding of what is current in order to establish what follows. Of course, literary scholars and other literary critics in their writings expose the strengths and weaknesses of the writers that make younger poets fashion their concepts of what their new generation should write about. The "alter/native" generation attempted to decolonize modern African literature with the writings of the likes of Chinweizu and other *bolekaja* critics. Other factors such as globalization may be leading younger contemporary African writers to rely less on their folkloric background and literary foreparents and to look to Western writing traditions.

Parody and Originality

It may sound ironical that parody could be a strategy to initiate orig-inality and revive an anemic contemporary African poetry. After all, parodying assumes an earlier version that the later writer attempts to use for a different effect. While on the drama side that paral-lels poetry, Femi Osofisan has done that with J. P. Clark's *The Raft* with *Another Raft,* there are examples in poetry. I have tried to mimic Wole Soyinka's *Shuttle in the Crypt* in "A Bottle in the Pit" (*Labyrinths of the Delta*). Parody in this sense means one writer's dissatisfaction with or interest in querying a viewpoint or form that has been used and attempting to use it in a different, perhaps more effective, way.

Parody thus involves creation and re-creation in creativity. It is a form of poetic reinvention, a poetic call-and-response, and not just being a hybrid. Two poetic techniques that parody might entail are irony and humor. This is inevitable as the poet parodying the work of another poet has to deflate the earlier version to affirm the necessity for parodying it. Irony and humor tend to go together in parody. This has been the case in modern African poetry. Odia Ofeimun's *The Poet Lied* is generally viewed as a response to and a critique of J. P. Clark's Nigerian Civil War poems, *Casualties.* With the possibility of linking the past with the present or the old and the new, parody will go a long way to revive poetry in the younger writer attempting to interrogate an earlier work with a new poetic or creative response.

Toward Revival and Originality

Modern African poetry has formed a tradition long enough to begin to lose excitement in the inexorable path to being worn out with-out radical strategies to continuously reinvigorate it with new forms, techniques, and thematic preoccupations. Contemporary African poets have to be more daring in all three areas of poetic endeavor to save their works from being of no relevance and not arresting enough for the reader to devote his or her time to.

Poets have to read what has been written before them in the tradi-tion they write in to garner what steps to take to continually renew that tradition. It will be to the detriment of younger writers if they do not know what has preceded them to write what will carry forward in a more energized form the genre which they have chosen to write in. Writing in a vacuum makes it difficult to locate an author in a specific or meaningful tradition.

The many media that have contributed to the shrinking of the reading space for poetry can also contribute to its resuscitation and revival. The media should sharpen the appetite for the consumption of poetry by reminding folks of the place of reading in a culture. Yes, there are many things that occupy people now in Africa but watching "Africa Magic" and European soccer should not be at the expense of developing their minds and culture of reading and consumption of poetry. Tastes have to change to accommodate poetry and a campaign should educate folks to know that it is not only material things that matter.

Also, those promoting poetry should go beyond specialized groups as book clubs and literary circles as the Abuja Writers' Forum and national writers' associations across the continent to enshrine poetry into the public space. Poetry should not be seen as a class marker, something only for the educated elites but something that everybody can enjoy. If poetry is read at the inauguration of the American president and the United States has a poet laureate and almost every state has its own laureate with April a Poetry Month and other state-sponsored institutions and events promoting poetry, why should African countries not do the same? If the United States has the National Endowment for the Arts promoting literature as a necessary part of American culture with funding for poetry, why should African states not do the same? There has to be a new beginning in Africa to revive poetry. I know South Africa has the position of poet laureate, since the late Mazisi Kunene was one. Other African countries should start in their own ways to promote poetry whether in their indigenous languages or the foreign languages they have adopted because developing the minds and imagination of their people is a worthy investment.

The space for poetry should be expanded to reach as many people as possible. In some Western countries, poems are posted on city buses, at airports, the underground/metro, and other public spaces. This could be done in most African countries to promote poetry by posting poems at airports. Even a hundred poems can be posted in strategic parts of the Murtala Muhammad Airport in Lagos, Nigeria, as both the Kotoka International Airport in Accra, Ghana, and the O. R. Tambo International Airport in Johannesburg, South Africa.

Conclusion

In the West, especially in the United States, critics have for decades since the latter part of the twentieth century talked about the death of poetry. Of course, poetry will not die. I may be raising an alarm about the demise of modern African poetry by talking about its exhaustion, aridity, anemic state, and its being on life support. I believe every generation has the resources to recoup from the exhaustion of a tradition and modern African poetry will rise out of its apparent demise and overcome its life-threatening condition. Poetry will never die in Africa and the writers, readers, and promoters should work toward a renaissance as Africa confronts its cultural challenges by converting hope and despair into inimitable jewels of poetry.

SECTION III

CHAPTER 11

The Imperative of Experience in Poetry: An African Perspective

African poetry that expresses specific types of experience appears no longer common as it used to be. Some, if not many, contemporary African poets now think that only the style or form matters and not the content or experience expressed. This could be a response to two generations of African poets, namely the second and third generations. On the one hand, while the generation of Christopher Okigbo and Wole Soyinka was said to have modernist tendencies of paying more attention to form than content, the generation of Kofi Anyidoho, Niyi Osundare, Tanure Ojaide, and Jack Mapanje was said to pay much attention to content at the expense of form. However, a careful reading of the two generations of poets shows that in their works, except in a few cases, there was much attention paid to content. As discussed with some examples, the best of poems as by J. P. Clark, Wole Soyinka, Dennis Brutus, Jack Mapanje, and Tijan M. Sallah, among so many African poets, have been poems based directly or specifically on one type of experience or the other. Contemporary African poetry will attract more readers the more new poetic works take into consideration the imperative of experience in poetry.

Poetry is not just playing with words without some experience to express. What is experience? Let me quote extensively from an earlier book of mine on creative writing:

> There are ... always two sides to a poem: the experience and its expression. The rightful fusion of experience and expression makes for a successful poem. If the writer employs an unusually fresh and creative way to express an experience, then the reader will relish the poem. If poetry were only expression, the writer would be a mere stylist involved in language use and rhetorical skill without a specific experience to explore. Poetry, thus, involves what is being communicated

and how it is communicated; *what* and *how*. A fine poem, therefore, seeks to merge two attributes into one—what is being said and how it is expressed into a unique artistic form...
This *what* is simply the experience being expressed. What is an experience? It can be described as a real or imagined encounter, factual or fictional, objective or subjective, to which a person responds. One can see experience too as what one goes through, and this is usually set in place and time. The physical/spatial and temporal settings of an experience are important. Experience is also knowledge—what we learn when we open ourselves to a particular situation. All our senses "experience" things and ideas. We see, hear, touch, taste, and feel things. What we go through, encounter, or experience enters our memory and guides us in responding to fresh realities. (Ojaide, 2005:2)

There are many types of experience: primarily private/personal and public/human. Private experience involves self-expression of one's feelings and ideas. While personal experience may be unique but it is so expressed in poetry or fiction to make it applicable to other humans. After all, what we express as individuals are feelings and thoughts that are human. Expressing human experience enriches poetry and makes the reader feel involved in sharing something— empathy or reiterating what draws a sense of shared humanity. People experience hunger, fear, and love, among so many other emotions. Any state of the human condition, sickness, happiness, or whatever we live through is also a form of experience. But, apart from the personal, one can use the alter ego by masking another. So, one can put oneself in the place of another person to express a feeling or thought. While this is often called masking, it is the Negative Capability that John Keats wrote about.

Experience involves individual or public response to the environment. The environment relates to nature, ecology, society, culture, politics, and economy. African writers have always responded to their environment in all its ramifications. From orature to the written medium, the artist has satirized negative practices such as greed, dishonesty, insensitivity, tyranny, oppression, exploitation, and more. Similarly, artists extol the virtues of sensitivity, generosity, kindness, selflessness, and more. From traditional songs of abuse to praise songs, African literature has moved to written poems, plays, and novels that deal with primarily exposing negative features in society so as to enthrone good virtues.

Experience makes for details, rather than generalizations. An experience tends to be specific and can be described or portrayed as such: specific time, place, and to someone or group. Since experience has to do with time and place, it goes into one's memory. Many poets tap on their memories of past experiences in their writings. Poetry itself makes the past experience come alive or even everlasting. Remember William Shakespeare's poem on the "fair lady"! Many African poets have paid everlasting tributes to loved, respected, and revered ones through their poems. Look at J. P. Clark-Bekederemo's "Night Rain" and "Agbor Dancer" too! Both poems explore specific experiences, a night rain and a dancer respectively. They are described in concrete terms to form a picture that the reader can imagine in the mind's eye. Let's quote from "Agbor Dancer" as an example of the pivotal role of experience in a poem:

> See her caught in the throb of a drum
> Tippling from hide-brimmed stem
> Down lineal veins to ancestral core
> Opening out in her supple tan
> Limbs like fresh foliage in the sun.
>
> See how entangled in the magic
> Maze of music
> In trance she treads the intricate
> Pattern rippling crest after crest
> To meet the green clouds of the forest. (*A Decade of Tongues*, 8)

The poet is directly describing an experience which appears ongoing and creates a sense of immediacy which makes the poem appeal to the reader. The same sense of immediacy of a real/concrete experience informs "Night Rain," a part of which reads thus:

> What time of night it is
> I do not know
> Except that like some fish
> Doped out of the deep
> I have bobbed up bellywise
> From stream of sleep
> And no cocks crow.
> It is drumming hard here
> And I suppose everywhere
> Droning with insistent ardour upon
> Our roof thatch and shed
> And through sheaves slit open
> To lightning and rafters
> I cannot quite make overhead
> Great water drops are dribbling

> Falling like orange or mango
> Fruits like beads I could in prayer tell
> Them on strings as they break
> In wooden bowls and earthenware
> Mother is busy now deploying
> About our roomlet and floor.
> Although it is so dark
> I know her practiced step as
> She moves her bins, bags and vats
> Out of the run of water. (*A Decade of Tongues*, 6)

In the poem one can find passion, details, a sense of immediacy, and dynamic action, which make the poem describe a concrete human experience that the reader can relate to irrespective of place, age, or gender but as a human being. It is from the one specific concrete experience that the reader can draw a philosophical idea or lesson. A concrete or specific focus of the poet thus allows for a deductive reasoning from the concrete, particular, and specific to the general, universal, and human.

However, for an experience to be poetic depends on how it is explored. There must be something in the experience to make it poetic and aesthetically pleasing to the reader. How does the writer choose or deploy this type of experience? The experience has to be compelling enough for the poet to use beautiful language to express it. As such, the experience itself has to be beautiful to be expressed beautifully. Again, I quote from my earlier elaboration on the poetic experience:

> The poet must "see" an experience *worth* expressing or communicating. It is worth communicating in the sense that it must signify a new vista in the poet's consciousness. It must be a special experience that stands out in contrast to other familiar or mundane experiences. It combines intellectual importance to emotional viability. This is the thought and feeling that artists and critics for ages have been articulating as the bedrock of good poetry. To be poetic there has to be artistic appropriateness to the thought or feeling in its specificity and specialty. Though specific, the experience tends to have universal and human dimensions that consequently enlarge (and deepen) humanity and the human consciousness. (Ojaide:2005: 8)

Thus, the experience that the poet writes about has to be *right* to be aesthetically pleasing. Does the experience show any irony or convey some figurative image of life? Examples are copious in African literatures. Most African poets have poems that will illustrate this point about the poetic experience. I have used as an example my poem, "Inside London," based on "London Ciki," a quarter of Maiduguri in Borno State of Nigeria that grew close to the Muslim cemetery that the people called "London." A rich alhaji had an impressive mansion that was fenced very high and guarded by three armed men apparently so that no thieves would break in to steal from the man or threaten his life. Despite the high walls and guards, the rich man suddenly died of a heart attack, which meant death stole through the guards and high walls to snatch him:

> In London Ciki alhaji's compound still stands
> the inside a mystery to passersby and neighbors
>
> the sky-imploring fence a fort of affluence without the lord
> still safe from the very shanty community he had shunned
>
> all gates closed at nightfall dark outside and inside
> all that remains of the fort without its commander. (*In the House of Words*, 45)

In this poem the irony that despite all the high fences, adamantine gates, and armed guards against thieves, death still stole in to take away the rich man's life. Death is the greatest thief or robber who comes in without being seen to snatch away the rich man into another world!

To sum up what experience means, it is a multiplicity of things with different terms in literary jargon. It is: thought and feeling, subject matter, theme, message, content, and viewpoint. All of the experience is subsumed in the content of a poem. The language/expression of the poem carries the experience. It is the language that clarifies, illuminates, beautifies, mystifies, and intensifies the poet's chosen experience. Language/expression transfers the feeling or thought of the experience to the reader!

I have given this long definition of experience to foreground the imperative of its consideration in poetic composition. A poem cannot be successful without expressing a meaningful experience. Of course, without a worthwhile experience the poem will lack concreteness and the attributes of specificity, passion, and other poetic features. Such a poem will be hollow, light, and not be easy for readers to identify with. A poem not based on a specific private or public experience will bring out the product of stylization in which form may take the place of the message.

Many of the poems of Dennis Brutus display the immediacy of experience in poetic expression. As a victim of the South African apartheid regime, Brutus suffered incarceration and other pains which come out in his poetry. The reader, wherever he or she is, can feel the atmosphere of the experience of what it takes to be nonwhite in apartheid South Africa. In "The sounds begin again":

> The sounds begin again;
> the siren in the night
> the thunder at the door
> the shriek of nerves in pain.
>
> Then the keening crescendo
> of faces split by pain
> the wordless, endless wail
> only the un-free know.
>
> Importunate as rain
> the wraiths exhale their woe
> over the sirens, knuckles, boots;
> my sounds begin again. (*The Heinemann Book of African Poetry in English*, 5)

Also in the prison poems, *Letters to Martha*, Brutus describes specific experiences he went through, and in one of them it is the guard's bark that he remembers rather than the star-lit skies he peeped through the window to see.

Wole Soyinka expresses similar experiences in the prison poems of *A Shuttle in the Crypt*. One of such poems is "Conversation at Night with a Cockroach" which begins thus:

> Come out. Oh have you found me even here
> Cockroach? grimed in gloss connivance
> Carapaced in age, in cunning, oiled
> As darkness, keyed in decoy rasps.
> Your subtle feelers probed prize chapters
> Drilled perforations on the magic words. (5)

The poets that follow J. P. Clark, Dennis Brutus, and Wole Soyinka also go for particular experiences to express their feelings and thought. A good example is Jack Mapanje's "The Cheerful Girls at Smiller's Bar, 1971," illustrative of his generation's work:

> The prostitutes at Smiller's Bar beside the dusty road
> Were only girls once in tremulous mini-skirts and oriental

Beads, cheerfully swigging Carlsbergs and bouncing to
Rusty simanje-manje and rumba booming in the juke-box.
They were striking virgins bored by our Presbyterian
Prudes until a true Presbyterian came one night. And like
To us all the girls offered him a seat on cheap planks
In the dark backyard room choked with diesel-oil clouds
From a tin-can lamp. Touched the official rolled his eyes
To one in style. She said no. Most girls only wanted
A husband to hook or the fruits of Independence to taste
But since then mini-skirts were banned and the girls
Of Smiller's Bar became "ugly prostitutes to boot!"

Today the girls still giggle about what came through
The megaphones: the preservation of our traditional
et cetera. (Ojaide and Sallah 33)

Here is a poem that pokes fun at the morality of the so-called morally
minded state officials who are even more corrupt, if not depraved, than
the common people and use personal denial of sexual favors to decree
against girls who wear mini-skirts and have the guts to say no to the
public officials. Contrary to the public perception of those girls in mini-
skirts as "prostitutes," they are ironically at the bar to look for husbands
and "fruits" of Independence and not there out of promiscuity.

Tijan M. Sallah's "Harrow Poems" that he wrote while confined
to a hospital bed after a car accident in London also tell the advantages of poems that address specific incidents, experiences. Here is my
favorite in the collection, "Next to God, the Doctor":

When in pain, next to God is the doctor.
The universe collapses when pain soars in the nerves and bones,
And all one could do is to summon the nurse as the proctor.
The doctor's words ring like God's trombones,
Every syllable must be weighed with an ounce of good measure.
And the prescription must be held with the sacredness of treasure.

When in pain, next to God is the doctor.
And one is reminded of Epicurus's dictum:
That Nature bestowed on humanity
Two sovereign principles—pain and pleasure.
It is in our nature to seek money, fame, wine and good posture,
And to avoid snakes, scorpions and pinches on the rectum. (141)

The point is that no poem works as well as a poem that is based on
a specific experience which forms the poetic content, subject matter,
feeling, or thought.

The younger poets of today appear split on the use of experience in poetry writing. Many of them such as Nduka Otiono, Ogaga Ifowodo, and Amatoritsero Ede focus on experience/content as the older poets. Going through their works, one comes across the specificity of experiences whether of travel, love, or happenings in the homeland and outside that they want to impress on their readers' minds. For instance, Ifowodo writes a poem on the oil pipe explosion at Jesse in Delta State of Nigeria that took the lives of over a thousand people in the early 1990s. He also wrote a series of poems on Nelson Mandela's 27 years in Robben Island.

Globalization and the deracination of other younger writers who have no knowledge of their indigenous backgrounds and have not cared to study them have driven such writers to propose preposterous concepts of poetry that make older writers cringe. It is not that the old cannot adjust to new ways; it is because the younger ones appear to be totally surrendering themselves to a foreign culture and totally ignoring their own culture or society that they should interrogate. The resort to, for the lack of a better term I choose to call, mere stylization will bring forth a generation of African poets rambling with words arranged with some rhetorical formula to fill a piece called a poem, a meaningless one for that matter.

While I have given examples from several poets of the 1960s, 1970s, and 1980s, the imperative of experience that touches the reader is the cornerstone of traditional African poetry or songs. In poetic performances such as the Ewe halo, Urhobo Udje, Yoruba ijala, and Zulu izibongo, it is not the mellifluous nature of the song alone but the message it carries. One can tell from traditional songs that are most popular tend to be those that express philosophical thoughts about life deriving from an experience. Thus, the imperative of meaning, message, and content is deeply embedded in traditional African poetry and transferred by the writers into written modern poetry.

This chapter is a plea for our younger writers to rethink their writing ideology and the tradition they write from. Experience as content matters much in poetry and the expression should carry it just as language carries the thought processes of a people. Whether real or imagined, a poetic experience carries the aesthetic considerations that give the reader something to take away after reading a poem. I am not saying every poet should base his or her poems on a specific experience, incident, happening, feeling, thought, but anything set in time and place and either addressed or described directly tends to have a special immediacy and passion than merely reflecting on abstract ideas will do.

CHAPTER 12

Indigenous Knowledge and Its Expression in the Folklore of Africa

INTRODUCTION

Knowledge has often been racialized by Europeans who want to claim it as only theirs. From the time the West started to see Africans and their descendants as the "Other," Africa has been depicted as a tabula rasa, which connotes that Africans have no civilization or imagination that carries any knowledge. The concept of the "Other" was perpetrated in imperialist and colonial discourses. In the binaries created by Westerners, they (Westerners) had knowledge and Africans were ignorant; the West was superior and Africa was inferior (Jarosz 1992; Bhabha 1994).

For these reasons, Africa-originated knowledge is often ignored or attributed to outsiders. Ancient Egyptian achievements are rarely seen as pre-Islamic and acknowledged as African. Similarly, Great Zimbabwe is claimed by those who deny African knowledge to have derived its civilization and architecture from Arabs as the great Benin bronze casting through the lost wax process was attributed to Portuguese influence. In art, Europeans place painting as high art and sculpture, which Africans are so adept at and have made what Frank Willet considers their greatest cultural contribution to the world, as low art.

The idea of indigenous knowledge of Africa is thus a way of countering Western hegemonic thinking and arrogance about their self-perceived monopoly of knowledge. As will be seen in the following discussion, knowledge should not be seen in the limited view of being material and technological alone; rather knowledge can be not only immaterial but also manifest in so many other ways, and Africans have abundance of indigenous and local knowledge.

According to Walter Brugger and Kenneth Baker, knowledge has to do with imagination, insight, experience, judgment, thinking, and knowing. To them, "the theory of knowledge is the philosophical investigation of our mind's *capacity for truth*" (216). Key to the meaning of "knowledge" in this study are words like "information," "experience," "education," and "awareness." This chapter discusses both the African aspect of what UNESCO describes as "the intangible heritage" of humanity and Thomas Aquinas speaks of as "immateriality" of knowledge (Brugger 212) as well as other material and technological aspects.

The indigenous knowledge of Africa needs to be exposed not only to affirm faith in but also to give authority to an Africa-centered civilization. In a recent book, *There Was a Country: A Personal History of Biafra*, Chinua Achebe, the renowned Nigerian writer, affirms that "we always knew of the beauty of our culture" as he describes an aspect of Igbo civilization in Nnokwa whose "townsfolk were particularly noted for their role in the transmission of the knowledge of Nsibidi, an ancient writing first invented by the Ejagham (Ekoi) people of southeastern Nigeria, and then adopted and used widely by their close neighbors—the Igbo, Efik, Anang, and Ibibio" (192). Achebe goes on to deduce from this that "The very existence of this alphabet dating back to the 1700s without any Latin or Arabic antecedent, is a rebuke to all those who have claimed over the centuries that Africa has no history, no writing, and no civilization!" (192) Contemporary Africans need to research into the indigenous knowledge of their forebears and the living to showcase it beside other contributions to knowledge in a universal assembly in the manner the great Senegalese poet and president, Leopold Sedar Senghor, conceptualized in Negritude.

While Western peoples flaunt their knowledge in books that are archived in libraries or other places, the indigenous knowledge of African people is generally archived in their oral traditions or other aspects of their folklore. This multidisciplinary knowledge is saved in oral texts in often invisible alphabets in different indigenous languages in Africa. African indigenous knowledge, therefore, is abundant and multidisciplinary. It ranges from proverbs, folktales, and other oral narratives to epics, chants, and other poetic forms to medicinal and spiritual cures. In Africa, indigenous knowledge is archived in the folklore whose oral traditions carry profound thoughts and practices.

This study is necessary because there is paucity of materials in the field to draw from about the indigenous knowledge of Africans. There have been numerous studies of oral traditions of Africa, as Isidore Okpewho, Ruth Finnegan, Thomas Hale, Graham Furniss, Kofi Awoonor, Timothy Wangusa, and many others have done, but their focus is not to bring out how these folkloric traditions are the media for the expression or preservation of African indigenous knowledge. Other scholars such as Wande Abimbola, Maurice T. Vambe, G. G. Darah, and Ode Ogede have studied the oral traditions of African groups as of the Yoruba, Urhobo, and Igede of Nigeria or nations such as Zimbabwe and Malawi and the use to which they have been put as a means of cultural resistance by contemporary writers. Some of the oral literature scholars such as G. G. Darah, Daniel Avorgbedor, and Tanure Ojaide have discussed the functions of specific genres of oral literature in certain traditional African communities or groups. However, again, these are not studies of the expression of indigenous knowledge or the bringing out of that knowledge from its medium of expression.

Toyin Falola and Christian Jennings in their coedited *Africanizing Knowledge: African Studies Across the Disciplines* attempt to indigenize either universal or Western knowledge. The focus on disciplines shows a Western orientation toward departmentalizing knowledge, unlike African knowledge that tends to be more compartmentalized and integrated. Thus, the scholarly effort so far has been more to make African scholarship more African than begin a discourse of the expressions and showcasing of African indigenous knowledge itself. It is in view of these lapses in African scholarship and the need for the African civilization to showcase its knowledge to the rest of the world that this modest effort is being made to discuss African indigenous knowledge and its expression in the folklore.

The Malian scholar of African folklore, Amadou Hampate Ba, once made a statement that has now become almost proverbial: "In Africa, when an old person dies, it is a library that is burnt down" (1960 at UNESCO). Traditional African culture is oral; the literature, in the forms of epic, legend, folktale, song, and other genres, is transmitted by word of mouth from one generation to another. In the nonliterate culture, a person can be a treasure of knowledge, experience, and wisdom. In other words, an old person, like a library, is a repository of knowledge and this is through the medium of oral tradition. Folklore is thus the repository of a people's indigenous and local knowledge in the forms of language, literature, legends, myths, epics, folktales, songs, proverbs, tongue-twisters, riddles, music, dance, art, religious beliefs and practices, medicinal treatments, and other customs and traditions. These are traditions that have been carried out over time, and include such practices as birth, marriage, burial and other rites and are passed through oral traditions. Embedded in these oral traditions are indigenous and local knowledge systems.

Put differently, folklore is a people's cultural memory, inherited wealth of knowledge and experience; in Africa it is the oral tradition. Through orality, African people vault immense knowledge and wisdom. In traditional African societies, there were/are no formal classes or schools as in modern society where knowledge is imparted to the young by teachers with college or university diplomas. Rather, at the end of the day's work, the elders gathered the young ones round the fireplace and taught them about their societies, ranging from how to relate to one another, making them know about their belief systems, to how to be good citizens of the community, be patriotic, and understand the nature of their environment and society. The teaching of knowledge is in the forms of legends, myths, epics, folktales, songs, proverbs, tongue-twisters, riddles, and so forth. The oral tradition is thus the medium through which indigenous and local African knowledge is not only preserved but also passed from one generation to another.

African Oratures

As Edward Sapir has put it, language carries the thought, ideas, and knowledge of a people. Foremost in the African language is the primacy of proverbs whose mastery proffers oratorical authority on the speaker. Proverbs are words of wisdom and they often encapsulate the knowledge and experience of the people. The proverb is so important in expression that, as Chinua Achebe says of it among his Igbo people of Nigeria, it is "the palm oil with which words are eaten." This is applicable to what obtains in most African ethnicities and societies. Proverbs and other wise sayings are copious in every African indigenous language. Knowing one's language or any of the African languages therefore is a means of acquiring not just the language skill of interpersonal communication but also a means of gaining knowledge about oneself, society, the world, and life itself. Through constant speaking of the language, Africans gain insight into so much knowledge that should guide them smoothly through life. If not so smoothly, language helps, as in the case of the use of proverbs, to soothe one's plight.

Let me give some examples of how knowledge is embedded in African proverbs. To the Yoruba people of Nigeria, Benin Republic, and in the diaspora, life is a market. This means we come to life, live it, and leave as in a market. Nobody sleeps in the market; one comes to either sell or buy and then leaves at the end of that market. It also has to do with the profit and loss of life. There is so much knowledge and wisdom in such a succinct saying. Igbo proverbs have been popularized by Chinua Achebe especially in both *Things Fall Apart* and *Arrow of God*. From the child that washes his hands clean and is able to eat with elders to when the moon is shining the cripple craves for a walk, and who lives by the river should not wash his hands with spittle, Igbo proverbs carry the Igbo philosophy of life.

From the examples of proverbs given, one can say that the elderly and the experienced in the African traditional society use proverbs to dispense knowledge to younger ones who will grow up to do the same. No gathering of men and women assembled to discuss important issues, as conflict resolution, marital problems, counseling, and others can go well without copious use of proverbs. Proverbs are used to advise, console, encourage, and do so many things. Riddles in Africa are vehicles of local knowledge. To the Hausa, an egg with thorns is a pineapple. An Urhobo riddle is *"Phughu phughu tueni!"* and it means that the fruits of a plant fall beside it. Answers to most riddles are based on local knowledge and many are metaphors or tropes of what is available in the environment.

Traditional African societies have special people who carry the task of passing indigenous knowledge from one generation to another. There are also those who guard the tradition to make sure that the knowledge is done professionally. I have chosen to call them "guardians of the sacred word," after Kofi Awoonor's title of his book on Anlo-Ewe oral poets. A few examples will suffice but these "guardians" are called by different names, the most distinguished among them are griots (griottes) of the Mali and Senegambian region, *ororile* of Nigeria's Urhobo people, and the *imbongi* of the Zulu and Xhosa groups of South Africa. While on the surface one can say that the griot is a professional singer of tales, his or her role goes far beyond that to include being the custodian of the people's oral constitution, the chronicler/historian, and one engaged in conflict resolution. The Urhobo *ororile* is a poet and composes songs that reflect the mores, ethics, and dos and don'ts of the community. He plays the role of the guardian of the community's ethics and morals and assists to maintain a cohesive corporate existence. The *imbongi*, an instantaneous poet, plays a similar role as the griot and *ororile* among different ethnic groups in South Africa. However, he goes beyond, like the Yoruba *ijala* chanter, to extol the virtues of the society.

In addition to those concerned with preserving and disseminating indigenous knowledge with words, there are others in the traditional African community with the responsibility of preserving indigenous knowledge. They include traditional rulers and chiefs, priests and priestesses, diviners, and others. For instance, traditional rulers and their chiefs know so much about the history of their land and people. One would expect that the Alaafin of Oyo, the Ooni of Ife, the Oba of Benin, the Asantehene of the Akan, the Kabaka of Buganda, and others have oral records and texts of their history and traditions that pass from one generation to another. In fact, in Oyo the repositories of such oral history are called *arokin* and they are the official historians in the service of the Alaafin.

African folktales are often seen as means of entertainment for the young. However, they play an even stronger role in educating the people, especially the young, about morality, ethics, and wisdom. Each folktale is an oral "text" taught by elders and studied by young ones for lessons of life and society. The stories could be about animals, birds, or even spirits but no-one is left in doubt that they behave as humans in society. African folktales are very didactic and have lessons embedded in them. The animals in the story promote a sense of communal existence and harmony while the individual exercises some rights and obligations. Each individual contributes to the well-being of society and any attempt to disrupt this sense of harmony is resisted by the sanctioning of the over-individualistic ones. The *ajakpa* tales of the Yoruba are a good example of the place of the individual in the community. The tortoise is greedy and goes against the spirit of communal cohesion. As John Mbiti says of the African view of oneself, "I am because we are."

People are socialized to know folktales to relate to other folks in the community and understand the environment. This kind of indigenous knowledge is very important for the individual and the community. The knowledge of an individual believing in a corporate existence is fundamental to the world created by African folktales. As Mazisi Kunene has emphasized, Africa may not be industrially and materially advanced but the Mother Continent is wealthy ethically. In Haitian folktales, opportunity is given to individuals to be mischievous and extreme but such actions or modes of behavior are not condoned. One who transgresses the communal ethos thus becomes a pariah and is often ridiculed to discourage extreme or radical behavior that promotes selfish interests instead of corporate ones.

Other forms of oral traditions are sources of indigenous knowledge. The epic is a repository of a group's knowledge. It teaches a people's history, culture, arts, and more. Of course the griot who sings the heroic tales is a human treasure and carries the experience of his or her people. From the various texts of *Sunjata, Ozidi,* and the epic of *Mwindo,* there is so much to learn about the African concept of hero. Isidore Okpewho in *The Epic in Africa* has done a thorough study of the features of the epic hero. In *Sunjata* such features include patience, courage, passion for justice and fairness, saving one's people from oppression and exploitation, and exercising of authority for the people's good. According to Okpewho, the hero represents the highest ideal to which society can aspire. The hero is a good citizen who has leadership qualities and has a passion for justice, fairness, and a sense of pride in the homeland. People of African descent imbibe knowledge of history, political science, civics, military tactics, psychology, sociology, the arts, and many others from their epics or heroic tales.

Similarly, myths and legends are also sources of knowledge. Myths may obscure scientific reasoning but they are meant to explain the nature of things and teach a lesson. I have used in my novel, *Matters of the Moment,* the myth of why man and woman are always quarrelling but cannot do without each other. As man alternates between desire and distrust for woman, God withdraws to an impossible height so as not to be bothered by humans who should resolve their problems themselves. This knowledge is more than any Western or church marriage counseling service will do for a couple who know that it is in the nature of humans for a man and a woman to quarrel now and then but they must understand themselves and live together as partners to be happy in the world that God has given them. Legends teach young ones to have a sense of destiny and a passion to be great. That greatness can only come through communal service.

A significant source of knowledge is African oral poetic performance traditions. *Udje, halo, ijala,* and *izibongo* are representatives of African oral poetic performances, the first two satiric genres and the latter two panegyrics. *Udje* expresses the worldview of the Urhobo people as *halo* does for the Ewe, *ijala* for the Yoruba, and *izibongo* for the Zulu and Xhosa worldviews. *Udje* involves satire and takes the form of highly articulated song sequences performed in a dramatic context. It is a unique type of Urhobo dance in which, on an appointed day, rival groups, representing quarters and even whole towns, perform songs composed from often exaggerated materials about the other. The dance songs strongly attack what the traditional society regards as vices: laziness, vanity, wretchedness, miserliness, flirtation, adultery, prostitution, wickedness, and greed, among others. The singers are intent upon upholding what they consider to be positive norms of the society. Central to the concept of *udje* are the principles of correction and determent through punishment with "wounding" words. These songs have an important social function, for they maintain a delicate balance between the general good of the society whose ethos must be upheld and respect for the law-abiding individual. The satirical content of the songs demonstrates the extent to which they are imbued with a distinctive moral awareness related to the collective life. There is thus a profound sense in which they bear out, in an arresting form, Henri Bergson's conception of "laughter" as an essential part of the mechanisms by which social life is regulated by ridiculing what in a particular society would be considered individual excesses or threats to collective harmony. The Urhobo *udje* tradition bears comparison to the genre known as *halo* among the Anlo-Ewe, an ethnic group that straddles the frontier between Ghana and Togo. As with *udje, halo* performances consist of satirical songs by rival groups who confront each other in a definite context of staged performances. On the other hand, both *ijala* and *izibongo* are praise poetry; they extol the virtues of courage, generosity, selflessness, and readiness to take on the community's tasks toward a harmonious society.

For sure, these satiric and panegyric genres of the oral tradition of Africa as of the African diaspora have so much knowledge in them to be learned by the listeners and audiences for whom they were and continue to be performed. As I explained elsewhere (Ojaide, 2003), there were no prisons in traditional Urhobo society. Thus serious crimes such as murder were punished with execution. However, lighter crimes as flirtation, stealing, and others were punished with satiric songs; hence the *udje* and *halo* took the place of ordinances and laws and made everybody to fall into line. While one can exercise one's individuality, it should not hurt others. As will be commented on later, many of these oral poetic genres were part of traditional festivals and were dedicated to tutelary gods. Knowing these songs helps one to navigate one's way in society with ease—avoid the don'ts and, as in the praise poetry, strive for the virtues of the society.

Music and Dance

Music and dance are also major vehicles of indigenous and local knowledge. As noted by, among others, J. K. Nketia and Francis Bebey, African kinds of music share common features. They include percussive instruments and rhythms, lead singer and chorus, and vitality of costume and expression.

Where is the indigenous knowledge in African music and dance? Let us take the example of the Shona instrument and music called *mbira*. It is infused with mythical beliefs and it is said that when you play the mbira you get your wish. It is a soothing music that is said to be divinely accompanied. Most African dance forms are artistic reenactments of myths, legends, and history. Music and dance are parts of festivals dedicated to gods to look with benevolence at their human underlings. Many prayers are in the forms of songs accompanied with drumming while the dances celebrate the communion of humans, ancestors, and gods. In fact, the drum calls the ancestors and gods to listen to human prayers and activities. Music and dance in traditional and even Christian worships in Africa result in spirit possession, a heightened form of spiritual consciousness. It appears African people, especially in religious circles, have long been aware of the impact of music on the brain that modern Western researchers are only now talking about. Music and dance are themselves artistic skills that are learned. In addition, they carry the belief systems of the people and give the people a cultural identity.

RELIGION, SPIRITUALITY, AND PHILOSOPHY

A people's knowledge involves their conceptualization of human existence. Spirituality is very important to peoples of Africa . To Joseph Holloway, "Religion forms the core foundation of the African world" (xiv). John Mbiti has, in his *African Religions and Philosophy*, described African religious/spiritual practices. It is significant to pursue the deep knowledge that is steeped in concepts in African religions and philosophy. Two examples that need further discussion are the Yoruba *Ase* and the Akan Sankofa. *Ase* involves the mystical power to will things to happen, the faith to have prayers fulfilled, and have a divinely ordained good life. One learns in praying from Yoruba folklore that "The transformative energy created in prayer allows one to change the conditions of their lives and thereby creating a place for one to grow and evolve. Prayer becomes a place to communicate with and realize with the love that Olofin has for us" (Quinones 10). Similarly, by consulting Ifa, "Orunmila will direct his akapo on what to do and on how to deal with such unique, spiritual needs" (FAMA iii).

On the other hand, the Akan Sankofa, represented by the image of a bird looking backward as it goes forward, has to do with reaching back and taking from the wealth of history (Kwakye 6). In other words, our future is the sum total of our past and present and it is the way that we make them that will determine our future and fate. Thus, human fate is a combination of what could be called destiny and one's agency of industry and perseverance. There cannot be deeper mystical, religious, and philosophical knowledge than what *Ase* and Sankofa stand for. Knowing the African folklore exposes one to indigenous knowledge that helps one to live a more meaningful life.

THE YORUBA EXAMPLE OF THE EXPRESSION OF INDIGENOUS KNOWLEDGE

Since the focus of the chapter is the expression of indigenous and local knowledge, let me use the Yoruba example of Ifa. Ifa is connected to Orunmila, who is next to Olodumare in the Yoruba pantheon. As described by Afolabi A. Epega, "The total body of instruction from Orunmila is called Ifa. The instruction consists of the art of divination, notation, interpretation, and application of the oracle of Ifa" (4). This system of indigenous knowledge involves the "babalawos (fathers of mysteries)," who are "disciples of Orunmila, or, as commonly called, Ifa priests" (Epega 4). It generally takes three to seven years to learn the art of the babalawo who consults Ifa by interpreting 16 palm nuts thrown on a divination tray (opon ifa) and through verse prescribing the sacrifice for desired blessings or averting mishap. Verses express each odu—as many as 256 odus in 1680 verses.

Signs and symbols are involved in Ifa divination, an indigenous Yoruba system of knowledge. First, colors are symbolically involved; Orunmila is said to be very black and Orisanla white, colors which relate to their different and respective roles as creator and cool personalities. Similarly, numbers define attributes of Yoruba deities. As known, "Odu Ifas are the writings, signs or symbols used by Orunmila himself to express the divination by Ifa Oracle and they are old" (Epega 43–44). One can say that "Ifa is the Ancient Wisdom of the Yorubas that applies to the past, the present, and the future. Hence some of the 430,000 ways of expression in Ifa or Odu Ifa are of quite recent date and some are of hoary antiquity, far older than the Pharaohs" (Epega 44). Ifa expresses indigenous wisdom by denoting imales or orishas with knowledge of the secrets of the world or heaven, knowledge of what the Creator has kept in store for the common good of mankind (Epega 50).

ARTS, CRAFTS, SCIENCE, AND TECHNOLOGY

African folklore and oral traditions embrace music and dance, religious and spiritual concerns, as well as the arts, crafts, and technology.

These different fields of knowledge are intricately bound in the belief systems and practices of the people in Africa. The artistic creations that deck religious shrines continue to be sculptural works of artistic excellence. Masks and figurines are copious. The representational abstract works of Africa form a field of knowledge that European artists such as Pablo Picasso and Matisse studied to start Cubism just as Western musicians have converted jazz to an American music. From Nok, Ife, Benin to Kongo, Akan, Baule, Bamana, Dogon, and many other artistic traditions in the Mother Continent, African artistic creations in the forms of sculpture, rock engraving and painting, and other newer media have their works encompass the experiences of their culture.

African influences are striking in many parts of the diaspora. The Mende people of Sierra Leone have close kinship relationship with the Gullahs of the Sea Islands of South Carolina and Georgia in their expert knowledge in the cultivation of rice, basket weaving, Gullah language, and religious practices. In the documentary, "The language you cry in," this kinship relationship is traced through the slave trading period to the ritual songs of burial that survive in an almost incomprehensible form in the United States of America.

Robert Farris Thompson has traced Kongo symbols in the diaspora in his classic *Flash of the Spirit*. The materials such as bottles hanging on trees, broken pots on top of graves, and Kongo mystical symbols and cosmography are evidence of Kongo residues in the New World. All these things involve belief systems and a sense of man having a relationship with God and the afterlife.

There is much indigenous technology in many aspects of production and consumption in Africa. There are local and indigenous ways of distillery or brewing of *akpeteshi*, *pito*, *sobo*, and other drinks. Looking back, one continues to marvel at how our forebears got to make starch to eat or get foods like garri and others produced in the first place. One cannot leave this section of our survey without mentioning the astrological knowledge of the Dogon people of West Africa and the indigenous knowledge that goes with iron smelting, copper and bronze works, and gold industries. From their isolated escarpment, the Dogon people have names for dozens of stars and knew the Sirius long before Western astrophysicists discovered it. From the Nok culture of Central Nigeria to the Dogon of Mali and the Fon of present-day Benin Republic and others, iron has been mined and smelted for weapons and artistic productions for centuries in Africa. In Central Nigeria and the Great Lakes region, iron smelting goes back to at least 800 BC, even preceding the adoption of iron in Europe (Schmidt and Childs 1995). We now know that

Africans not only invented the technology of iron production on their own but that the Haya people of Tanzania produced steel when such technology was missing in Europe (Schmidt and Avery 1978). Ife and Benin's use of bronze in the lost wax method for sculptures and figurines is legendary and for the latter continues till this moment. At Ife, geochemical analysis now tells us that the craftsmen of that ancient city produced primary glass beads and sold these beads across West Africa in the twelfth through the seventeenth centuries (Lankton et al., 2006). The Ashanti and their Akan brethren have over centuries perfected their gold mining and refining skills.

Talking of indigenous knowledge, there is much to learn from the Yoruba Orishas of Ogun and Aganju. In the Yoruba world, "Ogun represents the ability to take something from its rawest form and [to] create something miraculous and creative. Ogun has the ability to bring change to the world with the tools of the hand and mind and change the way civilization operates and labors" (Quinones 46). Similarly, Aganju "has the ability to propel us forward to think in new ways and challenge others and society" (Quinones 69). There is thus so much local and indigenous knowledge of technology among Africans to lift them into an advanced stage if contemporary minds take on these knowledge leads.

MEDICINE/HEALERS

Herbs and barks are sources of natural healing as well as mystical knowledge. Daniel A. Omoweh, writing on the adverse effect of Shell's oil exploration and exploitation in the Niger Delta of Nigeria, names many endangered herbs and barks of trees of the environment that have therapeutic value. He links a people's environment with their health, culture, and literature, saying that the "most viable form of storing knowledge on traditional medical skills, therefore, is still through incantations, ritual, songs and cult procedures which are memorized by the practitioners" (180). There is also spiritual healing combined with medications done by African medicine men across the continent.

CONCLUSION

African people have knowledge that goes far back in time and this means that not only one group or race has monopoly of a heritage of knowledge. Awareness of this gives psychological and emotional balance to black peoples knowing they have their own proud past which confers on them a sense of dignity. There is no doubt that oral traditions carry the indigenous and local knowledge of black peoples. It is in them that traditions are carried over to younger generations, and proverbs are the expressions of the knowledge, wisdom, and experiences that govern life and make life meaningful. A challenge for the current generation of Africans is why have we not done more to study these areas of knowledge, apply what is learned, and to make more visible African contributions to the contemporary world?

Furthermore, Africana Studies departments worldwide should incorporate folklore of Africa into their curriculum to make students aware of the indigenous and local knowledge. I also challenge scholars to make folklore an important field of research and philosophical reflection. I also direct this challenge at literary scholars of modern African literature. With major African authors highly influenced by the folklore of their people, the study of their folklore becomes an imperative. Many African literary creations such as Chinua Achebe's *Things Fall Apart* and *Arrow of God*, Wole Soyinka's *Idanre and Other Poems*, *The Interpreters*, and *Ogun Abibiman*, and Ngugi wa Thiongo's *The River Between*, *Weep Not, Child*, and *Petals of Blood* are better understood through the folklore. The same holds for the literary works of most African authors.

CHAPTER 13

Policy Studies, Activist Literature, and Pitching for the Masses in Nigeria

INTRODUCTION

Though political science, especially policy studies, and activist literature deal with politics, this is more so of policy studies than literature which may not have politics as its concern. Political science and literature are more closely related in their objectives than the often hostile appearance between writers and politicians. The activist writer, as a critic, tends to portray the politician as a reactionary and stumbling block to a progressive society as in Chinua Achebe's *A Man of the People* and Wole Soyinka's *The Interpreters*. Modern African literature generally reflects the history of the continent or individual nations, a point that G-C. Mutiso, Janheinz Jahn, Romanus N. Egudu, and others have emphasized at one point or the other during the past 50 years. "History" in African literature is a code name for politics. As such, modern African or Nigerian literature reflects the political experience of the continent or country. It is interesting to note that in the 1990s at The University of North Carolina at Charlotte, Chinua Achebe's *Things Fall Apart* was taught as literature in the then African and African American Studies Department (now Africana Studies) and also in the Departments of History and Political Science. This shows the subliminal relationship between literature, history, and political science. The emphasis in this chapter is both on the relationship between Nigerian literature and political science in the area of public policy at the local and community levels and the objectives of activist literature and public policy at the grassroots level.

This chapter has as its backcloth the intellectual contributions made by Oladimeji Aborisade in policy analysis in the areas of local government and community studies at Obafemi Awolowo University in Nigeria and at The University of North Carolina at Charlotte.

Aborisade has focused on local and grassroots politics in Nigeria, editing the following books: *Local Government and the Traditional Rulers in Nigeria* (1985), *On Being in Charge at the Grassroots Level in Nigeria* (1989), and *Nigerian Local Government Reformed* (1989). In the period of 1990–1994, Aborisade and Robert Mundt carried out intensive fieldwork in Nigeria and North Carolina in local government and also conducted workshops in Nigeria for the chairmen of local government commissions, the departments of local government in the governors' offices, the chairmen of local governments, the secretaries, treasurers, and their local government functionaries in Nigeria. This comparative research resulted in the publication of *Local Government in Nigeria and the United States: Learning from Comparison* (1995). Aborisade and Mundt have also authored *Politics in Nigeria* (2002), a seminal work in which they observe that political science is filled with the "mild polemic about the relative merits of a system approach as compared to a more state-centered analysis of political life" (xv). They take a middle road, which is "basically a system approach that views politics as a repetitive process involving individual relationships with institutions (institutionalized political roles), but also an approach in which the state is identified as a major actor and a major set of institutions, which has its own needs and makes its own demands on the system, even as it usually plays a central political system role in 'allocating scarce resources'" (vi). There is symmetry of sentiments in these two political scientists working on policy matters and two Nigerian active writers in their seeing politicians, military or civilian, as responsible for Nigeria's lack of economic growth. Here is part of the opening paragraph of the last chapter of the book:

> Under the Abacha regime, Wole Soyinka saw a "spiral of murder, torture, and leadership dementia that is surely leading to the disintegration of a once-proud nation." ... billions of desperately needed naira have been wasted, a few have grown rich at the expense of the poor ... In the words of poet Tanure Ojaide,
>
> > *We have lost it,*
> > *the country we were born into.*
> > *We can now sing dirges*
> > *of that commonwealth of yesterday—*
> > *we live in a country*
> > *that is no longer our own*
> > —"No Longer Our Own Country," 1986 (242)

Here activist writers and political scientists in their policy analysis put the blame for the failures of the Nigerian state on politicians. As already stated, the focus in this chapter will be on political science with particular reference to public policy at the local government and community levels and activist literature.

Public Policy at Local and Community Levels

Governance at the local or community level has always been an administrative mode of operation in Nigeria from colonial times till now. It started from administrative divisions created out of regional governments and then administrative districts, smaller units, created out of those divisions. This administrative splintering was primarily aimed at bringing government presence closer to the people. This model of government is conceptualized on the belief that government can cooperate with the governed as an agency of positive change and development and that the more the common people feel the presence of government, the more the combined efforts toward socioeconomic transformation and resolving other developmental issues will bear fruit. While this rationale has also been the aim of state creations since the Nigerian Civil War period, there has been an ever-increasing demand for the government to reach the people, or, put differently, for the people to feel the government. Moreover, since government is seen as a critical agent of wealth and social goods distribution, the closer a community is to the government, the higher the chances of gaining access to the state resources—jobs, roads, schools, health services, and so forth. Divisions created in colonial times have generally become states across Nigeria and the states have created more local government areas. It is the colonial districts, the smallest units of political governance, that later metamorphosed into councils, and then local government areas. As a third-tier governance structure, after federal and state governments, the local government is very important in the Nigerian political administrative structure. Each local government has a chairperson supported by supervisory councilors in charge of works, roads, schools, health, and other responsibilities. It is significant that the Nigerian Federal Government, through statutory allocations, assists local governments to pay the salaries of teachers in elementary schools that are entirely the responsibilities of local governments.

The important role of local governments is to take care of those responsibilities that the state and federal governments have ceded to them. This is thus a state-sanctioned creation to take care of local and community issues that are far from the center at the state and federal levels. Specifically, as outlined in *On Being in Charge at the Grassroots Level in Nigeria*, local governments are in charge of markets and motor parks, sanitary inspection, refuse disposal, control of vermin, slaughter houses, public conveniences, burial grounds, registration of births, deaths and marriages, provision of recreation centers, licensing, control of animals, control of advertisements, naming of roads and streets, collecting vehicle parking charges, and collection of property and other rates (444–45). Other responsibilities of local governments are "health centers, maternity centers, dispensaries and health clinics, ambulance services, preventive health services…and control of buildings and piped sewage systems" (Aborisade, 1989: 445).

Significantly, local and community studies relate to issues that bring the government and the people together at close proximity. The objective is to bring self-help and development to an area. Over many decades, it is evident that the creation of new local government areas has brought not only visible development but also made the problems of the common people to be seen at close quarters and their needs to be articulated, heard, and addressed. A drive through the country shows abundantly clear the physical dividends of the government at the grassroots level. It is another matter whether the local governments could have done far better were it not for the corruption and greed of the local government officials, some of whom do not even reside in the local government areas but in nearby cities and only return to "share" federal allocations. There is surely a conflict between theory and practice in Nigerian politics that policy analysis reveals.

What is important is that public policy expects the delivery of certain functions at the grassroots level. This may sound idealistic in the context of practical politics in Nigeria but it becomes a measure of success or failure at this level of government. Are individuals and groups assisted at the local level through community bank loans and other state-supported organs for development in the areas of education such as literacy, health in the forms of clinics, maternal care, immunization and other methods of health care delivery, and economic well-being through commerce, business, and financial assistance? Are water and light problems dealt with at the local government level with the sinking of boreholes and rural electrification projects respectively? Is the environment taken care of through sanitation, garbage collection, and other measures? Is poverty tackled also at the grassroots level with assistance to poor individuals or groups to exercise their agency to take care of themselves? The works of public policy scholars such as Aborisade and Mundt remind local governments to tackle the people's problems and to advance their struggle for social, economic, and environmental well-being.

The Masses as Concerns of Policy Studies and Activist Literature

It is my submission that political science through administration and analysis and activist literature work in tandem for the betterment of the lives of the common people. This chapter addresses how African literature has been used, through poetry, fiction, and theatre, to advance the cause of the common people, the same challenge that the local government is set up to tackle for individual and group progress. Literature and political science are different disciplines but they are theoretically, ideologically, and ideally linked in their commitment to human development. For example, Nigerian literature calls attention to the plight of the common people by exposing what they are denied and putting heat on politicians and rulers to care for the common people with the state-acquired resources from minerals, taxes, and other available means.

The subaltern concerns of the writers are the same principles that good political institutions at the local or community level are meant to guide: policies and actions for the common good. Often literature satirizes the politicians at the local government level (as at the state and federal levels) to embarrass the officials to use the financial resources available in a more equitable and prudent manner to benefit the people. Different genres of Nigerian literature have served to sensitize the reading public about the plight of the common people.

Subaltern Voices and Postcolonial and Marxist Theories

Postcolonial studies with emphasis on subaltern voices and silence provide a framework to address the complementary but often antagonistic relationship between literature and local community governance. Postcolonial literature and the Marxist concern for the masses and workers give voice to the silenced and bring to the center issues of the marginalized. They aim at bridging the class divide between the haves and the have-nots and, in doing so elevate the standard of living of the local "workers" who are primarily farmers and petty traders. In both literary works and public policy discourse, the plight of the common people falls within what G. C. Spivak describes as the "Other" and falling outside of the hegemonic structure and so have no way of having their voices heard or acknowledged through any form of self-representation. Since the Nigerian subaltern cannot speak at the federal level in Abuja or at the respective state capitals, the local and community level provides them a platform to be heard. It is the realization of this avenue that led to a Nigerian constitution that grants the local governments 22 percent of the entire national income to be shared equally among the 774 local governments in the federation.

Political inclusiveness demands that those who live outside the state and federal centers be not totally ignored or denied access to state support in human development and progress. This is because avenues have to be created for whatever is done at the federal level to filter to the state, and what is done at the state level to filter to the local government. It is only through this medium that there can be true national development. How, for instance, can a nation grapple with its health problems of infant mortality or maternal care without local government input? Issues of the environment often start at the local community level before they spiral to involve the state and the entire nation. It therefore makes administrative sense for those at the center and "others" at the periphery to meet somewhere for a cohesive growth. Nigeria's administrative units were either set up by the colonial British administration or, after independence, patterned after Western administrative units of provinces, councils/counties, and so forth to cater for those outside federal and state centers.

Traditional African literary aesthetics provide the Nigerian writer the sensibility to produce works that advance the plight of the common people. Literary artists and writers in Nigeria from oral tradition to modern times have assumed the role of guardians of the common people whose rights are capable of being trampled upon with impunity by the few rich and powerful in their midst. Literature in the African tradition is a means of questioning issues and problems toward their resolution for a salutary ethos. At the community or local level, the satiric *udje* of the Urhobo people, like the Ewe's *halo*, attacks negative social behaviors such as stealing, laziness, adultery, flirtation, and selfishness. The *ororile*/poet uses laughter as a means of regulating human behavior with the poetic songs. The songs are meant to correct bad behavior and also deter others by making them the butt of songs. These songs have an important social function, for they maintain a delicate balance between the general good of the society whose ethos must be upheld and respect for the law-abiding individual. The satirical content of the songs demonstrates the extent to which they are imbued with a distinctive moral awareness related to the collective life. Communal harmony and peace must be present for any human or other forms of development. Traditional literature such as the Yoruba *ijala* also promotes virtues in the community.

Peaceful coexistence and individual freedom are also promoted in folktales like the tortoise tales to show that there is room for extreme behavior but such disruptive behavior is never condoned.

Here's an example to show how Nigerian orature criticizes negative behavior and promotes social cohesion, hard work, and other virtues toward human development and progress of the area. In an Ughievwen *udje* song on local politics, the poet vehemently attacks overzealous local partisan supporters of both Chief Obafemi Awolowo and Dr. Nnamdi Azikiwe, party leaders of their respective Western Nigeria-based Action Group and the Eastern Nigeria-based National Council of Nigeria and Cameroon. The poet talks of their obsession with the cock and the palm tree, respective symbols of the two parties, without time for them to work and take care of their families and their community civic duties. In fact, the subject of the abuse song has become "kokoroko," a crowing cock and no longer a human being. Extremism could lead to political violence that will disrupt individual and group progress in the area. The Urhobo *udje* is representative of other satirical modes in Nigeria. Praise poetry genres as the *ijala* and *oriki* among the Yoruba extol virtues that promote good citizenship, good governance, and social harmony for local development. Also the Yoruba culture empowers women at certain times to sing derogatory and abusive songs at night targeting men. This is expected to shame and get them to change to positive habits and actions as during the Gelede performance.

Literature, as Terry Eagleton and other Marxist literary theorists and activist writers see it, has to range on the side of the common people, the masses. Literature in the African tradition is rarely art for art's sake and is often very utilitarian. In making literature functional, the Nigerian writer tends to use his or her work as a weapon to fight for the common people. Literature is placed at the service of the often disenfranchised, poor, or lower class, most in rural areas that the local governments target to improve their lot. The Nigerian society is generally divided between the haves and have-nots, which in the political context of the country is also a conflict of the rulers and the ruled, the military and the civilians, the powerful and the weak, and so forth. Thus, there is the class divide separating those at the center from those at the fringes.

Modern Nigerian poetry of the second generation draws attention to the gap between the haves and the have-nots to embarrass the rulers and generate sympathy for the masses. Niyi Osundare and Odia Ofeimun, among many poets, use their writings to expose the disparity between the haves and the have-nots and seek a resolution of the socioeconomic imbalance in society. Osundare's *Songs of the Marketplace* is a people-oriented collection that ranges on the side of the exploited, oppressed, and poor people against their social and economic predators at the state or federal centers.

Classism exists between those Nigerians at state and federal levels, often urban, and those in rural environments who are the target groups of local governments. Modern Nigerian poetry, taking a cue from the orature, attempts to reduce social disparity and inequality by attacking exploitation and marginalization of the weak, poor, and masses. This literature aims at representing the voice and concerns of those at the bottom of social hierarchies.

Gender Issues

One area in which literature and local and community studies have made great strides is in the area of women's health and economic access. Nigerian literature has for so long taken the condition of women and the pursuit of equality with men and self-actualization as one of its major subjects. Flora Nwapa's *Cassava Song and Rice Song* advocates recognition of economic crops that women produce; she notes that people survived on the same crops in war time when yams—the male crop—could not be produced by men who formed the armed forces. Many male writers have also taken the cause of women. Look at this poem, "For Mbwidiffu":

> I hear the agonizing cries of girls
> in flight from the flashing razor;
>
> I hear horrific howls of daughters
> against their parent-sanctioned rape.
>
> Who wants to be held down to wear the stigma
> of adult life, her ecstasy wrapped in a rag?
>
> Who wants her yams scorched before harvest,
> stripped of womanly pride for old times' sake?
>
> "And they have the nerves to cry out,"
> the patriarchs wonder in male-only joints;
>
> "after all, their mothers went through this
> without crying or complaining of cruelty!"
>
> These men do not count the army of divorcees—
> leaking women no man wants in the neighborhood;

they look down on their children's wrinkled mothers
morose and up to the neck in forced misery; wrecked.

Of course, the contented men take no count
of the multitude of brides dying at childbirth.

The girls fleeing, the old men complain,
have turned into animals without names.

There's no laughter in the girls that fall in line—
firebrands wipe out sunshine from their faces.

I still hear the chilling wails of the fugitive girls,
the benumbing silence of their ghostly presence

and now the goateed men ask the Maker why these girls
aren't made of the same stuff as their tamed mothers.

The simple answer: "Time has changed!
Time has changed. Time has since changed!" (*The Beauty I Have
    Seen*, 30–31)

This poem is one of so many literary works that address the deplorable situation of women who have been kept down for so long by patriarchal customs. Nigerian literature attempts to liberate women from male tutelage and make them regain their agency and live self-actualizing lives.

Health and Environmental Matters

Health and the environment are interrelated and have been common pursuits of local governments and community units as well as of literary writers. Scholars of Nigerian local politics such as Oladimeji Aborisade and Robert Mundt see the environment in terms of agriculture and marketing as well as health and disease as shown in their second chapter of *Politics in Nigeria*. On the other hand, many Nigerian writers in the past three decades have focused on the environment at local and community levels as literary critics deploy ecocriticism to study the new literature. Recent Nigerian literature deals with the ecology and environment in ways which also touch local and community politics in the areas of farming and fishing, the occupations of the people and their means of sustenance.

The writers whose works and activism have focused on the local environment include Ken Saro-Wiwa in his *On a Darkling Plain*, Niyi Osundare in his *The Eye of the Earth*, Tanure Ojaide in both

The Activist and *The Tale of the Harmattan*, Nnimmo Bassey in his poetry, Ogaga Ifowodo in *The Oil Lamp*, Kaine Agary in *Yello-Yello*, Ahmed Yerima in *Hard Ground*, and Ikoriko in *Oily Tears*. It is significant to note that the writers do not approach health the way local government and community institutions or units do directly by promoting maternal care, child immunization, and more. Rather, the writers have a biocentric approach—telling readers to understand the symbiotic relationship between nonhuman beings and humans for a balanced environment.

According to Rob Nixon, "bioregionalism" is the "responsiveness to one's local part of the earth whose boundaries are determined by a location's natural characteristics rather than arbitrary administrative boundaries" (Olaniyan 757). Bioregionalism advocates eco awareness and the need to maintain a harmony between humans and nonhuman forms in the environment (Branch xiii). On the surface level, bioregionalism and local government may seem at odds with each other; however whether a locality is determined by "natural characteristics" or by "administrative boundaries," they often overlay each other and are still local and are the context of activities of the common people.

Osundare has alerted Nigerians at all levels to the importance of taking care of our environment in "The Earth Will Not Die," one of the most direct poems in *The Eye of the Earth*. However, it is in the Niger Delta area of Nigeria that local and other writers have focused on how to address the fragrant environmental degradation resulting from oil and gas exploration and exploitation. The attempt by Niger Delta writers such as Isidore Okpewho in his *Tides*, Kaine Agary in her *Yello-Yello*, Ogaga Ifowodo in *The Oil Lamp*, Ebinyo Ogbowei in *Song of a Dying River*, and Ojaide in both *The Activist* and *The Tale of the Harmattan* to protect the environment and halt ecological damage has brought to the fore the role of activism in Niger Delta literature.

Specifically, Ogaga Ifowodo and Ojaide have addressed the explosion that resulted in the deaths of over a thousand people at Jesse, near Sapele, in Delta State in the mid-1990s where local folks collecting leaking fuel to sell were incinerated in the accidental blaze that broke out. Similar accidents have taken place in many parts of the Niger Delta. The environmental concern of writers is related to issues of minority status in a federation, sharing of economic wealth, marginalization, environmental justice, and others. It is at the local level that "resource rebels" such as the Egbesu Boys and other groups spring up. These issues, which are also political, are addressed by Niger Delta literature. Works such as Agary's *Yello-Yello* and my

Activist talk about the health, sociocultural, and economic fallouts of environmental damage.

It is significant that oil and gas explorers and exploiters deal with host communities in matters relating to compensations for their lands and damages to the environment. Often there are community groups—town and youth associations—that deal or negotiate with the multinationals that have departments of community services. In Delta State, for instance, Shell, Chevron, and other companies have paid compensations (usually meager) to their host communities. Many times the multinational oil corporations have made some contributions to the localities where they have their oil and gas facilities. Through agreements between the oil companies and host communities, Bonny in Rivers State and Brass in Bayelsa State, for example, have free electricity provided by Shell and Agip respectively. Many of the oil companies build roads, town halls, and clinics as well as sink bore holes, and renovate schools for their host communities. At a time, Shell established a cassava farm at Agbarho near Warri and a fish farm at Igbide in the Isoko area of Delta State. Oil companies also give scholarships to university students from communities in which they operate. Thus, communities in local government areas have demanded their share of development out of the high profits from the oil and gas exploitation from their lands. Writers in those areas have highlighted the environmental degradation and the need for the oil and gas exploiters to invest a fraction of their profits in not only restoring the environment but also in compensating the locals whose occupations of farming and fishing have been totally destroyed by their activities.

CONCLUSION

From the discussion, activist literature and public policy are theoretically aligned to improve the lot of the masses. The various traditional African and postcolonial approaches of literature have their parallels in local political management and public policy. As emphasized in this chapter, Nigerian literature has no problems with the theory of Nigerian local politics; the angst and mistrust are with the practice of politics. Activist literature attacks sociopolitical malpractices at the local or community level in squandering the resources that should be used to advance the development of the common people. In the tradition of African literature, it is common that literature responds to the history, politics, and other experiences of the people at the local and community levels. On the other hand, politics does not respond to literature except when rulers and their functionaries respond, often negatively, to what the writers write or do outside their works. But political science through public policy and policy studies shows the positive direction toward the development of local government areas.

Political institutions at the grassroots level and literature in Nigeria are geared toward the betterment of lives of rural people, the masses, and the marginalized. It is the writers' keen sensibility and outrage at rampant corruption and greed that deny the masses their humanity that make it look like literature is against political policies and actions. However, political science addresses policies of development. Policy studies and activist literature have similar goals in indicting politicians that from the Nigerian experience often corruptly enrich themselves at the expense of the masses. The problem literature and policy studies have with Nigerian politics arises from the disconnection between political theory and practice. Workshops and other avenues should be organized to train local government administrators and community leaders and workers to professionally contribute to the development of individuals and the areas. Oladimeji Aborisade has been involved in training local government workers for years and I salute his contribution to bridging the gap between political theory and practice at the local level. With his work, there is no doubt a meeting of objectives between political science and activist literature. In the end, political science and literature in Nigeria aim at creating a healthy environment in all its ramifications for the human development of the common people as they continue to be the watchdogs at the service of the common people.

CHAPTER 14

The Politics of African Literature: Production, Publishing, and Reception

INTRODUCTION

African literature is political and politicized as it contests political issues and proffers political visions. In this chapter, effort will be made to interrogate the politics in the production, publishing, and reception of contemporary African literature. This chapter is meant to complement the second chapter, "Contemporary Africa and the Politics in Literature." As emphasized in the second chapter, almost every human experience in Africa has become political or connected to politics in one way or another. Similarly, there are political issues involved in the production, publishing, and reception of literature written in Africa. Also, as in the second chapter, here politics intersects with the culture, society, economy, zeitgeist, and other aspects of contemporary African reality. Politics in literature, as used in this chapter, has to do with a conscious or unconscious effort, choice, strategy, or the lack of any determination to do something with particular results anticipated. Politics involves ideology, ideas, and notions of the African reality that writers, publishers, and readers have to deal with in relation to contemporary African literature.

In addition, there will be an attempt to engage the sociology of contemporary African literature as it relates to the production, publishing, and reception. Closely related to these areas is the literary reputation of the writers and their writings which is often related to politics. The main objective of this chapter, therefore, is to provide a scholarly platform that covers enough parameters of literary discourse to have a holistic discussion of politics in contemporary African literature. In fact, one can argue that until there is serious interrogation of such aspects of African literature as its production, publishing, readership, and reception, there can be no meaningful statement on its politics.

PRODUCTION

The production of a people's literature is anchored on their literary tradition, culture, society, history, economy, and other aspects of the people's lives. The experiences are expressed creatively in literary forms that preserve and exhort the values and culture embedded in the works. African literature thus is an African sociocultural production. With Africa's history of colonization, there has been the addition of the written to the oral in literature with each medium reinforcing the other. As scholarship in African literature shows, the oral and the written are not antithetical but complement each other (Irele and others). History thus has been a major factor in the dynamics of African literature, transforming from the traditional oral to the modern written. Both the oral and the written coexist in most African societies with the oral more practiced in rural traditional societies and the written in more urban Westernized societies of the continent.

Literacy in Africa is not uniform since there are some countries with a higher literacy rate than others with a dismal record of literacy. Tanzania, Ghana, and South Africa have a relatively high literacy rate compared to, among others, Chad and Niger. A country's literature may sometimes be a reflection of its literacy rate. The more literate and educated a community is, the more readers and writers it will have because the proliferation of the written literature inevitably relates to the writing and consumption rate of that literature. It is therefore understandable that the more Westernized larger countries or communities within countries tend to produce more writers than the less Westernized and smaller countries. In the cases of Tanzania and Ghana, one can see the effort made by foresighted political leaders like Julius Nyerere and Kwame Nkrumah in taking literacy and education seriously as a national challenge. There is a rich Tanzanian literature in Ki-Swahili. In any case, the Westernization perhaps explains the early ascendancy of Nigeria (and West Africa) in literary production in the 1960s that made Ngugi wa Thiongo to lament the "literary wilderness" of East Africa. Southern Africa, especially South Africa and Zimbabwe, has a higher literacy rate than East Africa and also has many writers. Today one barely reads works from Chad, Niger, Botswana, and Equatorial Guinea but there are writers there but not as many as, for example, in Senegal, Ghana, Nigeria, South Africa, and Zimbabwe.

Other factors that affect literacy rate in Africa include geography and gender. The closer a place is to the administrative/political headquarters or capital, the higher the literacy rate is likely to be. Residents of such a place tend to take advantage of state or private schools around to go to school. That explains the higher literacy rate in urban areas than in rural areas with the respective civil servant and professional population of the city and the primarily farming rural communities.

In most of Africa, men generally had a head start in Western education and that translated to being literate and becoming writers. During the colonial period, parents appeared to be more willing to send their male children to school than female ones. Many ethnic cultures that practiced early marriage for girls saw no benefit in sending girls to school. This gender disadvantage in acquiring Western education for women explains why most of the renowned early African writers are male: Leopold Sedar Senghor of Senegal, B. W. Vilakazi and Peter Abraham of South Africa, Chinua Achebe and Wole Soyinka of Nigeria, and Tchicaya U'Tamsi of Congo Brazzaville, among others. In fact, the first few poetry anthologies of modern African literature hardly featured any females and when done were wrongly presented as male. There was thus an erasure of women from the literary scene and their voices hardly heard at the beginning of modern African literature because women did not go to school as early as men did.

However, things have long changed in Africa. After many countries gained independence, especially from the 1970s onward, this colonial anomaly has been corrected and girls are being sent to school. The wave of female writers, including Ama Ata Aidoo from Ghana, Grace Ogot and Micere Mugo from Kenya, Flora Nwapa and Buchi Emecheta from Nigeria, Sindiwe Magona from South Africa, Nawal El Saadawi from Egypt, and Yvonne Vera from Zimbabwe coincides with women going to school at a high rate. In present-day Africa there are cases in universities and other tertiary institutions of more female undergraduates than male students and especially in the arts and humanities. Thus access to Western education through attendance of schools has bearing on the creation of African literature.

OTHER FACTORS AFFECTING PRODUCTION OF CONTEMPORARY AFRICAN LITERATURE

In addition to literacy rate, access to Western education, and gender, there are many other factors affecting the production of contemporary African literature. A major one is the demise of the multinational publishers such as Heinemann, Longman, and Macmillan that mid-wifed the birth and helped the growth of modern African literature in the 1960s and 1970s. African literature was new then to the world scene and produced such works as Chinua Achebe's *Things Fall Apart*, Ngugi wa Thiongo's *Weep Not Child*, Peter Abraham's *Tell Freedom*, and other classics. These big international companies headquartered in Europe but with branches in African countries had the resources and competence to publish many African literary works and also distribute them widely in and outside Africa. Their respective African Writers' Series went a long way to promote the production and distribution of literary works across Africa. Publishing encourages writing and the excitement about writing at the time was generated by the availability of ready publishers. The suspension of publishing African literature by those companies due to economic reasons has led to the drastic reduction of published literary works of a good quality in Africa.

Apart from denying easy access to publishing to African writers, that phenomenon also stopped writers and readers of one country from being very conversant with the literary works of other nations. There was a time when Heinemann was in vogue for a literary work by a Kenyan to be distributed and read in Ghana or Nigeria and vice versa. The avid literature reader read works of other nations. The economic decision for the withdrawal of multinational publishers from Africa also resulted from the bad economies in Africa which do not allow readers to buy enough books for the companies to make a profit. Without the economic resources to buy books, book production in Africa suffered a major setback from the period of austerity measures when the International Monetary Fund asked African nations to accept stringent economic policies that resulted in human suffering in the continent. Writing and buying books were relegated to the background when there was struggle for survival.

Overseas Publishing

Today, many African writers get published through international trade publishers such as Picador, Farrar, Giroux, and Strauss, Macmillan/ Routledge, smaller Western presses interested in African literature, University Presses of North America, and Black/African presses in North America and Europe. While generally the production of the literary works is superior in quality to those done by local publishers in Africa, the books are often expensive and rarely available in African bookshops. The irony of the matter is that it appears for a long time and perhaps up till now that getting published abroad gives an imprimatur of respect to African writers and the foreign published works. Some African writers get published abroad first before getting published within their own countries.

A good example of a press that introduced African writers to Africans from abroad is The Greenfield Review Press, a small publisher running about a thousand copies, managed from the attic by Joseph Bruchac in Greenfield Center, New York. The press published African writers including Kofi Awoonor, Ossie Enekwe, and Tanure Ojaide before their publishing in their respective Ghana and Nigeria. *The Greenfield Review*, also published by Bruchac, first introduced many African poets such as Syl Cheney-Coker and Niyi Osundare to African and non-African readers in the early 1970s.

Many of the African literary works that gain international acclaim appear to be published by Western publishers. For instance, works of the South African Zakes Mda, the Nigerian Chris Abani, Chimamanda Ngozi Adichie, Sefi Attah, Helen Oyeyemi, the Congolese Emmanuel Dongala, and the Ghanaian Benjamin Kwakye have trade imprimaturs of Picador. In addition, African/Black publishers overseas, especially Three Continents Press, Africa World Press, and African Heritage Press in the United States and Ayebia run by Nana Ayebia Clarke in the United Kingdom are examples of publishers of African creative works overseas. Africa World Press run by Kassahun Checole from Trenton, New Jersey, appears to have published more African creative works than any other press of that stature since Heinemann's separation from African literature. As already stated, there is respect for the foreign published works in Africa because they are professionally edited and produced, have the imprimatur of the Western academy, and are widely distributed.

While overseas publication of African literature has economic advantage to the writers who receive regular royalties, the works promoted, and stocked in foreign bookstores and libraries, there are still problems. Often the foreign publishers have their ideas of Africa that they want to promote in the manuscripts they choose to publish. Some African writers in the West that refuse to write bizarre things about Africa have complained that only the writers who write about a weird Africa, the global equivalent of Hegelian ideas, get published. While this may be a controversial accusation, there are elements of truth in it considering some of the African literature works published in the West. Uwem Akpan's *Say You Are One of Them* got rave reviews in the West and got included in Oprah Winfrey's Book Club list but did not generate as much interest within Africa. The short stories have all negative images of Africa, especially of violence. The point is that Westerners should not accept, as Adichie puts it, "the single story" of a negative Africa since the continent also has many positive experiences. Thus having a very bleak picture of Africa is not realistic but only confirms Western racist images of Africa.

The Western interest in child soldiers at the beginning of the new century has promoted works such as Ishmael Beah's *A Long Way Gone: Memoir of a Boy Soldier*, Uzodinma Iweala's *Beast of No Nation*, and Emmanuel Dongala's *Johnny Mad Dog*. In fact, Beah was interviewed on American Public Radio several times. Dongala's story was so popular that it was adapted into a film of the same name. These works deal with violence which accompanied civil war-ravaged parts of Africa and the part played by child soldiers who are cast as protagonists of the respective biographies and novels.

On a different level, Chris Abani's *GraceLand* with the negative image of urban Nigeria and a depressed rural Igbo land where homosexuality is practiced has not up till now (2014) been reissued by local Nigerian publishers. This situation is unlike Chimamanda Adichie's *Purple Hibiscus* and *Half of a Yellow Sun* that have been reissued by Farafina Press in Lagos. Calixthe Beyala has works published in Paris but, while there are few publishing houses in Cameroon, the sensationalism of sex in the West has added to the promotion of the works more in France than in the writer's home country.

The phenomenon of Western publishers issuing many African literary works that conform to their ideas of Africa has created two types of African literature: those produced overseas and those produced within the continent. Often the Africa-based writers do not have the advantage of good production, finances, editorial staff, and promotion that the Western publishers have. At the same time those writing in Africa do not seem to have freedom that the liberal societies of the West provide the African writers living there. The African writers having the West as their refuge can write about their societies and nations in very critical and sometimes exaggerated ways, especially on politics, sex and sexuality, without the challenges of their people at home but to the acclaim of Westerners affirming their distorted ideas of Africa. I have often drawn attention in my other scholarly writings on African literature to the works of Igbo Nigerian writers overseas and those within Nigeria in the works of Chris Abani, Tess Onwueme, Chimamanda Adichie, and Ernest Emenyonu versus works by those living and writing in Nigeria such as Akachi Ezeigbo, Ifeoma Okoye, and Adaora Ulasi, among others. The ones outside appear in the content of their works more radical especially concerning issues of sex and sexuality than those within Nigeria. Thus there is politics in the publishing industry as there appears to be a difference between works promoted abroad and works published in Africa. And also political is the stance of writers, depending on whether they write within Africa or in the liberal Western societies that a part of which still holds racist views about Africa.

NATIONAL AND LOCAL PUBLISHERS IN AFRICA

Publishing of African literature in Africa is primarily done by national and local presses. The times of the East African Publishing House that had all of East Africa as base have gone and in its place national or local publishers. Generally, the national and local publishers suffered from the economic hardship that started in the mid-1980s that made them to fold up or downsize. Local branches of Heinemann, Macmillan, and Longman have become shadows of their old selves in Nigeria. However, there is still a thriving African publishing culture however distressed and the major ones are Baobab in Zimbabwe, L'editions d'harmattan in mainly Senegal, Spectrum (Ibadan, Nigeria), and Fourth Dimension (Enugu, Nigeria). There is the emergence of Malthouse, Bookcraft, Kraft Books, Aboki, Farafina, Cassava Press, and Lantern presses, among others, in Nigeria that focus on literature. In recent times, Kraft Books has emerged as the leading publisher of literary books, especially poetry. Adewale Maja-Pearce, who once worked for Heinemann, has established in Lagos a cooperative of writers that funds the publishing of their works. From the works already produced, there appears to be good professionalism but since the resources are limited, the cooperative press is struggling to survive. However, as long as authors pay to get published, the practice makes their publishing outlets vanity presses. The editorial work, production, distribution, and other professional aspects of these presses appear poor because of the inadequately trained staff and limited resources.

South Africa has perhaps the most vibrant publishing culture of literary works in Africa. Among their major ones are Kwela, Snail Press, Philips, University of KwaZulu Natal Press, Cape Town University Press, and cooperatives like Vonani Bila's publishing outfit.

Self-Publishing and Vanity Presses in Contemporary Africa

Self-publishing is booming in many parts of Africa. One can explain it with the scarcity of publishers in the continent and more so after the withdrawal of the multinationals such as Heinemann, Longman, Macmillan, and a few others. Young writers needed an avenue to publish their works and many, especially in Nigeria and South Africa, resorted to self-publishing. This means the writers hand over their manuscripts without any professional editorial input to be printed. In the case of Kraft Books in Nigeria, the publisher, Steve Shaba, takes the manuscript from the writer after he has been paid the negotiated amount for the "publishing" and hands it over to a printer who produces the book. Starting with poor production, Kraft Books has improved considerably and focuses on poetry. Basically, in most of the self-publishing, the writer contracts with a printer to print his or her manuscript.

I have reservations about self-publishing especially because many young writers hurry to print their works and so miss professional editing of such works. Such books, in many cases, tend to present many errors ranging from grammatical through misspellings and typographical errors, to shoddy formatting and production. However, if the young or "beginner" writers need an outlet through self-publishing, they should give their works to someone who can edit the work professionally and rectify any grammatical or language problems that may arise. Such assistance is available in most English or Creative Arts Departments in the universities.

I am less averse to self-publishing by more experienced writers who may have ideological reasons not to be published by a national or international publisher but wish to self-publish. In a few cases, the writers themselves have their own imprints such as Femi Osofisan's Opon Ifa, Odia Ofeimun's Hornbill Press, and Vonani Bila's Press. The experience these writers have helps to raise their works to a good standard and there is less fear that without the publisher's editorial input the books will not be fine.

Self-publishing is a reality of the African literary scene and one can only advise writers to get their works to colleagues or language experts in the academy to read before taking such a work for printing. In addition, writers should choose an experienced publisher, who has the tools and professional wherewithal, including the knowledge of proper formatting of the different literary genres, to do the book production. Self-publishing is a phenomenon that is likely to increase and has to be improved upon since it will not go away. To be fair to many who self-publish, it is better to self-publish than allow the manuscript to rot in the closet when and where there are few outlets for younger writers. Many of the better known publishing houses in Africa, as elsewhere in the world, tend to publish known names rather than unknown names. To their credit, some self-published works have won national and international literary awards and I want to dispel the notion that every self-published work is weak. Ahmed Yerima's *Hard Ground*, published by Kraft Books, won the prestigious National Liquified Natural Gas Poetry Award in 2009. In 2013, Tade Adeola's *Sahara Testament* won the same award beating other works that were not self-published.

LITERARY PRIZES AND CONTEMPORARY AFRICAN LITERATURE

There is no doubt that winning a literary prize goes a long way to promote an author and his or her work. While many writers, readers, and literary scholars may quarrel with the politics of literary prizes, at the same time winning a literary award does great promotion for the writer since the media publish the news and the work and its writer get known. The institution of prizes tends to motivate writers in their effort to win fame and/or cash.

There are many prizes and awards open to African writers. Some are international and others national and local. Many American, British, and French literary prizes are open to citizens of any country. Sometimes the only requirement is that the entered book must be in English or French. Africans have won the British Booker Prize; Ben Okri for *The Famished Road* (1991) and J. M. Coetzee twice, for *Life and Times of Michael K* (1983) and for *Disgrace* (1999), and Chimamanda Adichie's *Half of a Yellow Sun* won the British-sponsored Orange Prize. The point is that some awards are worldwide and others are language-bound. Of course, the Nobel Prize tends to cite a writer's specific text that has informed the award. It is the ulti-mate canonization of a writer's opus and four Africans have won the prize since 1986 starting with Nigeria's Wole Soyinka, to include the Egyptian Naguib Mahfouz, and the South African Nadine Gordimer and J. M. Coetzee. A less known but popular award is the Neustadt Literary Award given by the University of Oklahoma at Norman and Mozambican Mia Couto won the 2013 edition of the prize. As a result of colonization which forced foreign languages on Africans, many contemporary writers win prizes in France, Britain, and the

United States, among other places. There are prizes linked to regions or international political associations such as the Commonwealth Poetry Prize, the Commonwealth Fiction Prize, and also the short story prize.

Within Africa, there is the Wole Soyinka Literature Prize administered by the Lumina Foundation based in Lagos. There are national literary prizes in most African countries for specific genres and such prizes promote the writing and production of more literary works. A poetry prize endowed by the Morocco-based Assilah Forum Foundation, a nonprofit organization, is awarded every two years to an African poet. The prize is named after Tchicaya U'Tamsi, the great Congolese (Brazzaville) poet, and started in 1989. Nigeria's Niyi Osundare won the award in 2008.

GLOBALIZATION AND THE NEW MEDIA

Publishing has gone beyond paper or hard copies to include online publishing. There are many online magazines and books. Online publishing or posting adds additional avenues and spaces for publication of African literary works. One can read many poems by Africans, including Ashur Etwebi of Libya, and a host of Ghanaian, Nigerian, and South African poets online. The appearance online of literary works not only makes them accessible but also promotes them. By subscribing to some programs, many read African novels and poems, for instance, from their Kindle. There are many African literary magazines published online. They include the Canada-based Amatsorise Ede's *Maple Leaf Supplement*, the Europe-based *New African Writing*, and many more thus creating avenues for writers to expose their works.

In addition to online publishing, many writers publish their works on Facebook and personal blogs. Chimamanda Adichie and many younger African writers have their fan clubs on Facebook or have someone else open a Facebook account to promote their works and activities. The Internet has succeeded to dematerialize publications by not having a hard copy of books but an online copy. And it has extended the possibilities of a literary work's audience because it no longer matters where a work is published. Barring the shenanigans of despotic or conservative governments, a literary work online can be accessed and read anywhere in the world. The new media could even affect text poetry in the shortened form and contracted language in which it is written.

POLITICS OF IDENTITY IN WRITING AND PUBLISHING

There are two observations worth noting on the politics of African creative writing: the stand of writers within the nation and the focus of many publishers. There is politics within the nation being expressed in writings and interviews by many writers who contest the nation in their specific countries. One can use contemporary Nigerian writers as examples but the phenomenon could be in many other African countries. Instead of seeing themselves as just Nigerian or African writers, some writers identify themselves on ethnic or regional lines. Chimalum Nwankwo has identified himself as an "Igbo poet" as other writers of Igbo extraction have called themselves "Biafran" writers. As a result of the traumatic Nigerian-Biafran War of 1967–1970, many writers of the area, especially those who experienced the civil war, see themselves as Igbo or Biafran. This is understandable because of the immense suffering which has left indelible scars on their collective psyche. Obi Nwakama and Obiwu Iwuanyanwu, two Nigerian writers currently living and writing in the United States, are examples of writers who see themselves as Igbo and Biafran. In scholarly writings on African literature, there have been essays on ethnic literature especially on Igbo literature which deal with works set in the area or by writers of the area. The same, on a smaller scale, has been done on Yoruba literature. There has been no self-proclaimed Yoruba writer that I know of and even Akinwumi Isola who writes in Yoruba could only be described as a writer in Yoruba, since the emphasis is on his use of the language and not the politics that Yoruba evokes.

In Nigeria, there has been an association with a yearly conference of Northern Nigerian Literature. This self-identity of these writers is meant to draw attention to works produced in the north which include oral as well as written Arabic, Hausa, and English works. The Islamic heritage which has inspired many creative works is interrogated. Works of Nana Asmau, the versatile daughter of Usman dan Fodio and other older works and modern works of Zaynab Alkali, Idris Amali, Idris Okpanachi, and others fall into the category of Northern Nigerian literature. Identifying as a Northern Nigerian writer is a political act.

There is a growing body of work which has attracted much attention the past decade and a half, especially since the death of Ken Saro-Wiwa, called Niger Delta literature. As defined and written in chapter 4, Niger Delta literature has to do with writers of the area and from outside responding to the Niger Delta experience and locality, especially the environmental degradation of the region because of oil

and gas exploitation by multinational oil corporations. It is a literature which politically contests the minority status of the people, their
exploitation and marginalization in the Nigerian nation in which the
wealth from their area is used to develop the rest of the country without much attention to the consequences of the oil and gas extraction.
Nothing could be more political than the manner that writers of sub-
groups choose to identify themselves, for instance, as Igbo or Biafran,
Northern Nigerian, or Niger Delta writers. While the examples here
are from Nigeria, there are possibly such identities in other parts of
Africa as in Anglophone and Francophone Cameroonian literatures.
In Kenya there are the writings of Gikuyu and non-Gikuyu writers.

The choice of identity of writers is reflected on the publishing
side too by the focus on specific regions, nations, and some will say
ethnic groups, in the choice of writers being published. The East
African Publishing House publishes only works from East Africa.
Many South African publishing houses, especially Kwela and Philips,
publish mainly works of South African writers and it was exceptional
for Kwela to publish the Nigerian poet Tanure Ojaide's *Tale of the
Harmattan* (2008). From the published works available, Spectrum
Publishers based in Ibadan focuses on writers from Nigeria's Western
region and some will say Yoruba writers. Fourth Dimension focuses
on writers of Nigeria's Eastern region and some will say Igbo writers.
Also Aboki publishes writers from the Middle Belt of Nigeria. The
situation of these publishing houses and the proximity of those writers in the area might be the reason why they appear ethnic and not a
conscious effort to limit publishing to the region or ethnic group in
which they are established.

So political is this situation in Nigeria that there is a so-called
Lagos-Ibadan axis of publishers and writers as there is an Eastern
Axis. Those outside those areas feel abandoned and left on their own
and Ken Saro-Wiwa of the Niger Delta might have decided to start
Saros International Publishers to counter the dominance of seemingly
Western and Eastern Nigerian publishers in Nigeria. His publishing
outfit located in Port Harcourt focuses on his work and writings of
Niger Delta writers.

Red Sea Press run by Kassahun Checole, himself an Eritrean in
the United States, publishes only works on Eritrea and issued Reesom
Haile's *We Invented the Wheels* and the anthology of Eritrean poetry
edited by Charles Cantalupo. From the works published by Ayebia,
there is an overwhelming emphasis on Akan and Ghanaian works.
Again, this shows the political decision of publishers to choose what
to and what not to publish. While I have mentioned some specific

publishers here, there are many others doing the same selection or emphasis in their publishing decisions across the African continent.

LITERARY REPUTATION OF CONTEMPORARY AFRICAN WRITERS

The literary reputation of African writers or their works, as elsewhere in the world, is difficult to establish. There is the quality of a writer's work, the accessibility by the public, contribution to the literary tradition of the culture, and the exposure to the media and readers. In contemporary Africa, the writers themselves, their agents, or admirers create glossy blogs or websites and use a lot of media outlets to promote works. Thus, a writer's accessibility or popularity might not match the quality of the works produced. Many writers have elaborate and glossy websites that draw attention to their works. The point being made is that while the quality of the work is important, some writers court the new and old media and exploit the new media for self-promotion. Checking the Internet for the websites, blogs, and Facebook of many writers will confirm this observation.

Local, national, continental, and international prizes, as stated earlier, help to promote a writer and the works and also raise the profile and literary reputation of the writer. Almost every literary prize has its promotion machine and when someone wins the prize, the author enjoys the limelight by appearing in the organization's website, Facebook, newspapers, television and radio, and award ceremonies. As also stated earlier in this chapter, writers published by major publishers in the West receive higher promotion that builds up a literary reputation than those published in Africa. It is more difficult for a self-publishing author within or outside Africa to expose himself or herself by the hand-to-hand or limited sale of the work compared to major publishers that distribute the books to major bookstores and libraries, send out catalogues every quarter or six months, and promote the books at the African Literature Association and African Studies Association conferences where participants hunt for new books. At the same time some publishers, more than most others, spend more resources and effort at promoting works and also taking books to book fairs especially in Africa (Zimbabwe, Cape Town, and Port Harcourt, among others), Frankfurt (Europe) and many cities in the United States. A major event that promoted writers and their works was the Africa's Best One Hundred Books initiative that came through the Zimbabwe Book Fair. The creative works listed there and their writers enjoyed a boost in sales and promotion across the continent and overseas. Self-published authors and major publishers sell books through Amazon.com.

One must not forget the phenomenon of African writers in the diaspora. Since they publish overseas and their books are not distributed in Africa where they are often too expensive to buy, such diaspora writers get known outside but not in their homelands or continent, a situation that has been described as "hear-say writers." Readers and scholars "hear" about such writers but have not read any of their works. Thus African writers, especially in Europe and North America, who are not published by major houses but small or obscure foreign publishers risk being labelled as "hear-say writers." One example is Uche Nduka who first resided in The Netherlands and Germany before relocating to the United States. Though he has published fine poetry collections such as *The Bremen Poems* (New Leaf Press, 1995) and *Chiaroscuro* (Yeti Press, 1997), he is hardly talked about in Nigeria.

Nothing works for a writer's reputation better than the quality of the work itself. Classics such as Achebe's *Things Fall Apart*, Mahfouz's works, Soyinka's *Death and the King's Horseman*, and Coetzee's *Disgrace* speak for themselves. The longer a writer writes the more readers and scholars are exposed to his or her name and work. So, on one level, the older writers who have been writing consistently for a long time get known and recognized. Examples include Ngugi wa Thiongo, Syl Cheney-Coker, and Niyi Osundare. At the same time a young writer who wins a major award gets a splash in the media. A good example of this is Chimamanda Ngozi Adichie who won the British Orange Prize with her *Half of a Yellow Sun*. It is normal in any literary tradition for the writers that have for long written to be better known.

Sometimes the writer's national or overall reputation is reinforced by extra-literary activities such as social and political activism. While many writers are activist in one way or the other, there are some writers who are more visibly so and that notion of their activism helps to boost their reputation as writers. During the apartheid period in South Africa, the writers that protested openly and got arrested or sought after by the apartheid government such as Dennis Brutus and Sandile Dikeni rubbed off on their literary works. Those who were in the Black Consciousness Movement or the African National Congress got some promotion through their political activities. Similarly, Ken Saro-Wiwa's activism on minority rights and environmental degradation of the Niger Delta by the multinational oil companies raised his literary profile to the extent that he was recommended for the Nobel Prize for Literature.

A writer's literary reputation can be very local, national, or world-wide. Often, as a teacher of African literature, one hears at the very local level teachers who want to promote their local heroes who may not be known outside their limited locality. I personally observed this at Niger Delta University, Amassoma, in Nigeria where students talked very highly of local poets who were not known outside their states or region. A student repeatedly praised Ikiriko's *Oily Tears*, which I sought and read. It no doubt adds to the literature of environmental pollution of the Niger Delta but its being self-published apparently limited its circulation beyond where the writer could reach. Self-publishing as in Nigeria leads the writers to lobby for their texts to be adopted in literature courses and raise profiles of works that may not be of a superior quality.

I have a final observation to make on the literary reputation of writers and their works. The writer's reputation changes as it waxes and wanes from time to time. One's literary reputation depends upon the writer's activities or sometimes death. Many writers have attention drawn to their works when they die, as happened recently to Chinua Achebe, Kofi Awoonor, and Festus Iyayi. However, on the whole, writers who publish often tend to remain on the literary radar than those that issue single works or have literarily "menopaused." Many writers whether in Ghana, Nigeria, Kenya, or South Africa had at one time or the other enjoyed some fame when first published but once they do not bring out any new publications over the years, such writers get off the radar and almost get forgotten even though they are still alive. While reluctant to give examples here, one can think of the South African Oswald Mtshali whose *Sounds of a Cowhide Drum* was popular in the 1970s but the writer did not follow up and the poet is rarely mentioned now when discussing contemporary South African or African poetry. The Nigerian Molara Ogundipe and Harry Garuba raised interest in their respective *Sew the Old Days and Other Poems* (1985) and *Shadows* in the 1980s but appear not to have followed up with more writings for over three decades. Sometimes a writer is not able to continue with the vigor or quality of earlier publications as perhaps Ben Okri and Nurudin Farrar, who were some two decades ago mentioned for the Nobel Prize but whose reputations have either slipped or been surpassed by newer writers.

CONCLUSION

African literature continues to be a political and politicized sociocultural production. The political or politicized nature is a complex of factors that intersect ranging from the writer's experience or ideology and personal decision on his or her work and the role played by publishers, readers, and literary scholars, and others. One can safely say that everything about contemporary African literature is political whether it is what the writers write about, their choice of identity and what to write about, where they write from, and so forth. Writing itself is political. The same thing could be said on the publishing which in fact could be very political in the decisions taken by the publishers. So, as humans and societies have become increasingly sucked into politics so are the works of the writers, publishers, critics, and readers political or politicized.

SECTION IV

Inviting the World into the House of Words: The Writer, His Place, People, and Audience

It is a very long way from Ibada Village (which no longer exists) to Charlotte, North Carolina. I was not even born there, but at Igberhe Village, so-named after the plantain plants that sustained the people. This hole, as my grandmother would describe it, was evacuated for Ibada Village, named after Ibadan, Nigeria's Western Region's capital then. And to my child's eyes our new village was "Ibadan." The houses all had corrugated iron sheets, which bedazzled with their silvery shine when new, especially in sunlight. There was a pliable earth road through it connecting Okpara Inland (Otorho Okpara) and Okpara Waterside (Erho Okpara). My two hands are both of Okpara, the subclan of Agbon. It is said that Okpara is slippery in the dry season, if you take the town for granted! I was born and raised in my maternal side; hence I begin from my mother's village. I am an Okurunoh man (really from Enemarho Village) but I am Ibada-born.

My father who had lost all three boys from his earlier marriage and had only a daughter before marrying my mother asked her to go to her own mother's home for delivery. He was there at the right time and after I was delivered at Igberhe Village and he knew that I was a boy, he rode his rusty Raleigh bicycle to tell his people that I was a girl! This story I heard only when already grownup and credit my father for his strategy. He feared for my survival and did what he felt would save me. Unlike my maternal uncles, my paternal uncles were not on good terms with each other. I was already five before I visited Enemarho Village, my father's home, for the first time. It was my grandmother, Amreghe, of the great Isaba family who raised me. She was the Mother Hen that covered me with her wings. There also were my grandfather and uncles Otota (Peter) and Onosigho. Grandfather Odjegba covered tedious miles on foot to Okpara Inland and other places to parties and wherever there was a ritual feast (*iye*) or free drinks. Many funny things popped out of his head when drunk but he was the spirit of the party. He was a great fisherman and farmer and remains a pride to us all. Onosigho, a cloth merchant, was a prosperous man who was thrifty despite his relative wealth. Otata, whose real name is Ofobrukueta, often acted as my father and today lives with my mother in Okurekpo. It was the childish way that I called Ofobrukueta that stuck to him as "Otata." It is the elder that gives the child a name but I, as a child, gave my maternal uncle his name!

I am the son of farmer-parents. My father had many rubber plantations. He tapped his own rubber trees and prepared Grade-A rubber sheets. He was also a palm nut collector and had a local palm oil press in which he prepared first-grade oil. He was a man who perfected the art of whatever he set out to do and took all the care and time required for the highest quality. He had a small cocoa plantation in which he also planted coffee trees and bananas. He was a great fisherman too. My mother was a farmer and planted yams and cassava. She did some fishing too, but later was more of a retail seller of meat. It is from this rural and humble origin that I came.

I went to school early, but the white priest would not allow me to be registered because my right hand could not cross over the head to touch my left ear. I still followed my cousin Okpoto (Samuel Onosigho) to school till the following year (1955) when I was no longer too small. St. Charles Catholic Primary School still stands there, but it was no longer the small "mission" that priests preferred to live in rather than in the bigger towns of Okpara Inland, Eku, and even Sapele. The old saying persists: "The reverend father knows what keeps him in Okurekpo." The early converts there were overgenerous to their Irish guests! Of my primary school days, I remember with fondness the versatile HM James Emucha whose enthusiasm inspired me to be a teacher. Pius Orovwuje was also a great teacher. So were both Omonogbo and Samuel Eshigbe.

After my elementary school days at St. Charles, I attended St. George's Grammar School at Obinomba. It was the first time that I left Urhoboland and was excited seeing Abraka (Bareki) and Obiaruku. I was scared at Obigbo, the village of coffin makers, before Obinomba. It appears I was always the smallest (perhaps the youngest) in my classes and Father Cunningham might have wanted to protect me from the bullying big boys by making me the altar boy and bellboy. For four years, I was the cock that woke the school. I also served at daily Mass for years. Though I disliked the banning of local languages, then called vernaculars, St. George's was a good education for me, the education that included Latin and English grammar.

It was while at St. George's that I visited Sapele for the first time and saw the African Timber & Plywood Company's Sawmill, heard its programmed siren, saw television for the first time, watched a movie, saw "boma" boys, and crossed the Ethiope River in a pontoon. During vacations we not only went to hook but also to tap rubber. On weekends we, "Grammarians," eagerly went to "social gatherings." We lived the adage of working and playing at the same time. We indulged in different dances and riddles and took "guy names" that have been shed since adulthood. I was small and innocent and wrote love letters for big girls to their boyfriends. The girls tried to give me gifts and were always around me to cover themselves from their real friends in public. After two girls died in a secret bid to abort conception, I refused to write love letters.

Mine is a story of moving from a hole, so to say, into exposure; from the interior into the open. I was one of two students (the other Patrick Erhiye) from Obinomba admitted into the three newly created Federal Government Colleges in the country. I then went to Sokoto as a pioneer student of Federal Government College. But the ethnic disturbances of 1966 brought me back, first to King's College, Lagos, and then to Federal Government College, Warri. I was there when the civil war broke out. I was on vacation at 10 Radio Road, Warri, when Biafran troops came to occupy Midwest. My guardian, Charles Edemenaha, moved us to Orerokpe during the occupation. The Federal troops soon came to flush out the Biafrans. Both armies were barbarous and sectional.

After the two-year program, I chose to attend University of Ibadan rather than University of Lagos that first sent me an admission letter. My father, Dafetanure, was nonliterate (and illiterate) but knew the value of Western education. He had learned from the frequent land disputes and subsequent litigations the importance of having a lawyer in the family. Also when sick, he wanted me to become a doctor. He rode his bicycle to Warri in a delegation to see a lawyer and the good life he saw confirmed his faith in a good education. Like in the Higher School Certificate program with two scholarships (State and Federal), I had three scholarships (State, Federal, and Catholic) for my university education.

I studied English, French, and German. The civil war was on and several times we had to sleep at roadblocks at the outskirts of Ibadan to be in class the first day of the term. Some of my colleagues had to take tortuous creek ways to reach Lagos before going to Ibadan. I took part in many demonstrations and about twice bussed to Lagos for demonstrations. It was in my final year in 1971 that the Apampa-Must-Go demonstration took place and a student was shot dead. I had started writing in Warri and continued in Ibadan, where I published in student magazines such as *The Beacon* and the *Pelican*. I wrote most of the poems in my first collection, *Children of Iroko*, while at the University of Ibadan. My first collection is titled after my nativity, Okurunoh. I had moved from Ibada Village to the real Ibadan! After I graduated from Ibadan, I became the first ex-student of Federal Government College, Warri, to go back to teach there. I had had a stint at teaching during vacations at St. Kevin's Grammar School, Kokori. I had briefly worked at the Federal Ministry of Education, Lagos, before asking to be posted to teach—an insane decision to many people. So was also my decision to turn down a scholarship to do MEd and rather wait to do an MA in Creative Writing in Syracuse or MLitt at Leeds.

There was the lure of greener pastures at the newly opened Petroleum Training Institute, Effurun, where I officially taught for two years—officially because we were bussed to Ughelli and after a subsidized lunch came back to Warri. It was not challenging enough for me teaching technical communication and writing. Professor Essien Udom, who had been my Independence Hall Master at Ibadan, invited me to Maiduguri where he was the Vice Chancellor. He later sent me for graduate studies at Syracuse University in the United States, where I got an MA in Creative Writing and a PhD in English. It was a great exposure and big boost to my writing career. After the PhD, I returned to Maiduguri on December 18, 1981 to teach there for nine years.

At the time the Urhobo Social Club was very vibrant nationwide and I was involved in the Maiduguri Chapter. I immersed myself in my writing and it was the years in Maiduguri that I started winning literary prizes, which include the Commonwealth Poetry Prize for the Africa Region in 1987. I went to receive the prize in London and at the Commonwealth Center (in the company of Chinua Achebe) lunched with Queen Elizabeth II. I also won the Association of Nigerian Authors' Prize for Poetry, the BBC Arts and Africa Poetry Prize, and the All-Africa Okigbo Prize for Poetry. Those were glorious years for me despite the economic austerity.

I took sabbatical leave to Whitman College, Walla Walla, Washington, where I was the Visiting Johnston Professor in 1989/90. After that year, I took up an appointment at The University of North Carolina at Charlotte, where I still teach. While abroad, I try to visit my Delta home regularly to reconnect with my roots. I have written more collections of poetry, as well as a memoir, short stories, and in recent times a novel. I have chosen the writing life and I am putting everything into it. In all my writing, my early upbringing in the Niger Delta continues to feed and fuel my imagination. Since being away from home, I have been drawn more to home than when there. My Urhobo is more fluent and stronger than what it was while I was living in Nigeria. I have opportunities here to go home and research on the Udje dance songs and published a book on it—*Poetry, Art, and Performance: Udje Dance Songs of the Urhobo People* (2003). I have set many collections of poetry on the Niger Delta and they include *Labyrinths of the Delta* (1976), *Delta Blues and Home Songs* (1995), *Invoking the Warrior Spirit* (2001), and *In the Kingdom of Songs* (2002). I have used my Urhobo heritage to poetic advantage in many of these poems by exploring the *Ivwri* philosophy and using Urhobo folklore as a backdrop. Ours is a very rich heritage that gives confidence to one and propels one to the top of one's profession. That is what *Ivwri* does. References to Urhobo historical, mythical, and legendary figures such as Mukoro Mowoe, Essi, Ogidigbo, and Arhuaran populate my poetic landscape. In recent years I have been writing some poems in Urhobo. One cannot be luckier than be enriched considerably by one's own heritage

I must pay tribute to my wife, Anne, and children who have enhanced my writing life. I believe strongly in the family and Osonobrughwe has blessed me with a happy one.

*   *   *

This is a writer's dream and blessed is the one who lives to experience it: see the world gather in an auditorium to celebrate and discuss one's work! I am overwhelmed by the generous sentiments expressed and the size of scholars, readers, writers, students, and others from far and near. I want to pay tribute to my literary elders, the trailblazers—Chinua Achebe, JP (Clark), Kongi (Wole Soyinka), and others. I do not forget the oral artists nationwide, including the famous Omokomoko Osokpan who has been singing since my childhood up till now. At the same time, I am not the only writer of my generation, sometimes called second and at other times third, that one of us, Funso Aiyejina, calls the "alter/native generation." Many of my generation are here including Ezenwa-Ohaeto, Odia Ofeimun, and Tayo Olafioye and I welcome them as colleagues and kindred spirits. My good friend Niyi Osundare has not been able to make it here today.

I have won many literary prizes and been honored many times for my writing at home and abroad, including at the Commonwealth Office in London where I had lunch with the Queen of Britain and many prime ministers. But good as the past honors, nothing compares with this: your own people's and readers' recognition of your writings and deeming it relevant to invite the world to assemble in the Niger Delta that has been the focus of my work for the past 35 years for a conference. Neither an Agbon chieftaincy nor a Nigerian national honor can give as much fulfillment to me as this conference. Thanks to Professor Onookome Okome of the University of Alberta at Edmonton who not only initiated the idea but also worked hard for its realization. Thanks also to Professor G. G. Darah and Dr. Sunny Awhefeada who helped to put this together. And thank you all from Botswana, Cameroon, South Africa, the United States, and from all over Nigeria for your honor in attending this conference.

Here where I stand at Delta State University, Abraka, is at the heart of the Niger Delta in which I am deeply rooted. My father's village of Okurunoh, after which I titled *Children of Iroko*, and Ibada Village where I was born and raised by my maternal Grandmother Amreghe are in this Ethiope East Local Government of Delta State. Okurekpo where I had my primary school education, trekking there from Ibada Village dry or wet is some eight kilometers away. Where I had my first literature class in secondary school is about five kilometers away—St. George's Grammar School Obinomba. Also, Federal Government College, Warri, where I had my Higher School Certificate program, is only about 30 kilometers away from here. Many of the experiences I talk about in my memoir, *Great Boys: An African Childhood*, took place in this vicinity. It is in this area that I grew up.

It is on this Bareki, the colonial name of Abraka, so-named after the police barracks, that the poem "Abracadabra at Abraka" is based. "Ughelli," perhaps my first political poem, is based on Ughelli, producing oil and gas but without electricity then; what I felt as a youth about marginalization. The Electrical Corporation of Nigeria (ECN) and later renamed NEPA (National Electric Power Authority) was based in Ekakpamre, near Ughelli, and both towns had no electricity then while the company generated electricity that was enjoyed across the southern part of the country, especially Lagos. And Agbarha, "where everybody is king," is also nearby. If you look outside, you will see the lush tropical foliage that in *Delta Blues and Home Songs* speaks the "lingua franca of green," The *udje* songs, after which several poems are modeled in the "Home Songs" section of that poetry collection, are composed and performed by the Ughievwen and Udu peoples, who are also nearby.

The Niger Delta's images, landscape, folklore, and people's concerns all enter my writings. Put simply, I see the world and life through Niger Delta eyes. One needs to be deeply rooted to be strong and I believe the Niger Delta gives me not only my strength and stability but also lights me up for the world. This honor of a conference thus takes place in a most fitting setting that gives me a lot of fulfillment.

Much as I am steeped in the Niger Delta, I am part of the Nigerian nation, which my living abroad in no way diminishes. After all, I schooled or worked in Sokoto, Lagos, Ibadan, and Maiduguri. I must have been in up to 32 of the 36 states in the country. I spent a good part of my life in Maiduguri, which strengthened my talent and many of my poems, including "Savannah Suites," arise from that experience. My loyal friends from Borno and Adamawa States are testimonies of this bond. I have always loved Jos, the "city in my heart." I have traveled very far and extensively to more than a dozen countries in about five continents and lived in the United States for long, but I remain body, mind, heart, and soul Nigerian and African.

Two points I want to make at this juncture. One is the need for complementary relationship of peoples. No one person, group, or nation has everything; there are strengths and weaknesses and we need to be strengthened by others too. I do not want to be seen as incapable of going beyond my Urhobo ethnic group, my Niger Delta region, my Nigerian nation, and my African race. I am a human being and those things that nurture me can come from any parts of the universe. It is because I am deeply rooted in the Niger Delta that I am a strong Nigerian, proud African, and a determined humanist.

The second point is that in the attempt to benefit from complementarity, especially in an age of globalization, one should not always be conceding one's identity and embracing only other people's ways, aesthetics, or lifestyles. One should be rooted deeply enough to sell one's self to others. There is the need for the local (here the Niger Delta) to be boldly inscribed in the global; hence I will always continue to put the Niger Delta at the forefront of the world in my creative works. Globalization should be a two-way traffic and not just a one-way from the Western world of Europe and North America. There is need for the local to be globalized and the global to be localized in a "glocal" world.

The world is changing fast as our culture, society, and environment and we have to adapt. Many of us cannot speak our own languages and do not know the folklore and ways of our people. While we should not cling to the past for the sake of ethnic identity, we have to be selective to retain those aspects that strengthen us and leave behind what is no longer relevant or cumbersome. I am bothered that many artistic and creative aspects of our culture are being destroyed by the blinding zealotry of new foreign religious groups that promote the destruction of our culture. We make fools of ourselves if we say we practice Christianity and so do not have to perform those cultural traditions that in their own ways helped to create a healthy social, moral, and ethical ethos in the past. It is very instructive that despite the Pentecostal wave and new religiosity, our people are more devious morally and ethically than at any time before! If Haloween were a Nigerian tradition, the zealots would have fought against it and canvassed for its elimination as a satanic tradition. But in the United States, it is seen as just a tradition and children of Christians and pastors proudly take part in its celebration. We should be proud of our oral traditions that should be recorded and passed on with new technological tools for future generations. I think of udje song performances that brought the best in artistic and moral achievements that have virtually been abandoned. Many times I have been told that the practice of oral poetic composition and performance is linked to gods and goddesses and so unchristian! We need to protect our folkloric heritage and save it from zealots and shallow minds.

Similarly, we should pay attention to the environment that has been a refuge and a sustainer of our lives and heritage. We need conscious effort to prevent it from being destroyed by greedy oil companies and our own hands. We should resist the oil companies prospecting for and exploiting oil and gas in our lands from degrading the environment that is not only our provider but also a source of spiritual solace. We should also stop practices based on nonscientific and ignorant ways that make us destroy our own environment. We should not cut down trees because witches have them as covens. Rather, we should plant trees in our villages and towns. We can see that the beans, yams, groundnuts, fish, and game that made us an agricultural people are either gone or depleted, even as we have more mouths to feed.

Let me go back to my writing. Let this celebration be the beginning of more things to come. I already have more poetry and fiction manuscripts ready to place with publishers. Whom do I write for? I have been studied, read, or quoted by students, scholars, and writers in the United States, South Africa, Iran, Malaysia, India, and many other places. I started as "a child of the iroko" in "the labyrinths of the delta" and attempting "the eagle's vision" in imaginative flights as I sing "the endless song." I had "the daydream of ants" after seeing "the fate of vultures" in Nigerian national politics. In recent times I invoke the "warrior spirit" of Iphri as I sing "in the kingdom of songs." "I want to dance." I have also viewed "matters of the moment" as "the activist" attempts to change things. As I wait for "the hatching of the cockerel," I also indulge in "water passion and oil remedies."

Now I am a house of words in the Niger Delta to which all humans are invited. It is open to all peoples in pursuit of justice, fairness, equality, freedom, and sensitivity to the plight of the under-privileged, marginalized, persecuted, disabled, and others discrimi-nated against. We all have to join hands to fight against oppression, corruption, dictatorship, lies, dishonesty, and other negative prac-tices that diminish our sense of humanity in the Niger Delta, as in Nigeria, Africa, and anywhere in the world. We are all connected as human beings and should not feel that what happens in one place does not affect us. Somehow, what affects others however distant, also affects us. When justice is assaulted somewhere it affects every human being. As I reiterate, I write through the prism of the Niger Delta for all humanity. We must not be blinded by love not to be self-critical. We will do injustice to ourselves and the people we love if we excuse them from following the human code; in fact, if you read my work carefully I am more critical of myself and the Niger Delta and Nigeria than the rest of the world. You can call it tough love, what I practice.

To whom much is given, the adage goes, much is also expected. The Niger Delta, Nigeria, Africa, and the world have given me so much—I am truly blessed. I accept your honor as a challenge to work even harder with your inspiration and also to reciprocate the Niger Delta's generosity to me with a gift that will touch the minds of its people. I will be presenting in a moment a copy of all my books to Delta State University, Abraka. I also want to honor my commitment to continue to endow the annual Ojaide Poetry Prize for the Delta State Branch of the Association of Nigerian Authors.

In conclusion, may this goodness done to me spread to all, espe-cially the writers of my generation whose works also deserve to be studied and their respective talents deserve honoring. I want to thank again Professor Okome whose dynamism brought this conference about. Also thanks to Professor Darah, Dr. Sunny Awhefeada, the Vice Chancellor Professor Enaohwo, Chief Michael Omeru, and all of you friends, relatives, fellow writers, scholars, students, and well-wishers. You give me the compelling reason and divine inspiration to write. I thank you all.

CHAPTER 16

Personally Speaking: *The Beauty I Have Seen*

INTRODUCTION

Here I write about my poetry work, *The Beauty I Have Seen*. Here are two poems from the collection: "When the muse gives the minstrel a nod" (51) and "For Mbwidiffu" (30).

WHEN THE MUSE GIVES THE MINSTREL A NOD

When the muse gives the minstrel a nod,
no bead ever competes with his diamond.

The minstrel gets his share of pain and joy
that he converts into songs of the season—

with the gift, an elixir, he cures migraines of misery;
for sure a wizard he sees without strain in the dark.

He takes the impassable road to the pagoda within,
knowing the wide road without a sign runs into peril.

He matches divine favors with a record sacrifice,
carries what is light to lift but heavy on the head.

Transported into primeval rapture by zeal for song,
he knocks out others for a singular vision of beauty.

There is only one moon, the world's munificent bride;
beside her legions of attendants in their livery of light.

Since there is only one muse in the pantheon
and music comes from the breath of her love

when the muse gives the minstrel a nod,
no bead ever competes with his diamond.

For Mbwidiffu

(after reading "Ecstasy")

I hear the agonizing cries of girls
in flight from the flashing razor;

I hear horrific howls of daughters
against their parent-sanctioned rape.

Who wants to be held down to wear the stigma
of adult life, her ecstasy wrapped in a rag?

Who wants her yams scorched before harvest,
stripped of womanly pride for old times' sake?

"And they have the nerves to cry out,"
the patriarchs wonder in male-only joints;

"after all, their mothers went through this
without crying or complaining of cruelty!"

These men do not count the army of divorcees—
leaking women no man wants in the neighborhood;

they look down on their children's wrinkled mothers
morose and up to the neck in forced misery; wrecked.

Of course, the contented men take no count
of the multitude of brides dying at childbirth.

The girls fleeing, the old men complain,
have turned into animals without names.

There's no laughter in the girls that fall in line—
firebrands wipe out sunshine from their faces.

I still hear the chilling wails of the fugitive girls,
the benumbing silence of their ghostly presence

and now the goateed men ask the Maker why these girls
aren't made of the same stuff as their tamed mothers.

The simple answer: "Time has changed!
Time has changed. Time has since changed!"

Long after my Grandmother sang to me at home and I constantly heard
other forms of indigenous poetry, I took a BA in English from the
University of Ibadan, an MA in Creative Writing and a PhD in English
from Syracuse University. I am also a Fellow of the Iowa International
Writing Program. I thus straddle two poetic traditions: the African oral
poetic tradition and the Western written poetic tradition.

The Writer Is not an air-plant

I have been quoted as saying that the writer is not an air-plant but someone deeply rooted in time and place. I am not sure this idea is originally mine but I first expressed it in the late 1980s. Original or not, I stand by the opinion that a writer is strongly influenced by or attached to his or her time and place. The writer's time involves having a sense of history with its society and politics, literary tradition, and prevailing aesthetics. When T. S. Eliot wrote about tradition and the individual talent, he was very much aware that a writer always writes from a sense of time, the zeitgeist, and gives a personal stamp or uniqueness to the experiences he or she chooses to express. By place, in the context of a writer's work, I mean the environment, geography, nationality, society, and culture. These aspects of place, like those of time, condition the writer to produce his or her own type of writing by responding to current realities. Harold Bloom's "anxiety of influence" comes to mind here. An awareness of one's literary precursors and their time and place, rather than be simply following a preceding tradition, could lead to new types of writing, which might involve a different literary form or strategy. In most cases, one generation attempts to go counter in form, style, or some other way to the preceding generation; a phenomenon compared to the son killing his father to be a man! Oftentimes the writer, especially the poet, responds to reality through the prisms of time and place and consequently fashions a viewpoint or philosophy in the writings that promote the virtues or values that the time and place hold dear. The experiences the writer articulates are individual perceptions of reality as it relates to time and place. I am not saying that the writer/poet is imprisoned and so cannot write outside of the phenomena conditioned by time and place. Human nature is so varied that it provides ample experiences for the writer to explore. Also, there are local and universal/global experiences that the poet can express as individual/ personal or public experiences. There is so much out there to attract the poet's attention in human nature and the world—human desires, foibles, virtues, travels, daily happenings, sociopolitical events, and climate change, to name a few subjects. Thus, one can define poetry as a personal or individual meditation on or exploration of the multifarious aspects of life through special use of language. The poet does not take the ordinary or the typical for granted but continues to reassess truths, behaviors, and ways of being, seeing, and knowing. My writing can be seen in the contexts of time and place and my experiences relate to my Niger Delta background, Urhobo/Pan-Edo folklore, Nigerian, African, global, and human issues.

Time and History

My growing up in a period of history from colonization through independence to postindependence rule (from my elementary school days of the later1950s to the present, 2013) has influenced my poetry. Though Janheinz Jahn had for long said that modern African literature is a reflection of history and politics, a point that postcolonial theorists (Homi Bhabha, Gayatri Chakravorty Spivak, etc.) have affirmed, as one cannot live outside history in Africa, so too can one not write outside of history. For me, the periods of the failed nascent democracy in Nigeria, civil unrests, military takeovers, civil wars, and postcolonial misrule have their presence in the human experience that I express in my poems. In *The Beauty I Have Seen*, many poems in the "Flow & Other Poems" section such as "I Sing Out of Silence," "Contribution to the National Debate," "Testimony to the Nation's Wealth," and "After the Riots, in Jos," among others, deal with sociopolitical issues that are related to Nigeria's history. The writer in Africa is political out of historical necessity.

My Background

Similarly, my background is very significant in the poetry I write. I was raised by my maternal Grandmother in a closely knit village community with certain moral imperatives. Everybody was the other person's keeper so that when as a small boy I went fishing with my age-mates, Godwin and Iboyi, there was a thunderstorm that disoriented us with a flash flood, the entire village adults went to seek and rescue us from drowning! As I went to elementary and then secondary school and later the university, my two uncles and their multiple wives and others in the village contributed to my education by giving me pennies and shillings whenever I was going back to school. In our compound my uncles so cared for me that I received more gifts at festivals than their own biological children and my wise Grandma often gave back some of the things I got to their children to avoid jealousy and malice. I thus grew up to know that I belong to an interdependent community in which the advantaged in wealth, strength, or other blessings had to assist others with their talents, since "I am because we are." I believe that whatever advantage of language I have as a writer I should give voice to the voiceless, use my words as a shield for the weak or helpless, and do whatever I can to uplift the common folks of the increasingly growing "community" to which I have become a member.

Born and raised in Nigeria's Niger Delta area, the tropical rainforest of rubber trees, palm trees, lush plants, greenery, and copious water form the backdrop of my poetry, especially in the images I employ to express my experiences. My geographical background provides me a repository of images, including the iroko, rivers, eagle, sunbird, tortoise, antelope, porcupine, vulture, and other fauna and flora of the area, from which I draw to express my feelings and ideas. In my writing, these images assume a symbolic connotation deriving from the oral tradition. "Doors of the Forest" and "I hoped to climb a ladder to the sky" express my nostalgia for the pristine natural environment of the Niger Delta of my youth.

As if the vegetation of the Niger Delta is not enough, the presence of oil and natural gas has compounded the sense of place of the region. The discovery of oil there in 1958 and the subsequent environmental pollution of the area through oil spills, blowouts, sabotage, and equipment failure of the multinational oil corporations such as Shell, Chevron, and Agip-Total have made life extremely difficult for the indigenes of the area who traditionally rely on farming and fishing for sustenance. The irony of being among the poorest people in the world despite the vast oil and gas resources that net the Federal Government and the multinational oil companies hundreds of billions of dollars annually showcases exploitation, marginalization, and unfairness. Since the Niger Delta people are minorities in the Nigerian federation, their resources have been taken to develop Lagos and now Abuja while their area remains highly undeveloped. Also the massive environmental degradation and pollution have given an activist and protest edge to the literature of the area, including mine. As I told *World Literature Today*:

> My Delta years have become the touchstone with which I measure the rest of my life. Even when I wander outside to the many places I have experienced, that land remains indelible in my memory and imprinted in my thought. Home remains for me the Delta, where I continue to anchor myself. (*WLT,* 15, 1994)

Also, as written earlier,

> The Niger Delta is not just physical space but a spiritual, mystical, and psychological setting. It evokes ideas of public and private space in me: the physical and the psychic Delta are fused in my individual being. I foreground the Delta both consciously and unconsciously because it is the place I know best and I am most familiar with and consciously because I have so imbibed its spirit that it speaks in me even when I

am not aware of it. It is the backcloth, so to say, of my experience as a writer. It is the driving spirit of the Delta that shapes the vision and provides the images in my writing. (*Ordering the African Imagination*, 2007, 36–7)

Literature as a Cultural Production

I have expressed this so often but still need to state it in this crucial presentation: literature is a cultural production. As such, literature is part of a people's culture. Thus, the literature, whether oral or written, has a tradition, canon, aesthetics, and other aspects that are conditioned by the people's culture, experience, and sense of reality. One cannot separate a people's literature from their culture even in the postcolonial context of the African experience. Africans may use a European language (English, French, or Portuguese) but that foreign language is informed by the writer's indigenous African language, culture, worldview, sensibility, experience, and reality. *The Beauty I Have Seen* is thus a contemporary African cultural production despite being written in English.

The Language of the Postcolonial Poet

Part of the influence of time and place is the postcolonial nature of the modern or contemporary African writer, especially in the area of language. I am Urhobo and most members of my ethnic group live in the Niger Delta area of Nigeria. I speak Urhobo and have a smattering of several other Nigerian languages as well as French and German that I studied at school. Of course, there is "the extra-territorial" English (after Abiola Irele) of which my variant of many Englishes is the West African/Nigerian English. I write in English and sometimes in Urhobo. Urhobo and English, two different languages, involve two different ways of looking at reality; what Ania Spyra calls "two pairs of glasses, each offering a different focus" (*WLT*, January/February, 2012, vol. 86, no. 1, p.21). When I write in English, I do not translate from Urhobo and while writing in Urhobo I do not translate from English. However, I am highly influenced by Urhobo oral traditions that give not only poetic profundity but also a cultural identity to my writing in English. My assumption of the persona of the minstrel in *The Beauty I Have Seen* derives from the minstrelsy tradition in Urhobo orature. The minstrel tells not just his own tale but the collective tale of his people. The first part of the book explores this tradition to talk about sociocultural, political, and other issues that affect the minstrel's community. The poet I represent, the contemporary minstrel, is thus a public figure, a traveler and observer of humanity, and one grounded in the landscape and fate of his native land and people.

Let me expatiate on diction and connotations in Urhobo and English. As Edward Sapir, Benjamin Lee Whorf, and other language experts have emphasized for decades, language carries the culture of a people and conditions their thought. What do I borrow from Urhobo in my writings as in *The Beauty I Have Seen*? How does Urhobo/African folklore give depth and cultural identity to my poetry? Some specific examples will suffice to illustrate this point. As already explained, the minstrel tradition used here is that from Urhobo folklore. Aridon is the Urhobo god of memory and my muse in these poems. Also, "The Tortoise Trainer" draws from Urhobo/African folklore of the tortoise as greedy and cunning and trying to disrupt the corporate existence that ensures communal harmony.

The Imperative of Content/Experience

I try to use simple language as much as I can because I believe that what makes excellent poetry is the unusual turn given to words to generate fresh meaning and not the use of obscure words or playing with form. In *The Beauty I Have Seen* I have tried to communicate feelings and ideas and so make the content of poems accessible. I have attempted to use a poetic style from the oral tradition, which uses repetition, proverbs, metaphor, irony, and other tropes that convey meaning in a startling manner. I endeavor to experiment with other poetic traditions of Africa and elsewhere that can strengthen my poetic articulation.

The Poet as an Activist

A writer or artist has the freedom to create what he or she likes. I have chosen to embrace the African concept of art as functional and not art for art's sake. To me the most significant aspect of writing is to contribute in making the world better than we met or find it; mending the world and creating an atmosphere that will nurture human virtues and values—honesty, fairness, justice, sensitivity, peace, and so forth. A work of literary art that fails to aim at that and only indulges in aesthetic pursuit fails in a society that needs people to be sensitized toward higher ideals to make life more tolerable and humane. As a result of the backward nature of most African nations in the context of human development, it is incumbent on the writers to promote literacy and those virtues that will reduce, if not eliminate, greed, corruption, social injustice, and religious fanaticism, among others, that keep them down. I range on the side of the poor, the oppressed, the marginalized and other deprived and disadvantaged groups for social and political change. To me, the poet should be a transformer of society for good. I attempt to follow this activist tradition in *The Beauty I Have Seen.*

THE SCHOLAR-POET

I am an African writer and scholar and both aspects of me reinforce each other. I write in the African tradition even though I open myself to experiences from anywhere in the world that will help to strengthen my Africanity or artistic craft. I have thus been influenced by Latin American, Caribbean, Modern Greek, and Russian poets to hone my craft. In aspects of human nature, I borrow from others outside Africa to make my primary readers more human.

THE BEAUTY I HAVE SEEN AS "SONG OF MYSELF" (SELF-CRITICISM)

Here are three poems from the collection: "The cows of Mt. San Angelo" (86), "Traveler" (144), and "You don't have to be" (146):

THE COWS OF MT. SAN ANGELO

Groomed as royal, the cows of Mt. San Angelo
have the abundant pastures of the mountain
to themselves; evergreen grass all year round.
Plump and healthy, no cows can be bigger
than these multi-ethnic crop of Virginia cows.
Black, brown and white-faced like a mask,
they mow the grass gracefully; no hostile figures
or irritants to worry about. Young ones
prance to their mothers when I come close,
but there's no fear of poachers in this pasture.

The cows of Mt. San Angelo cannot cover
the entire meadow green with abundance.
They know not that outside famine kills a number
and rinderpest and poachers are on the loose.
They are half-covered in lush grass without bother

of ticks—above, birds sing their hearts away
in the paradise they share. There's no Fulani
herdsman lashing at them to take the right course
in the lines they always create in the open space.
They yawn at night from the day's plentiful food.

They have the garden world to themselves—
they know not the harsh struggle or sweat
that each day brings; they are self-assured.
They share the road and their shit bothers none.
If one should be a cow, wouldn't one wish to be
one of the selected cows grazing Mt. San Angelo?
But, after all the pleasures, will the butcher
spare them the fate of other cows envious of them?
The cows of Mt. San Angelo belong to a class
of their own—treated royally for the king's table.

Traveller

In Kuala Lumpur
carry an umbrella

in Syracuse
wear snow boots

in the Sahara
tie a face swath

in Burutu
row a boat

in space
keep a life jacket

on earth
you are a traveler.

You Don't Have to Be

You don't have to be Jewish
to shiver at the nightmare of Auschwitz

you don't have to be black
to feel the agony and shame of slavery

you don't have to be native
to be hurt by the arrogance of discovery

you don't have to be foreign

to know what discrimination means

you don't have to be minority
to understand the dominion of big numbers

you don't have to be homeless
to go through the vagaries of life

you don't have to be rich
to fear the uncertainty of tomorrow

you don't have to be crippled
to suffer the pain of the handicapped

you don't have to be a star
to stare at the volatility of the weather

you just have to be human
to know the plight of others.

Tradition and modernity are combined in this collection. It is the practice in Urhobo poetry, especially the *udje* tradition, to start by laughing at your own self before venturing to laugh at others. In this collection, the poet assumes the persona of the minstrel. The minstrel persona is used as a figure familiar with the society as a means of knowing, seeing, and questioning truths. Poetry, to me, should function as a questioner of habits, actions, and happenings in the society toward a salutary ethos. The sense of community that the minstrel represents is underscored by the title poem, "The beauty I have seen," which ironically shows him better appreciated and received outside than in his own homeland. Singing about oneself also involves self-criticism, a role which my Nigerian generation of poets assumed, contrary to the earlier generation that blamed outsiders, Europeans, for Africa's troubles. My generation strongly believes Africans are now responsible for their own present condition, which they should exercise their agency to ameliorate and not whine over because of the happenings of the past however painful they were.

Many poems in the collection, especially in the second and third sections, deal with experiences outside either my primary home of the Niger Delta or my other home, the United States of America. I highlight the Akosombo Dam that "decapitated" the Volta River into the Volta Lake in Ghana; my embracing the wonderful diva, an untouchable/low caste beauty and dancer extraordinary whom I called the "pride of Bengal" in India; the ganja peddlers at the beach of Negril in Jamaica; watching fasting Muslims waiting for the call to eat dinner at a restaurant in Kuala Lumpur with mouth-watering dishes in front of them; and seeing where Shaka Zulu was buried in South Africa; among many experiences. These poems arising out of travels are meant to widen and deepen one's humanity toward a contribution to one's homeland. Above all, they are parts of "the beauty I have seen."

The poems are in three sections, the first using the minstrel persona; the second and third about travels as well as Nigerian and American experiences. I attempted to use unrhymed couplets to establish some formal discipline. The title poem, "The beauty I have seen," relates to the exhilaration the poet goes through in the process of creativity. Here, the "beauty" of experiencing one's homeland as well as the rest of the world is remarkable for the writer. It is a series of epiphanies, illuminations about life, society, and the world. "The beauty I have seen" is that experience that is so exhilarating that it cannot be replicated and it is only in memory that one relives it.

Here are three more poems before conclusion: "Durban" (58), "The Beauty I Have Seen" (67–8), and "The muse won't let me quit" (69):

In Durban, KwaZulu-Natal

(on the occasion of Poetry Africa 2005)

Fabled land of Shaka that yields to no one,
your imbongi voice reverberates across Africa.

Your soil carries a current that fortifies my soles;
your ocean-flushed air fills me with youthful zest.

In your soil the stump grows back into a stout trunk.
Your entire landscape glows with a proud heritage.

I invoke your warrior spirit of centuries
to reinforce my ancestral vigilance.

Without guard, freedom can slip away;
without vision, fortune can fritter into nothing.

Without memory, the trail will be lost
to the life-sustaining springs of famished times.

You brandished the assegai to keep your own—
the giant's presence protects the entire neighborhood.

I invoke your warrior spirit of centuries
to reinforce my ancestral vigilance.

In the streets the beads and fabrics that costume you
into only one of a majestic kind worldwide.

The elephant only brings forth a big offspring—
sons and daughters of the lightning spear stand upright!

Beauty garments the mountains, plains, and veldts
into one body whose spectacle takes the breath away.

I invoke your warrior spirit of centuries
to reinforce my ancestral vigilance.

You no longer tiptoe in your own land.
You stride with the majesty of the giraffe.

Ama-Zulu, who does not know that you
people not only the earth but also the heavens?

Who attempts to hold you down (and many
tried it with regret) thrusts his hands into fire.

I invoke your warrior spirit of centuries
to reinforce my ancestral vigilance.

In the kingdom of songs we share one standard:
you praise as I abuse; both necessities of life.

In the house of words we speak the same lingua franca
of love but will not allow guests to seize our inheritance.

One smears a rival, but I revere you.
One pulls down a challenger, but I raise you to the sun.

I invoke your warrior spirit of centuries
to reinforce my ancestral vigilance.

We, scions of the same sturdy loins,
our bloods coalesce into an invincible force;

our birthrights surpass others' measures of wealth;
our thundering chants drown the roar of lions.

In Durban the dark shadow dissolves into a warm-hearted host
and all languages of the world become one human song.

I invoke your warrior spirit of centuries
to reinforce my ancestral vigilance.

The Beauty I Have Seen

The beauty I have seen in abundance abroad
no picture however embellished can capture;

the million stars that shone their hearts for me
the same brilliance they can never replicate for the world.

I know why Akpalu brags that the Hausa have picked up
his Ewe songs; the thrill in his heart beats an ecstatic drum—

the homeboy freezes the thousand witnesses
that saw his coronation as chieftain of songs.

Who will find the remains of that day and know
what spell the spectacle held for the thronging eyes?

The lucent face beaming smiles to the packed ballroom
salutes the muse for the zeal they share for words;

nobody can be richer than the fortunate minstrel whose
every gesture of a grand masquerade receives applause.

Only once the gods of the hour convene in conclave
for this spectacle they brighten with their bellows.

The cannonade has rolled over mountain and valley
and the muse has given a nod to the minstrel—

the ululations that rock the stars enter the echoes
that bridge far and near in transmuted songs.
How can the minstrel display the effervescence of
the present to outlive the very moment that blooms?

The magic pageant has won the day;
let the minstrel put the day into song—

memory nudges on with its constellations
but that beauty's hour can't relive its prime.

The beauty I have seen in its fullest radiance
no picture however embellished can capture.

THE MUSE WON'T LET ME QUIT

Even if I wanted, Aridon wouldn't
leave me alone—the tasks of the caste

cannot be cast away by the minstrel at will;
minstrelsy I now know is a lifelong path.

Sometimes you are everybody's envy, applauded
at home and abroad; heart lifted out of the world.

At other times the tribulations too crushing,
the minstrel cries in bed from the burden he bears.

Even if I vow to lay down the costume,
Aridon won't let me quit the caste of my life.

For the shame of losing his most ardent worshiper,
the god of songs will never let me quit.

Conclusion

For me the poet is a tailor ant that gathers materials from different sources to build its home; also like a bird building a nest with different materials. The poem becomes an artistic refuge that is meant to provide comfort to the poet and reader/audience. *The Beauty I Have Seen* is a stage in the unending poetic journey. The more I journey and the more discoveries, the more the beauty of life I seek. The farther I travel, the more I learn that the Niger Delta is a microcosm of the universe. There are many gains of travel, whether physical or imaginative, and poetry brings that beauty to those who experience it.

As a cultural producer and critic, a scholar-poet, my scholarly side tells me to warn you not to accept everything the writer says about his or her work. I may not fully understand what I have written and so may not be the best interpreter of that work because the text is autonomous. I am not saying that you are wasting your time listening to me; rather, I am saying you have to read *The Beauty I Have Seen* and interpret it as you *feel* it.

In the oral tradition of *udje* poetic performance among my Urhobo people, a poem/song is not complete until it has been performed before an audience. Today the poems of *The Beauty I Have Seen* are completed and come to life since I have had the opportunity to read/perform them to different audiences.

CHAPTER 17

Revisiting an African Oral Poetic Performance: *Udje* Today

Ororile ta vberen phrun
Sieyen obuole o ki yovb' urhuru
(*The song-maker must first compose beautifully*
Before the vocalist can sing melodiously) [*from an udje song qtd. in*
Okpewho:1990:32]

INTRODUCTION

One should not give or get the impression that traditional African poetry is dead or no longer practiced with the coming of literacy and the emergence of modern written African literature. Of course, there are social, economic, modern, and other reasons that started to undermine *udje* from colonial times. With modern economic activities and the need for money to take care of families, there has been little leisure time left for the pursuit of the *udje* tradition. In addition, with the coming of the British colonialists, composing exaggerated and scandalous songs against members of the society had become increasingly unacceptable with many Urhobo going to court to settle cases that used to be taken as part of entertainment. One might feel that the condition of traditional African literature in contemporary times has been exacerbated by the forces of globalization which threaten its very existence. The new literature that arose from literacy did not stop the composition and performance of traditional literature.

However, in many parts of Africa, traditional and modern, also described as oral and written, African literatures thrive together in the same community and in many cases the modern feeds on aspects of the traditional as demonstrated in modern writers borrowing from the oral tradition. While the *udje* tradition of oral poetry and performance has no doubt declined and is only performed on special occasions such as traditional festivals, the death of great singers and important personalities in the community, sociocultural parties and installation of chiefs and kings, or the visit of foreign dignitaries, the oral poetic performance survives through new forms and strategies. Newer oral poets have over the years gone to studios first to record on vinyl/gramophones, then on cassettes, and now on DVDs, much of the performance tends to be of older songs. As a mark of change and continuity, contemporary African poets are adapting their rhythms and poetic strategies to the oral poetic performance style to elicit good delivery.

In this chapter, I use the *udje* oral poetic tradition of Nigeria's Urhobo people as an example of an African oral poetic performance that survives and still needs to be studied as it manifests today with the technological tools available to enhance its delivery. This study is very necessary as contemporary African writers continue to incorporate aspects of the oral tradition in their respective poetry, fiction, or drama. Space will be given in the following chapter to demonstrate the writer's poetry's indebtedness to the *udje* poetry and performance tradition. Most significant is that in a discussion of contemporary African literature, the oral literature, especially in its performance considerations, is integral to it. And, of course, it engages in politics at the local level in the politics of the songs and their performance. On a broader level, *udje* songs and their performance have entered the discourse of globalization in response to forces threatening its survival since the highly poetic nature of the songs ought to recommend the tradition more to critics than the attention it now receives.

UDJE ORAL POETRY AND PERFORMANCE

Udje is an integrative performance that involves singing and dancing by specially costumed performers. It is not only among the most prominent and poetic genres, with a continuing vitality in the areas of expression, but it also illustrates the formal characteristics and the social and cultural functions of oral poetry in Nigeria. As described earlier, *udje* involves satire and takes the form of highly articulated song sequences performed in a dramatic context. It is a unique type of Urhobo dance in which, on an appointed day, rival groups, representing quarters and even whole towns, perform songs composed from often exaggerated materials about the other. The dance songs strongly attack what the traditional society regards as vices: laziness, vanity, wretchedness, miserliness, flirtation, adultery, prostitution, wickedness, and greed, among others.

The singers are intent upon upholding what they consider to be positive norms of the society. Central to the concept of *udje* are the principles of correction and determent through punishment with "wounding" words. Once a performance is over, preparations begin for another. Thus, each side has at least a year to prepare since the songs performed by one side are often responses to those of the other side. As in war, each side also endeavors to spring up fresh surprises at every performance. These songs have a significant social function, for they maintain a delicate balance between the general good of the society whose ethos must be upheld and respect for the law-abiding individual. The satirical content of the songs demonstrates the extent to which they are imbued with a distinctive moral awareness related to the collective life. There is thus a profound sense in which they bear out, in an arresting form, Henri Bergson's conception of "laughter" as an essential part of the mechanisms by which social life is regulated by ridiculing what in a particular society would be considered individual excesses or threats to collective harmony.

UDJE PERFORMANCE

The aesthetic dimension is as important as the social meaning of *udje*. In the tradition, the song is not completed until it has been performed. As such, everything about the *udje* tradition is connected: the song and its performance. This also means that from its composition, the song/poem has performance features built into it since the song will be judged both on its poetry and its performance. The poet (*ororile*) composes with a communal workshop to edit his work and then the song is given to a sweet-voiced performer (*obo-ole*) to deliver to the public on an appointed day after several sessions of strict rehearsals. There are cases of talented persons who are poets and performers in one. Some of the best known in the category are Okitiakpe of Ekakpamre, Memerume of Edjophe, Oloya of Iwhrekan, and Vphophen of Okwagbe.

In the *udje* tradition, it is said that "Echadia oye udje." As such, it is the spectacle that makes *udje* appeal to the audience/spectators. The statement highlights the visual effects expected of *udje* performance. The performers resort to costumes that will enhance their appeal in vigorous but graceful dancing. The spatial arrangement and the ensemble of the performance also have their spectacular side. The lead performer (*obo-ile*, plural, *ebo-ile*) stays in the middle of the group, assisted by two junior ones; the dancers, who are also generally younger, surround the *ebo-ile*, while the drummers and women who clap take the rear. Drumming is a major part of the performance. The *udje* performance is also a visual art form. The body is adorned with costumes specially chosen to enhance the performer's overall appeal. The arrangement of singers, dancers, drummers, women clappers, and the audience creates a traditional amphitheater that brings communities together to enjoy moments of intense creativity. Because these visual effects are left out in audio recordings of the songs, they cannot be properly considered in their study as poetry. This divorce of the oral material from its context of performance thus leads to its impoverishment. The videotaping and DVD format of *udje* brings together the art, ensemble, spatial organization, dance, and songs of *udje* performance.

The full appreciation of performance poetry such as *udje* depends on distinctive linguistic and paralinguistic features like idiophones, tonal patterns, and gestures. The multimedia component is indispensable in recreating the dynamics of performance, as well as projecting the background settings and audience feedback that form an essential part of the performance. As a performance genre, *udje* unites several dimensions of sound events, namely spoken forms, heightened speech, chant, song, and formulaic interpolations. These sound events are in turn rendered meaningful and effective in performance through employment of related mediums of expressions such as varied gestural and motional dispositions, which may sometimes involve dramaturgy. Its mere representation in the print mode thus leaves it incomplete.

In addition, the performance gains momentum through active audience participation, which is achieved mostly through sound and movement states. Because of these sound, motional, and visual aspects that are central to oral poetry, the use of performance paradigm will inform the scope of my study on a more comprehensive approach to *udje* performance. The study with the DVD seems the ideal way of capturing not only the essence of the performance but also of presenting it to audiences at different times and places.

POLITICS AND *UDJE*

Udje has always had politics injected into the composition of the songs and their performance and is still very much so. In years of nationalist struggle and the heydays of Action Group and NCNC, a song satirizes poor party supporters who instead of farming or looking for ways to make money were always crowing like the cock! The cock was the symbol of the Eastern Region-based NCNC. A majority of Urhobo voters then belonged to the Western Region-based AG. In addition to a blatant case as just mentioned, there are other subtle political shots at rivals in songs.

Today the politics in *udje* tradition is not in the songs but in their performance. *Udje* performance helps to define one's roots through participation either in performance or as audience. With many migrating from the heartlands of *udje* into urban areas, festivals in which *udje* is performed is one way of cultural assertion. Thus, many in the urban areas come to their rural homes to associate with a well-known tradition. Many performers of *udje*, especially as young ones who later migrated to urban areas or distant lands, return to perform it especially during festival times. In addition to the nostalgic feeling, many urban folks in Warri, Ughelli, Port Harcourt, Lagos, Abuja, and Asaba, among others, use the occasion of *udje* performance to identify with their people in enjoying vibrant sociocultural moments of artistic performance. Those who come home, if they are politicians, will be rewarded with votes when elections come because the people feel they will be better represented by those who associate with them and share the same sociocultural background.

Closely related to folks going to their roots to identify with and watch *udje* performance is the phenomenon of those who hire *udje* troupes to perform at functions in their areas or in the city. The conscious decision to have an *udje* troupe is a political decision of taste and making a statement as there are so many Urhobo disco groups that are there for hire. An effort to keep *udje* tradition alive informs such conscious efforts to hire the groups to perform. Other political intersections in *udje* performance include being Christian born-again and being traditional. This dichotomy in the identity of people of the same family, clan, or ethnic group tells the strategizing that goes on in the society. Often those who perform *udje* are never the born-again or fanatical Christians who believe that *udje* performance or dancing *udje* is not Christian; whatever they mean by it. *Udje* politics goes beyond the local Urhobo and Delta politics into the national and global spheres.

Urhobo Music, Dance, and Performance Traditions

The Urhobo people have a strong tradition of music, dance, and performance that is embedded in the *udje* genre. A song is composed to be performed by one who has the qualities of vocalization which include voice quality and a demonstrative ability to render the song through musical, dramatic, and other performance aptitudes. A song has to be present to be performed, and it has to be accompanied with music and has to be danced to. The music is provided by instruments that include idiophones, membranophones, chordophones, and aerophones. Often stick clappers, drums, bells, and *isorogu* (thumb piano) accompany an *udje* song during its performance. The performance is rated very important as the accoutrements of costume and other dress modes add to the color and liveliness of the performance.

Udje remains the iconic Urhobo performance art. Many Urhobo expressions are connected to *udje* to show its vitality and demonstrative form. *Onudje* means dancing with excitement. It has to do with jubilation and celebration as the original *udje* dance convention was meant to encompass as a mark of victory over defeated rivals. In many parts of Urhobo land, *onudje* now signifies rejoicing. Similarly, *ogbudje* means celebrating, jubilation, and rejoicing. At the same time when one hears in Urhobo land that "udje she re," it means that jubilation, rejoicing, or celebrating has started. These *udje*-related terms in Urhobo show the degree to which the performance aspects of the genre are pervasive in the society and culture. *Udje* is performed traditionally during festival periods and so has to do with celebration and feasting. While two sides are set against each other in the competitive performance, each group performs in a carnival atmosphere and there is something carnivalesque about *udje* performance in its colorfulness and liveliness. *Udje* has to be pleasantly musical, graceful, and dignified.

Drumming plays a major role in *udje* performance. As noted in the performances, often when the *obo-ile* is performing, the songs are short, simple, and the singing is done in a low tone. Usually the chief *obo-ile* stays free from singing when it comes to serious dexterous types of dance movements. Drumming goes down in tone when a very poetic song is on and the performers want the audience to get the message. At other times the drumming is intense and dancers and nondancers are on their feet. The drumming, handclapping, and playing of other instruments are meant to stir the motor senses in the body for the dance. With Uhaghwa, the god of performance, served, great drumming, and singing elicit a possessing spirit that enraptures the performers. The prominence of *obo-ile*, the cantor/performer, results from the side's public display of its artistic skills and craft.

Urhobo Performance Aesthetics

One has to go to Urhobo aesthetics to judge the place of oral performance today of *udje* songs. Central to Urhobo aesthetics of song, music, and performance is the concept of "avwerhen," "sweetness." Atiboroko Uyovbukherhi has done a detailed study of Urhobo aesthetics based on the concept of "avwerhen" in "Avwerhen: the concept of sweetness in Urhobo aesthetics" (*Nigeria Magazine* 54 (4), October-December 1986, pp. 29–36). It has to do with what is mellifluous and pleasing, sonorous, vibrant, clear, and so on. For an Urhobo performance to enjoy "avwerhen," it has to please all the senses, including those of hearing, seeing, and feeling.

The writer has also written on Urhobo aesthetics in the article "How Urhobo people see the world through art" (*Where Gods and Mortals Meet: Continuity and Change in Urhobo Art* (pp. 72–79). Among the features discussed on what the Urhobo expect of art are *udidi* and the personality of the performer. It must have *udidi*, a certain awe and charisma that make the performance moving. Urhobo aesthetics demand that the performer be handsome, graceful, and dignified since he is expected to bare his upper trunk during performance. There is a saying in the Ughievwen and Udu areas of Urhobo where *udje* is performed that an ugly man does not perform *udje*! Though Okitiakpe of Ekakpamre was said in his rivals' songs to be ugly and yet such a talented performer, he was an exception.

This underlies the importance attached to the performer as a figure with the appropriate costume and comportment. The body is decorated with white chalk and the hair styled for the occasion. The ability of the performer to interpret the rhythm into dance movements, gesticulations, and creative performance tells his overall talent and craft.

African Musical Drama Practice

According to J. Kwabena Nketia, traditional African musical drama takes the form of drama of worship, memorial drama, and social drama. Drama of worship has to do with festivals as the Ogbaurhie Festival of the Ughievwen people who devote a traditional week of four or eight days to their festival during which *udje* is performed. On the other hand, memorial musical drama is performed when a member of a cultic association as of chiefs, hunters, priests/priestesses, or other association dies and is being buried. Often when an *udje* composer or performer dies, his or her burial is accompanied with *udje* performance. Social drama involves reenacting social relationships. In its satiric mode, *udje* songs and performance deal with social issues as of prostitution, adultery, miserliness, and other activities or kinds of behavior that threaten collective harmony. *Udje* performance involves all three major categories that Nketia has set for the drama of music.

RECENT FIELD RESEARCH CASES/*UDJE* PERFORMANCE TODAY

My recent research on the performance of *udje* songs constitutes this chapter. I have summarized the experience of the performance of songs in different parts of Urhobo but especially from the Ughievwen area of Ughelli South Local Government Area and the Udu people of Udu Local Government Area, both in Nigeria's Delta State. Ughievwen, now broken into two kingdoms and Udu have always been the bastions of *udje* composition and performance in Urhobo land. It is from these two areas that in its heyday that *udje* spread to other parts of Urhobo land.

The following are the occasions, places, and dates of *udje* performance that this study is based on:

1. Two different years of Orhughworun festival (March 2004 and March 2012 respectively);
2. Egbo-Ide *udje* performance (2012);
3. Otokutu *Udje* Group at Madam Agatha Nomuoja's burial in Orhughworun in 2004;
4. Esaba *Udje* Group at the Conference opening for Professor G. G. Darah's sixtieth birthday at Wellington Hotel, Effurun, 2007;
5. Installation of Chief Dozen Ogbariemu as Okapako Orere of Iwhrekan on May 7, 2011; and
6. Social parties and burial ceremonies held in which *udje* troupes are invited to perform.

ORHUGHWORUN FESTIVAL AND SOCIAL *UDJE* PERFORMANCE

Three Orhughworun performances, two annual festival performances and one performance at the burial of Madam Okoko Ighogbohwofua (nee Biagboron Darah) at Esaba in Ughelli South Local Government on Saturday, February 8, 2014, inform this discussion of *udje* performance.

Today the paired "battle of songs" of the past has become a single or rather unipolar performance of old songs from different rival quarters now performed by a troupe made up of those interested and can perform the songs irrespective of their quarters. I have observed that about the same performers feature in the three taped performances.

The more complete performance of the festival has a larger audience or more spectators (*inughe*) in attendance than the social performances at burial ceremonies. In every performance the spectators' response to the performers creates its own theatrical dynamics. Applauding tends to make the dancers put in more energy and introduce more creative steps. In the two festival performances, the performers are led by a chief priest and the *obo-ile* (the lead performer) in a procession that goes into the shrine of Uhaghwa, the god of performance, in a grove. Only few spectators, apparently indigenes of Orhughworun connected to the shrine, are allowed entry. Outsiders are not allowed to enter or videotape the proceedings at the Uhaghwa shrine in the grove to avoid the deity being defiled and also apparently for Orhughworun priests and performers to keep their town's spiritual secrets. The priest on behalf of the performers serves Uhaghwa, asking for a hitch-free performance. After the service, water from a bowl in which mystical herbs have been squeezed or washed is sprinkled on the performers and other members of the troupe. After that ritual is done, the performers move out again in a procession to perform at different parts of the town.

Unlike the performance in situ in the past, today's performance moves through the main streets of Orhughworun and stops at different parts to perform and move on until they arrive at the king's or chief's house where the last performance is done before they disperse. So the performance is a mixture of what Kwabena Nketia describes as a stroll and performance in situ. The Orhughworun troupe's performance at Esaba at the burial ceremony is different in the sense that there is a permanent "stage" set for the performance with the drummers seated. However, on two occasions the performers left their apportioned space to dance to the front tables where important guests sat. During their performance, the dignitaries "sprayed" money on them in appreciation of their performance.

Orhughworun Performance Style and Features

Orhughworun *udje* performers have retained the style and dance patterns of their forebears. Whether during the festival or on a sociocultural occasion as a burial of an elderly person, the dance steps are similar. However, there seems to be more time given to a specific song and its performance in cases where the performance is in situ. This also has more of the flavor of the old style of *udje* in its hey-days when performance was spread out for days with each day one group or side performing. The one-day performance nowadays tends to make things hurried. The competitive edge has also been removed since there is only one group and is pitched against no other group, unlike the "battle" of the past in which two sides are traditionally competing against each other on a yearly basis.

There are simple and intricate dance steps which seem to depend on the song being performed. Simple dance steps are performed when the performers want the meaning of the song to be clearly under-stood. The drumming is low. However, the more vigorous and ath-letic dance steps are reserved for when highly percussive drumming is involved and the song is low. I have observed several dance steps that Orhughworun shares with Otokutu.

Unlike in the olden days when an *udje* group performed sur-rounded by *ihwowhile* (song messengers) and women clappers before the performers, the *udje* performers at the Orhughworun festivals of 2004 and 2012 do not have that organized arrangement. The festival performance is fluid and a few of the dancers themselves or volunteers among the spectators clear the crowd to create space for the perfor-mance. It is thus a little disorganized and each stop for performance needs fresh efforts to create space for performance in the streets of surging crowds. The spectators follow the movement of the perform-ers and at temporary performance sessions "spray" different denomi-nations of naira on the performers. In the two festivals, a young boy of about twelve years received loud ovations for his dexterous dance interpreting the drum rhythms. The young boy is able to dance very well and is very colorful in the singlet worn on a traditional wrapper with rattles tied to his wrists, ankles, and waist. His face is powdered and he holds a traditional fan in his right hand to accentuate his dance steps. Members of the audience dance in any space they can create for themselves. The performance thus draws in the audience to partici-pate as the known performers.

OTOKUTU *UDJE* GROUP

I have witnessed Otokutu *Udje* Group perform several times: at the burial of my mother-in-law, Madam Agatha Nomuoja, at Orhughworun; at the opening of the First Tanure Ojaide International Conference at Delta State University, Abraka; and at the Second Tanure Ojaide Conference also at Delta State University, Abraka. Today it is perhaps the most visible and applauded as far as performance is concerned. The group is led by Sekondi, a man in his sixties, who had performed from his youth, and now lives in Warri from where he takes the group to wherever invited. Also, like the Orhughworun group, it is a uniform group that performs songs of different quarters of the past. The group is out to please the audience but also the competitive edge of the past is also not there.

The troupe sets up its performance "stage" where the performance takes place. They have ample time to perform different dance steps fully and go through a repertoire that exhibits closeness to the songs and dance styles Otokutu has been known for the past century. Dressed with a white T-shirt with "Otokutu *Udje* Group" inscribed on it, the performers tie a colorful wrapper . Some of the performers wear coral beads and they also have a head gear that includes white feathers and a head band that holds the feathers in place.

OTOKUTU PERFORMANCE STYLE AND FEATURES

From the three performances taped, the Otokutu *Udje* Group is a highly athletic group of much older and bigger men than the Orhughworun group but whose style and dance patterns demonstrate their versatility in the performance. During their performance at Orhughworun during the burial of Madam Agatha Nomuoja, the orator (otota), Ofua, applauded their dexterity despite their age and weight and said that one who is not well fed and very strong could not execute the vigorous dance steps they performed with such ease. One has to add that one has to have the experience, talent, and good physique to perform so well.

I can compare some of the dance steps to gym exercise movements. Three most daring moves need description. In one, after the lead performer had used his fan to indicate the ample space for the performance, blows a whistle to coordinate the group into a spacious circle. Since this is a vigorous and intricate dance, the performers/dancers not only space themselves from each other but are also given space by the spectators. The rhythm of the drums increases in tempo and each performer whirls himself into the air and downs on his feet in a stooping posture. This happens so fast that the ecstatic drumming makes every other attempt faster and more energetic. In another step with a staccato of drums and percussive instruments, the performers fall into a linear pattern. In pair after pair, the performers hop two steps one way and then throw the right leg into the air before downing it. Sometimes the dance step is repeated with the left leg thrown into the air after a two-step hop in another direction. And in the third dexterous move, the dancer somersaults. Usually the troupe forms a circle and two performers take the inside of the circle to perform a special dance step at a time. After the two, another duo enters to perform until all members have taken their turns. Since somersaulting could disorient most performers, the others form a ring to hold up any performer that is about to fall.

The performance at the burial ceremony of my mother-in-law had special peculiarities. The group was given a place with a view in front of the special guests' canopy. The troupe formed an amphitheater with seated drummers, standing female clappers, and the performers themselves surrounding the *obo-ile* (lead performer). Since they were the only group invited to perform, they had the entire gathering to please. After several performances, the spectators came up to "spray" naira on the performers in appreciation of their beautiful performance. This was perhaps the most memorable performance of the Otokutu *Udje* Group that I have witnessed in the past 20 or so years.

Esaba *Udje* Group

This group performed during the Literature Conference to mark Professor G. G. Darah's sixtieth birthday at Wellington Hotel, Effurun, Delta State, Nigeria. Made up of fairly young men dancers and female clappers, they ranged in age from the late teens to the late twenties. What they might gain in agility because of youth is lost through their inexperience, unlike the Otokutu group that is elderly but vigorous and experienced. The performers at Wellington Hotel in Effurun were not given good space to exhibit themselves because of the arrangement of the gathering round a swimming pool. Their singing was not very clear and only "Odaro," which I had been familiar with came out with meaning. It was the subject of the song responding on why his own townsfolk should pick on him as an old bachelor when there were others older than him who were not yet married. It is a critique of the society's selective way of apportioning blame. The rendition of the song could be better if the "stage" were better set.

A significant point to be made on this is that each performance even of the same known song could yield different results. Each occasion has its own atmosphere, nature of the crowd, singing and dancing ability of the performers, and other factors at play. What could be successful in one performance may not be the same in another. While generally the competitive aspect that led to the use of strong medicines against rivals might have gone, each performance has its own dynamics today as in the olden days.

Udje Features in Urhobo Music/Songs Today

Today, very few communities or individual artists compose *udje* songs as in the olden days. Peter Toroh of Egini, Lady Rose Orarume, Ogute Ottan and his associates, and Chief Dozen Ogbariemu are some of those who have carried the practice to recent and contemporary times in different songs. With the death of Ogute Ottan, Lady Rose Orarume, and Chief Ogbariemu, the phenomenon of new songs is getting rarer and rarer. Performers are compelled to perform old songs composed by their forebears and ancestors. Some of the songs could be as old as 150 years. The situation means that spectators can no longer identify with the songs as in the past when they were based on sociopolitical happenings. If *udje* composers were there today, there would be so much material to sing against—the material greed, the place of Pentecostal religion, the liberal sex, and other issues that make today laughable to the originators of the tradition.However, what obtains today is the diffusion of *udje* features in different songs, especially by Johson Adjan, Okpan Aribo, and a host of Urhobo disco song composers.

Aesthetics of Udje *Song Performance*

The following are observed trademarks of the aesthetics of *udje* song performance:

- The language. Urhobo terms used—one needs to understand the language to understand the aesthetic considerations of the *udje* performance tradition.
- "Egbudje"—in the Urhobo language, "egbudje"; in other words, one performs or dances *udje*. In the kingdoms of songs and the rest of Urhobo land, performing *udje* is associated with festivities, jubilation, rejoicing, expression of happiness, etc. This meaning tallies with the origin of the *udje* tradition in which after a contest those who win "gbudje" (jubilate) to humiliate the defeated side who go back to prepare to fight back the following year so as to win and humiliate their rival with *udje*. From the Urhobo meaning, *Udje* performance is energetic and vigorous.

- "Echadia oye udje"—Again, as is said by those familiar with the tradition, "echadia oye udje". This means that the spectacle or outward presentation makes *udje* most appealing. Thus, udje is primarily a performance tradition and the poetry aspect enriches the performance through the songs, voice quality, and deep meaning of the poetry.
- Personality of the udje performer: It is said that an ugly person does not perform *udje*. Thus, somebody with an imposing personality and affable is usually selected at the workshop as the cantor or lead performer. On many occasions the poet (obo ole) may not be the performer of his song or songs if his personality does not fit who should be the lead performer. Usually a handsome man like Memerume of Edjophe is selected. This is because the lead performer has to bare his body/trunk. In many anecdotes of udje performance in its heydays as told me by Chief Dozen Ogbariemu, many women get so mesmerized by the obo-ile (the performer) that they go and embrace him. Memerume had three wives and many mistresses and casual lovers as a result of his handsomeness and talent as a performer. Okitiakpe was said to be old and "ugly" but remained a great performer because of his athleticism. His rivals composed songs to sing about him and he responded with blistering and memorable songs against his rivals and praise for himself. Of his songs is the memorable "Mevwen Odjelabo." Even in "old" age, he still performed vigorously and beautifully. A measure of Urhobo concept of masculinity has to do with a man's dignity, handsomeness, mien, and affable personality. *Udje* aesthetics demand a talented/ flawless/spotless/ complete gentleman as performer. In a tradition of abuse songs, a group's best has to be shown in physical handsomeness, imaginative talent, and flawless performance.
- Costume: This is a very important aspect of the performance. The members of the group put on a colorful uniform. They pay attention to their hair style and often use feathers to deck their head gear. Transgender and cross dressing occur because done on a festival period and humorous and unconventional ways of dressing are condoned. Many of the male dancers have their bodies powdered.
- Incorporating Abstract Art: The effigy of the subject of the song is carried around to be recognized. Since this is done in abstract art form, nobody could be convicted of libel or defamation but it is done in such a manner as the subject of the art and song to be recognized. After all, he or she should be a member of

the community or neighbor. The effigy is rarely used in a fierce rivalry/competition in **Iten**/masking because conflict within the family is more destructive than conflict with outsiders/rival groups. The exhibition of the effigy allows for the merging of the poetic, the visual, and the theatrical that make the *udje* tradition highly artistic.

- Dance configurations: circular, linear, double linear, etc.
- Dance formations: group, team, individual, and mixed formations.
- Dance steps: vigorous, graceful. There is emphasis on different parts of the body in performance. Simple and intricate—simple when drumming is low to focus on the song. Drumming more rhythmic-percussive when intricate dance steps are being performed.
- Movement-kinesthetic, athleticism, vitality: There are many dance styles and they include twist-and-kick, airborne-and-landing, kicking the air, etc. The *udje* performance says much about the Urhobo body—a physiological exploration of the body that dances and performs.
- A hungry, sick, feeble person does not dance *udje*: he has to be well-fed, healthy, robust, athletic, and physically fit. This is because it is a draining and energy-sapping exercise.
- Singing in performance: the sweet-voiced, the character qualities of the performer—friendly with crowds, no shyness, etc. The singer addresses the crowd "Wa doo!" The singer and the dancer may not be one but could be one in exceptional talents.
- Music is a very important aspect of the performance in the drumming, singing, and dancing. The drum is used as a tone instrument to not only "talk" but also provide the percussive rhythm for the dance. There is great coordination between the drummers and the singers. In most of the thoughtful songs, the singers almost sing uninterrupted by the drummers who beat at a low pitch so that listeners/spectators can capture the meaning of the songs. It is after a very meaningful song is over that the drumming becomes loud. Where dancing is emphasized and the poetry of the songs is known in an earlier part, there is intense drumming.
- Drumming is very important in *udje* performance. As Kwabena Nketia says of African music, so is music for *udje* performance: "It would seem, therefore, that an examination of the aesthetics of African music reveals a distinct bias toward percussion and the use of percussion techniques, not only because of the structural

functions of such instruments, but also because of a preference for musical textures that embody percussive sounds or sounds that increase the ratio of noise to pitch" (J.H.Kwabena Nketia, *The Music of* Africa. NY: Norton, 1974; 115). Nketia further elaborates:

> Music for the dance thus performs two major functions: it must create the right atmosphere or mood or stimulate and maintain the initial urge for expressive movements; and it must provide the rhythmic basis to be articulated in movement or regulate the scope, quality, speed, and dynamics of movement through its choice of sounds, internal structural changes, or details of design.

> Obviously, the aesthetics of music traditionally integrated with dance are bound to be different from that of music not designed primarily with movement in mind. When considering the form, structure, and content of African music, therefore, we must relate these to an aesthetic concept which makes the qualities of sound related to movement its primary focus of attention (217).

- There is a tradition of *udje* drumming—percussive. Pace dictates the drumming. Dancers pay homage to musicians because good music could make the performer bring out the best in him and a bad drummer could mess up a good dancer's dance steps! There is communication between the lead dancer and the lead musician to synchronize the music and the dance.
- Possession: Chief Dozen Ogbariemu told me an anecdote of an *obo-ole* dancing before an audience that included his lover. The lead performer was possessed and danced on tirelessly because he was captured by the spirit of *udje* and Uhaghwa as he found himself on another plane of consciousness. This lead performed is often compared to the legendary stilt dancer of Urhievwron who performed like a spirit! The anecdote of the obo-ile who performed when his love/mistress was around and had to dance on and on and forgot to be the emcee that he was supposed to be and coordinate with the drummers. Of course, the audience noticed it and he was greeted with thunderous applause when at long last the dance ended. His lover, without inhibition, ran into the circle of dancers to embrace him, thereby giving the rival side material for a possible song the next season. As they say in *udje* tradition, "the dancer is never tired when the dance is on."

CONCLUSION

Udje, the Urhobo oral poetic performance, may not be as vibrant today as it was some 60 or more years ago. However, the composition and performance of the songs still continue in Urhobo land in different ways. At the same time contemporary writers, including the writer, incorporate aspects into their own writings and performance. This aspect of incorporation and indebtedness will be the subject of the following chapter. *Udje* performance is no doubt undergoing reinvention and metamorphosis in its performance today. *Udje* in its poetic tradition and performance will thrive in new ways but likely be subsumed in new literary forms that are oral and written.

CHAPTER 18

Performance, the New African Poetry, and My Poetry: A Commentary

Since poetry is a literary genre and literature is a cultural production, the performance or reading of poetry has its cultural dimension.
I have personally observed from readings or performances of poets
from different parts of the world a diversity of reading or performing modes. It must be noted from the beginning that reading itself
is a type of performance as the inflection, voice modulation, pitch of
voice, speed of articulation, choice of stressed and unstressed words or
phrases, and others are pertinent features of performance. In this way,
performance goes beyond Isidore Okpewho's definition of "the total
act as well as the context or environment involved in the delivery of
oral literature" (1990:16) to include the writing itself which includes
those devices of expression that make the "delivery" possible.

African poets are very demonstrative compared to poets of other
cultural groups. Western readers of European and North American
origin tend to read in a rather conventional reading manner without much demonstrativeness. However, poets of countries of the
former Soviet Union and Yugoslavia tend to declaim their poetry
and thus make their articulated poetry far livelier than poetry read
by poets of other parts of the West as in Britain, France, Canada,
and the United States. Similarly, I have seen poets of Israel and Arab
nations do readings/performances of their own as poets of Latin
America. Thus, there are various literary, especially poetry writing,
and performance traditions that are informed by cultural implications. I have drawn these conclusions from poetry festivals in which
I have participated. They include World Poetry Festival, Rotterdam
(Holland), Harbourfront, Toronto (Canada), Poetry Africa, Durban
(South Africa), Pan-African Poetry Festival, Accra (Ghana), and the
International Poetry Festival, Medellin (Colombia). At readings in

artists' colonies in many parts of the world and other international events, I have seen these observations validated.

Long before I went to school and read literature and later began to write poems, I had witnessed poetry as a performance art in my community. I observed this in the annual or long-spaced festivals which brought about the reenactments of history, legends, and myths in poetic performances. In my Okpara in today's Delta State in Nigeria, whether it is Edjenu (the Sky God) Festival, Eni (the Elephant) Festival, or Gun Powder Festival, the festival event is meant to be expressed through song, music, and performance. This holds true of many festivals in different parts of Nigeria and sub-Saharan Africa whether it is among the Bini and Yoruba of Nigeria, the Akan of Ghana, or others in different parts of the continent.

There is very little generic differentiation in traditional fiction/ storytelling, drama, and poetry. An aspect of each is incorporated into the other to make that specific genre effective and successful. Songs, which are oral poems, are essential parts of the folktale where they are sung at critical times in the narration and are usually refrains to give variety to the narrative mode. At the same time, each storytelling has its dramatic moments enacted by the minstrel. For instance, the good storyteller of a folktale mimics the behavior and action of the animals that form characters of the stories. Also, in a masquerade performance, which is drama, there are poetic songs enhanced by the drumming to propel the masqueraders in their dramatic craft. A poetic kind like the epic, a narrative of a historical or legendary hero such as Sunjata and Ozidi, among others, is a song performed to the accompaniment of music. This point shows how integrated traditional African literature is. There appears to be the integration of aspects of different genres that enhance performance, vitality, and aesthetic considerations.

The integrative quality of the oral tradition is carried by many African writers versed in their indigenous literatures into the written mode to enrich their poetry. A modern African poem appears to be a written work transcribed from being read internally. In other words, the modern African poet incorporates dramatic elements into his or her poetry to enhance its reading or performance quality. In many African oral cultures, the poem is only completed after its performance and that means that the composer is very much aware of the rendering of the poem into a performance mode with an audience in attendance.

Put differently, in the poetry of many writers of my generation in Nigeria and Africa, there are oral voices in the written poetry to underscore the influence of the oral tradition in our written modern poetries. This is at the core of what Funso Aiyejina describes as the "alter/native" tradition in the incorporation of oral traditional features into the written poetry. This also reinforces Abiola Irele's view that modern African literature is a "written oral literature" in the orality of the written literature. To many members of my generation of African poets the poem is not a modernist construct as the Western modernists or their African adherents saw it—something obscure, difficult, and fragmented in the vein of T. S. Eliot, Gerald Manly Hopkins, and the early Wole Soyinka, J. P. Clark, and Christopher Okigbo. To, among others, Kofi Anyidoho, Niyi Osundare, Chimalum Nwankwo, and me, the poem carries the form of orality that is meant to accentuate meaning. In other words, the poem is meant to be performative in form and simple in the sense of a syntax that is not much different from that of prose. One should not denigrate the simple nature of this poetry which validates itself in its use of fresh metaphors and other tropes to express feelings and thought. What makes good poetry is not its difficulty or obscurity but its expressive mode anchored on figurative language.

I hope it is understood that I am talking about modern/contemporary mainstream poetry and not the poetry meant for poetry slams and jams which tends to rely on mainly voice manipulation and not on what is essentially figurative language that is the main determinant of literary poetry. There is thus a big difference between the poetry of those slam contests and the poetry that I write and talk about. While the two have something to do with performance, the slam poetry overrelies on performance and theatricality rather than language and form in the more literary poetry. After watching the Ivorian/ Cameroonian Werewere Liking perform at the International Poetry Festival in Medellin, Colombia, in July 2013, I find her poetry in its performance as a bridge between slam poetry and literary poetry. She sings, dances, and uses other performance techniques to accentuate her poetry in a most lively manner. In this chapter I talk about two aspects of performance in the written poetry. The performance techniques, as part of orality, are built into the written poem while the other aspect is the physical performance through reading and other means of public presentation of the poem.

Udje is my model of not only the oral poetic tradition but also of poetry as a whole. The *udje* tradition among the Urhobo in Nigeria bears comparison with the genre known as *halò* among the Anlo-Ewe, an ethnic group that straddles the frontier between Ghana and Togo. As with *udje, halò* performances consist of satirical songs by rival groups who confront each other in a definite context of staged performances. As analyzed by Daniel Avogbedor, who has emphasized the character of *hal*ó as social drama, performances often involve violent conflict between contending parties; *hal*ó may thus assume a tragic dimension that is absent from *udje*. However, in both cases, the satirical thrust of the verbal content is sustained and enforced, as it were, by the performance mode through which it is actualized.

Whether the Yoruba *ijala* and *oriki*, the Zulu and Tswana *izibongo* or theUrhobo *udje* and Ewe *halo*, many modern African poets have studied and absorbed some of their features into their own writings. Poets such as the Ghanaian Kofi Awoonor and Anyidoho, the Nigerian Niyi Osundare, Ademola Dasylva, Akeem Lasisi, and Remi-Raji Oyelade, and various South African poets have imbibed the traditional oral poetic performance features into their poetry and performance.

I lived with this traditional oral poetry that was performed in many parts of Urhobo land before I went to school and started reading English literature in secondary school. I took literature more seriously in my Higher School Certificate program at Federal Government College, Warri, and then entered the University of Ibadan to study English, with emphasis on literature, as my major. The literature I studied at school was foreign in the sense that it was British and often reading the poems, plays, and novels set in a different place, culture, society, sensibility, and age, it was difficult for me to relate to what I read. Scoring an A in the West African Examinations Council-administered exam and also an A in the HSC only meant I studied hard what I was taught and not that I necessarily enjoyed or related to what I read.

I started writing seriously from my undergraduate days at Ibadan and all the poems that went into my first collection, *Children of Iroko and Other Poems*, were all written while an undergraduate. There is the Western background to modern African literature, and modern African poetry is a blend of both literary traditions of the West and African oral literature. In the West the poet is asked to read the poem; in traditional Africa, the poet is more of a performer of his or her song or chant. The rendition of a poem by an African seems to derive culturally from a different source than for the Western poet. Being exposed to traditional poetry and later researching into it has given my poetry elements of an oral voice in its written form.

I have learned lessons from my experience of the *udje* poetic form which somehow informs the creative process of my poems. I learn that the poem creation process takes into consideration its performance;

hence I try to vocalize internally and externally any poem I now write. The poem, though written, has to pass the test of performance before it is completed. So, there is an oral voice, so to say, in my written poem. The poem itself has to do with expression in language and it is left for the poet to use the oral or written mode. In this delicate balance of the modern African writer thrust into the postcolonial predicament, the answer is an oral voice in a written mode. It may sound complicated but it is not so. Even Western poets or those of other cultures read their poetries. However, what we are talking about here is different in the sense that there is some degree of conscious alignment of the writing process to orality in its vocalization. While every type of poetry, in whatever mode, has elements of vocalization in its aural nature that is meant to be vocalized and heard, orality has a specific, or rather unique voice. Thus, the oral voice in a written poem is more specialized than the aural in written poetry which is always there. Every written poem is somehow in the Western tradition meant to be read not only by the writer but also by the reader! I focus here on the African poet borrowing from the performance aspect of the African oral tradition to inform or enhance the written poetry. Poetry, like literature of which it is a part, is a cultural production, and what I am driving at is that a poem's rendition has its cultural sources and ramifications.

From my experience of reading among American and European poets at international poetry festivals, artists' colonies, or other occasions, there appears to be a great difference in the reading. This difference I can only relate to the orality of the African tradition which marks the poet out from those of other cultures. Werewere Liking's reading of her poetry, as of Kofi Anyidoho's, Gabriel Okoundji's, Niyi Osundare's, Odia Ofeimun's, and that of many other African poets is highly influenced by the indigenous orality despite the writing in French or English. It is generally livelier, more colorful, and performative than the Western mode. The African mode of poetry reading or performance derives from what Leopold Sedar Senghor attributes to the Agisymban quality of African orature that informs the modern poet. The stamping of feet, shaking of the head, the dance movements, and other gestures belong to this African cultural tradition of poetic performance.

Orality in written poetry has specific features that drive it. These features of performance poetry include repetition, strong lines, and memorable images. While the poem in the African oral tradition has formulaic language and techniques, there tends to be a lot of repetition of different kinds in the modern written poem. Thus, the presence of repetition, refrains, formulas, parallelism, and piling up detail in traditional poetry or songs also obtains in the written poetry of the African poet. While the traditional poem is a song or chant and is directly musical, the written poem with those features borrowed from the oral tradition also attempts to be musical in a unique African manner. There are other elements of performance which may not appear on the written poem or page but come out in the poem's performance or "reading." There are aspects of the language invisible in the writing that come out when read out or performed by the poet as expected. The tonality is very much a part of the performance or reading. As in the oral tradition, each performance or reading has its special "text" or oral voice depending upon the context of the performance or event, as in Isidore Okpewho, Daniel Avorgbedor, Tejumola Olaniyan, and others.

The performance aspects that come out of the written poem derive from oral performance techniques, craft, or skills. Again, these elements "come out" of the poem or page when the poet, now as performer in the classic *udje* tradition, brings outdoors the poem! While the composer (*ororile*) and performer (*obo-ile*) may be different people in the *udje* tradition, the same composer could perform his work as the great Memerume of Edjophe, Oloya of Iwhrekan, and Okitiakpe of Ekakpamre in the Ughievwen area of Ughelli South Local Government of Nigeria's Delta State. However, in modern times, the poet is invited to read his or her work; so, the writer and the performer are one and the same person. This should not blind the public from knowing that a poet could be a very fine poet but may be a poor performer of his or her poetry. In some cases, the poet and performer could be fantastic in their complementary roles, as I have seen of colleagues like Kofi Anyidoho, Odia Ofeimun, Niyi Osundare, and Gabriel Okoundji, among others.

It is significant to know that the full appreciation of performance poetry such as *udje* depends on distinctive linguistic and paralinguistic features like idiophones, tonal patterns, and gestures. The dynamics of performance affect projecting the background settings and audience feedback that form an essential part of the performance. As a performance genre, *udje* unites several dimensions of sound events, namely spoken forms, heightened speech, chant, song, and formulaic interpolations. These sound events are in turn rendered meaningful and effective in performance through employment of related mediums of expressions such as varied gestural and motional dispositions, which may sometimes involve dramaturgy. Its mere representation in the print mode thus leaves it incomplete. In addition, the performance gains momentum through active audience participation, which is achieved mostly through sound and movement states.

Because of these sound, motional, and visual aspects that are central to oral poetry, the use of performance paradigm informs the scope of any poetry that I write for eventual performance.

It is also important to note that while sub-Saharan African languages are tonal, the European languages of English, French, and Portuguese are nontonal. The modern African poet writing in English or French thus has to reconcile the indigenous tonal rhythms, speech tones, and musical mode to accommodate the English iambic or French alexandrine rhythms. In reading what could be like a chant, the African poet could be superimposing an African musical structure on the European language and its conventional rhythm.

I have noticed that many African poets superimpose their poems on an African poetic or musical structure. This can be seen in some Yoruba-speaking poets as Wole Soyinka in a poem like "Muhammad Ali at the Ringside, 1985," Niyi Osundare, Ademola Dasylva, Remi-Raji Oyelade, and Akeem Lasisi in poems that are modeled on *oriki* or *ijala* rhythms. I have attempted modeling some poems on *udje* form and rhythms in *Delta Blues and Home Songs*. Kofi Anyidoho has modeled many of his poems on Ewe poetic rhythms which are specifically written for performance.

The traditional song involves voice, instrumental accompaniment, and audience participation; so does the written African poem being performed, since there could be accompaniment of music (drums or percussive instruments) and dance. These considerations will influence the poem's rhythm and architecture. Learning from Leopold Sedar Senghor's use of accompaniments of the kora and other musical instruments, Niyi Osundare, Abdulrasheed Na'Allah, Kofi Anyidoho, and some other poets accompany their poetry performance with musical instruments. Some poets/performers have their works accompanied with drumming; others use the bell or some other percussive sounds. I have tried to accompany my "American Wonder" with dance because the rhythm of the poem engages the performer to move the body artistically in consonance with its flow.

The poem goes through different stages in its production and being written down is one of them. The poem is only complete when it is performed or read out before an audience. This means that the poem from its initial composition, "workshop" stage, to its being written and performed has performance features informing it. A performance that thrills the audience in the diction, meaning, and performance skills tells the poem as successful.

As in the oral poetic tradition like *udje*, written poetry's aesthetic dimension is as important as the social meaning of a poem. In the tradition, it is said that "Echadia oye udje." In other words, it is the spectacle that makes *udje* appeal to the audience. The statement highlights the visual effects expected of *udje* or any poetry performance. The performance event brings communities together to enjoy moments of intense creativity. Since costume is important in traditional African poetic performance, I have always used African attire when reading or performing my poetry. I want what I wear to culturally accentuate my poetry and its performance. I have seen a poet-performer like Werewere Liking dress in a very traditionally dignified manner in performing her poetry. The use of African attire adds to the spectacle of the performance and the pleasure the audience gets from the reading or performance.

Before ending this discussion of the oral voice and performance considerations in my poetry, it is important to know the function of poetry performance. It creates vitality and enthralls the audience. I have consciously modeled many poems on the *udje* poetic tradition in an effort to infuse vitality into the work. The most conscious of such poems are those in the "Home Songs" section of *Delta Blues and Home Songs* in which the poems "Professor Kuta," "My Townsman in the Army," and "Odebala" are in classic *udje* song form but written in English. In structure, language, satiric mode, and other aspects, these poems fall into the corpus of poems in Urhobo called *udje*. The form has given me the opportunity to look at the Nigerian society then and make fun of representative characters that epitomize the Nigerian sociopolitical malaise.

Here are three poems, two very recent and one older, that I wrote with their eventual performance or "public outing" informing them:

GENTLY

Dede-e dede-e
Dede-e dede-e

Dede-e dede-e
Dede-e dede-e

Gently and steadily the old man pulls the thread of the loom.

Dede-e dede-e
Dede-e dede-e

He limps his way through the rugged terrain that stretches before him
but outpaces strides of those without age or other kinds of challenges.

Dede-e dede-e
Dede-e dede-e

The cotton tree stands unnoticed amidst iroko and palm trees
but its soft sheets of fabric cover the entire world's nakedness.

Dede-e dede-e
Dede-e dede-e

It's not only years that confer wisdom, says the young crocodile that has
already dug its hole with the sharp tools of its mouth and having its
fill of fish.

Dede-e dede-e
Dede-e dede-e

It's not one's hulk that gives power, boasts the black ant
that can stab the elephant's butt and bring down the bush giant.

Dede-e dede-e
Dede-e dede-e

Speed comes not from just being endowed with a multiplicity of
limbs,
the two-legged mock the millipede that it races past in a lightning flash.

Dede-e dede-e
Dede-e dede-e

More than thrice at dawn the cock crows to the cacophonous accompaniment of its tribe,
but only once a day does the cheerful but taciturn sun rise and wake
the entire world.

Dede-e dede-e
Dede-e dede-e

I am not a priest but have built a beautiful temple on the mountain's top
where daily I chant prayers and praises to my non-sectarian goddess.

Dede-e dede-e
Dede-e dede-e

Nor am I a king with all the paraphernalia that weighs down the
unwary
but wear a crown of songs whose comfort assuages every ache that
afflicts the head.

Dede-e dede-e
Dede-e dede-e

Gently and steadily the old man pulls the thread of the loom.

Dede-e dede-e
Dede-e dede-e

Dede-e dede-e
Dede-e dede-e

For Youths

Omo Okogbe
Okogbe

Omo Okogbe
Okogbe

He entered with the gait of one spoiling for a fight.
He came in wearing charms on his arms and feet.

Omo Okogbe
Okogbe

He shouted down everyone he came to meet at the gathering.
He had no patience for anybody wearing charms as he did.

Omo Okogbe
Okogbe

Nobody knew where he came from, not to talk of his name.
Nobody remembered his grandfather had been a warrior chief.

Omo Okogbe
Okogbe

Who cared whether he was a messenger from a commander?
He did not bring the pride of whoever sent him to this place.

Omo Okogbe
Okogbe

So he hastily took on the kind of fight he had never trained for.
It took no time to settle his status on the arena—he lost his life.

Omo Okogbe
Okogbe

Now a song mocks the youth rushing in to challenge
those already out in the field or coming in with tight lips:

Omo Okogbe
Okogbe

Omo Okogbe
Okogbe

American Wonder

Come and see American wonder
Come and see American wonder

Come and see American wonder
Come and see American wonder

The local magician in my elementary school days sang
"American wonder" before pulling off a hard trick

Come and see American wonder
Come and see American wonder

The cake disappeared from a closed fist.
A simple thread turned into a silk scarf.

Come and see American wonder
Come and see American wonder

The tar beauty talcumed white has become
a moon flower flaring night into incandescence.

Come and see American wonder
Come and see American wonder

I threw the mermaid's serpentine necklace into the air
and a black-and-white bird landed on my right palm.

Come and see American wonder
Come and see American wonder

The candle I lit in my dark hermitage
surrounds me with mirrors of hope

Come and see American wonder
Come and see American wonder

My book of nights is a love-filled lamp
that gives out the hide-and-seek bride

Come and see American wonder
Come and see American wonder

I took chitlings that Mami Sara prepared with spices
and have never since been hungry for another food.

Come and see American wonder
Come and see American wonder

Come and see American wonder
Come and see American wonder

CHAPTER 19

Two Tributes: Chinua Achebe and Kofi Awoonor

Chinua Achebe (1930–2013): A Tribute

Chinua Achebe's place as one of Africa's greatest writers is not contestable. He bestrode the African literature world like a colossus and he would be remembered not only by us but by generations to come in Africa and elsewhere. In his work he restored pride to the African whose postcolonial condition had tried to rob him of human dignity because of Western colonial policies denigrating African culture. In fact, one of his most impressionable convictions was that "African peoples did not hear of culture for the first time from Europeans...their societies were not mindless but frequently had a philosophy of great depth and value and beauty...they had poetry and, above all, they had dignity." He thus inscribed African culture boldly on the world literary stage. And he spent his writing career exhorting his African society to regain "belief in itself" since colonialism attempted to strip its self-confidence away. At the same time, he castigated his Nigerian society for its obsessive corruption and ineptitude that made a nation so abundantly endowed to be still wallowing in poverty. To him, the major problem with Nigeria was that of lack of good political leadership. He inspired African writers to write not art for art's sake or pure art as done by Western writers but "applied art" to make them "teachers" working toward changing their societies for the better. He thus espoused a transformative ideology of art. He was our champion wrestler in the global literary stage and the Eagle on the Iroko made us very proud.

While I have always been familiar with Achebe through his work—novels, essays, and poetry—that I have to read as a student, teacher, and writer, I had the opportunity to be very close to him on one major occasion. It was when I won the Commonwealth Poetry Prize for the Africa Region in 1987 and we were together in London at the Queen's reception for Commonwealth leaders and poetry award-winners from different regions of the world. I experienced Achebe's admirable humility. An iconic writer he already was and I a "budding" poet, he related to me as if like a comrade of equal status. He was cheerful and always exuded subdued humor with his trademark shy smile. When the Queen quoted him in her speech, he turned to me, smiling shyly and said: "Tanure, you are my witness!" Now I am his witness and bear testimony to the great man known all over the world and respected by the Queen of Great Britain and the presidents and prime ministers present. All his life, he remained humble and those young and old who came to him always testified to the humility that made him tower so high today in my memory.

Chinua Achebe taught me to be principled and truthful, especially as a writer, since one is bound to be involved in controversies. He was not controversial for the sake of being so or to gain cheap popularity but he said things and took action based upon deep convictions. His anticolonial stance made him write a counter narrative to Joseph Conrad's *Heart of Darkness* and other works of European writers who portrayed Africans as one-dimensional characters. Achebe insists that Africans are a people who are neither angels nor devils. His stand during the Nigerian Civil War should be seen in the context of one with a keen sensibility who responded to events following the pogroms of 1966. He was an emissary of Biafra, the secessionist state, and worked for it and was never apologetic about his role during the war. His last book, *There Was a Country: A Personal History of Biafra* (New York: Penguin, 2012), has been controversial in Nigeria and has offended many groups and people on the opposite side—including me—during the war but he aired his views frankly. He was a courageous man who did not hide his position on crucial issues.

A great inspirer who sparked the literary imagination of young Africans to take writing seriously, Achebe was among the chief writers who blazed the trail of modern African literature. His writings have helped to build a canon of modern African literature that younger writers are today working hard to reinforce with their respective works. There has been so much talk about his not winning the Nobel Prize for Literature but that should not in any way diminish his literary reputation. Literature is a cultural production and one does not expect him to be rewarded by the culture whose literary philosophy and cultural genocide he denounced by pricking the conscience of the West on colonialism! Achebe was not just an Ogidi man, an Igbo, a Nigerian, an African; he was a man with a deep humanity. He has joined the ancestors but will forever be with us in spirit.

Kofi Awoonor (1935–2013): A Tribute

I first came across him as George Awoonor-Williams while foraging modern African poetry to learn to write my own poetry after my Higher School Certificate program in 1967. So, I read "Songs of Sorrow," one of his signature poems, before encountering him at the University of Ibadan, where Professor Dan Izevbaye taught us his poetry as part of modern African poetry. Yes, Kofi Awoonor belonged to that canonical generation of modern African poets that include J. P. Clark, Wole Soyinka, Christopher Okigbo, and Lenrie Peters, among others. He stood out from his peers in his special use of English which was almost a transliteration of his native Ewe. That was a time when modern African poets were experimenting with the English language on how best to capture the modern African experience with the colonial language. The young Awoonor had to use a type of English which was informed in syntax, structure, and semantics by his indigenous African language and in his case Ewe, the language spoken by his people of the same name that straddle between Ghana and Togo. In his "Songs of Sorrow," for instance, the speaker of the poem compares the affairs of this world to chameleon feces which he attempts to "clean" but "will not go." The speaker is also not in the "middle" but in the "corner" of life. Awoonor's poetic language in his early poems registers the tension of a modern African poet expressing an African experience in the foreign language of his English colonizer. This effort sometimes results in the direct translation from the Ewe to English as done in *Rediscovery* and *Night of My Blood*, his early collections of poetry.

It was while in my last year at the University of Ibadan that Joseph Bruchac, the self-identified Native American poet and publisher of *The Greenfield Review*, introduced me to George Awoonor-Williams whose poems he had published. Bruchac had been a Peace Corp volunteer in Ghana where they had met. I was fortunate that my *Children of Iroko* and later *Labyrinths of the Delta* would be published by Awoonor's publisher. It was at this time that I started corresponding with the Ghanaian poet and we exchanged letters for quite some time in the 1970s. Before I arrived in Syracuse, New York, in 1978, Kofi Awoonor had already left Stony Brook in New York in 1975 to teach at the University of Cape Coast, where he would become entangled in the Ghanaian political upheavals of the time. After being detained for treason as one of the perpetrators of a failed military coup, he was later released without trial.

Kofi Awoonor was my mentor in many ways. He was a poet, folk-lorist, novelist, and scholar which I can now claim to be. He made it possible for younger African writers to combine many things in one as he did. It is as a poet and a folklorist that I see myself most indebted to the illustrious Ghanaian writer. His experimentation with English in attempting to indigenize it rubbed on me as I did the same using my Urhobo folklore as in my *Children of Iroko*. Awoonor made me see something good in my minority culture to tap from to enrich the English language. His poetry has an African identity through his use of Ewe folklore. While I read his poetry as an undergraduate and con-tinued reading his later publications—*The House by the Sea, Comes the Voyager at Last, This Earth, My Brother*, and *The Breast of the Earth*, among others—I taught his poetry in African Poetry courses at The University of Maiduguri in the 1980s.

Kofi Awoonor might have been a strong factor in my not only researching into the *udje* dance songs of the Urhobo people but also modeling poems on the *udje* poetic tradition itself in his man-ner on the *halo* of the Ewe. His *Guardians of the Sacred Word* fea-tured Ewe traditional poets, Hesino Akpalu, Amega Dunyo, and Komi Ekpe as I later do of *udje* poets such as Oloya, Memerume, and Okitiakpe. Awoonor's "Songs of Sorrow" is modeled significantly on one of Akpalu's songs. The Ewe of Ghana and Togo bear many cultural resemblances to the Urhobo of the Delta area of Nigeria. From their respective folklores, they might have been related to Old Ife. I see their tyrannical Agokoli comparable to the Urhobo Ogiso whose immediate source is Benin. But it is in their respective *halo* and *udje*—fiercely competitive satirical oral poetic performances—that the cultural similarity bears out the closeness of the two groups. Just as Kofi Awoonor inscribed the folklore of a minority group into the national literature of Ghana, similarly I have attempted to inscribe *udje* of the minority Urhobo into Nigerian literature.

Kofi Awoonor was a man of many distinguished parts. He was not only a poet and novelist but also a scholar in his teachings at Stony Brook and Cape Coast and his bringing to limelight the highly poetic works of Ewe oral poets. He was a diplomat in the tradition of Pablo Neruda—he was Ghana's ambassador to Brazil and Cuba and a per-manent representative to the United Nations at a time. He was always involved in his nation's politics and trying to shape its democratic direction. Until recently he chaired an advisory committee to the

Ghanaian government. In whatever role he played in life, he advanced humanity through his poetic sensibility.

Though I have read most of his writings, ranging from poetry publications to his poetic novel, critical works, and his publication of Ewe traditional poets, I met the man in person only once—in Accra during the last Pan-African Poetry Festival organized by Atukwei Okai in early November 2008. He attended a poetry reading session in which I participated and I told him I felt honored. A great man's influence is strongly felt from a distance and not necessarily from close proximity and that is what Kofi Awoonor's enduring influence on my creative and scholarly work has been. It is deeply sad that his earthly life should end in his gruesome murder at the hands of Al Shabaab Islamist terrorists at the Westgate Mall in Nairobi, Kenya. But life is full of ironies. He may be gone physically but he lives forever in his numerous works that many will continue to read and cherish. Kofi Awoonor "touched" and nurtured me and others into what we are today whether creative writers, scholars, or in other pursuits. He lived a worthy life and will remain a proud ancestor.

References

Abani, Chris. *GraceLand*. New York: Farrar, Straus & Giroux, 2003.

Aborisade, Oladimeji, ed. *Nigerian Local Government Reformed*. Ile-Ife, Nigeria: Local Government Publications, Obafemi Awolowo University, 1989.

———, ed. *On Being in Charge at the Grassroots Level in Nigeria*. Ile-Ife, Nigeria: Local Government Publications, Obafemi Awolowo University, 1989.

———, ed. *Local Government and the Traditional Rulers in Nigeria*. Ile-Ife, Nigeria: University of Ife Press, 1985.

Aborisade, Oladimeji and Robert J. Mundt. *Politics in Nigeria*. New York: Longman, 2002.

———, eds. *Local Government in Nigeria and the United States: Learning from Comparison*. Ile-Ife, Nigeria: Local Government Publications, Obafemi Awolowo University, 1995.

Abrahams, Peter. *Tell Freedom*. London: Heinemann, 1970.

Achebe, Chinua. *There Was a Country: A Personal History of Biafra*. New York: Penguin, 2012.

———. *Hopes and Impediments*. New York: Doubleday, 1989.

———. *Morning Yet on Creation Day: Essays*. New York: Anchor, 1975.

———. *Arrow of God*. London: Heinemann 1960.

———. *Things Fall Apart*. London: Heinemann, 1958.

Adamson, Joni. *American Indian Literature, Environmental Justice, and Ecocriticism: The Middle Passage*. Tucson: University of Arizona Press, 2001.

Adesanmi, Pius. "Post-centenary Nigeria: New literatures, new leaders, new nation." Being keynote speech presented by Professor Pius Adesanmi on November 13 at the 2014 MBA International Literary Colloquium in Minna, Niger State.

Adichie, Chimamanda Ngozi. *Americanah*. New York: Picador, 2012.

———. *Half of a Yellow Sun*. Lagos: Farafina, 2007.

———. *Purple Hibiscus*. New York: Anchor, 2004.

———. "The Single Story." http://www.ted.com/talks/lang/eng/chimam anda_adichie_the_danger_of_a_single_story.html.

Agary, Kaine. *Yellow-Yellow*. Lagos: Dtalkshop, 2006.

Aiyejina, Funso. "Recent Nigerian Poetry in English: An Alter/Native Tradition," ed. Yeni Ogunbiyi, *Perspectives on Nigerian Literature*, vol. 1. Lagos: Guardian Books, 1988. pp. 112–128.

Akpan, Uwem. *Say You're One of Them*. New York: Little, Brown, 2009.

———. *Say You Are One of Them*. New York: Farrar, Straus, & Giraux, 2005.

Amadi, Elechi. *The Concubine*. London: Heinemann, 1966.

Anderson, Lorraine, Scott Slovic, and John O'Grady, eds. *Literature and the Environment: A Reader on Nature and Culture*. New York: Longman, 1999.

Anderson, M. G and P. M. Peek. *Ways of the Rivers: Arts and Environment of the Niger Delta*. UCLA, LA: Fowler Museum of Cultural History, 2002.

Appadurai, Arjun. "Disjuncture and difference in the global cultural economy," in *Modernity at Large: Cultural Dimensions of Globalization*. Minneapolis: University of Minnesota Press, 1996. pp. 27–47.

———. *Modernity at Large: Cultural Dimensions of Globalization* (Minneapolis: University of Minnesota Press, 1996.

Atta, Sefi. *Everything Good Will Come*. Boston: Intercontinental, 2005.

Avorgbedor, Daniel. "The Turner-Schechner Model of Performance As Social Drama: A Re-Examination in the Light of Anlo-Ewe *Halō*." *Research in African Literatures*, vol. 30, no. 4, Winter, 1999, 144–155.

Awoonor, Kofi. *Guardians of the Sacred Word: Ewe Poetry*. New York: Nok Publishers, 1974.

Azevedo, Mario, ed. *Africana Studies: A Survey of Africa and the African Diaspora*. Durham, NC: Carolina Academic Press, 2005.

Baker, Kenneth. *Philosophical Dictionary*. Spokane, WA: Gozaga University Press, 1974.

Barber, Karin. *The Anthropology of Texts, Persons and Publics: Oral and Written Cultures in Africa and Beyond*. Cambridge: Cambridge University Press, 2007.

———, ed. *Readings in African Popular Culture*. London and Bloomington: James Currey and Indiana University Press, 1997.

———. *I Could Speak Until Tomorrow: Oriki, Women and the Past in a Yoruba Town*. Edinburgh: Edinburgh University Press, 1991.

Bauman, Richard. *Story, Performance, and Event: Contextual Studies of Oral Narrative*. Cambridge: Cambridge University Press, 1986.

Beah, Ishmael. *A Long Way Gone: Memoir of a Boy Soldier*. New York: Farrar, Straus, & Giraux, 2007.

Beier, Uli. "Interview: Soyinka." *Isokan Yoruba Magazine* (Summer 1997), vol. III, no. III.

Bergson, Henri. *Le Rire*. 1940. Paris: Presses Universitaires de France, 2004.

Beyala, Calixthe. *Femme nue femme noire* (*Naked woman Black woman*). Paris: Albin Michel, 2003.

Bhabha, H. *The Location of Culture*. New York: Routledge, 1994.

Bloom, Harold. *The Anxiety of Influence: A Theory of Poetry*. New York: Oxford University Press, 1997.

——. *The Anxieties of Influence: A Theory of Poetry.* New York: Oxford University Press, 1973.

Branch, Michael, Rochelle Johnson, Daniel Patterson, and Scott Slovic. *Reading the Earth: New Directions in the Study of Literature and the Environment.* Moscow, Idaho: University of Idaho Press, 1998.

Brockes, Emma. Teju Cole: 'Two Drafts of Tweet? Insuffereable. But when I tweet I'm still a writer.' Saturday, 21 June 2014.

Brutus, Dennis. *A Simple Lust.* Oxford, UK: Heinemann, 1990.

Bukar, Idi. *The Desert Came and Then the Torturer.* Zaria, Nigeria: RAG, 1986.

Butcher, William, ed. and trans. *Julius Verne: The Definitive Biography.* London/New York: Oxford World Classics, 1995.

Cheney-Coker, Syl. *The Last Harmattan of Alusin Dunbar.* Oxford, UK: Heinemann, 1990.

Chinweizu, Jemie O. and I. Madubuike. *Toward the Decolonization of African Literature,* vol. 1. Washington, DC: Howard University Press, 1983.

——. *Towards the Decolonization of Modern African Literature.* New York/Enugu: NOK Publishers, 1980.

Chinweizu, Madubuike and Jemie. *Towards the Decolonization of Modern African Literature.* Enugu/New York: NOK, 1984.

Clark-Bekederemo, J. P. *Full Tide: Collected Poems.* Ibadan, Nigeria: Mosuro, 2010.

——. *All for Oil.* 2009. Lagos: Malthouse, 2000.

——, ed. *The Ozidi Saga: Collected and Translated from the Oral Ijo Version of Okabou Ojobolo.* Washington, DC: Howard University Press, 1991.

——. *The Bikoroa Plays: The Boat, The Return Home, and Full Circle.* Ibadan: University Press, 1985.

——. *A Decade of Tongues: Selected Poems: 1958–1968.* London: Longman, 1981.

——. *A Decade of Tongues.* Ikeja: Longman, 1981.

——. *The Raft.* London: Longman, 1978.

——. *The Ozidi Saga.* Ibadan: Ibadan UP, 1975.

——. *Casualties.* London: Longman, 1972.

——. *Ozidi.* Ibadan: Oxford UP, 1966.

——. "Poetry of the Urhobo Dance Udje," *Nigeria Magazine,* no. 87, 1965.

——. *A Reed in the Tide.* London: Longman, 1965.

——. *Song of a Goat.* London: Longman, 1965.

Conteh-Morgan, John and Tejumola Olaniyan, eds. *African Drama and Performance.* Bloomington and Indianapolis: Indiana University Press, 2004.

Cope, Trevor, ed. *Izibongo: Zulu Praise Poems.* Oxford: Oxford University Press, 1968.

Courlander, Harold. *A Treasury of Afro-American Folklore.* New York: Marlowe and Company, 1996.

Darah, G. G. *Battles of Songs: Udje Tradition of the Urhobo*. Lagos: Malthouse, 2005.

D'Azevedo, Warren., ed. *The Traditional Artist in African Societies*. Bloomington, Indiana: UP, 1989.

Dominabo, Amayamabo O. *Ken Saro-Wiwa 1941–1995: His Life and Legacies*. Buguma, Nigeria: Hanging Gardens Publishers, 2005.

Dongala, Emmanuel. *Johnny Mad Dog*. New York, Picador, 2005.

Donkor, Martha. "Marching to the Tune of Colonization, Globalization, Immigration, and the Ghanaian Diaspora," *Africa Today*, vol. 52, no. 1 (Fall 2005) 27–44.

Drewal, Henry John, ed. *Sacred Waters: Arts for Mami Wata and Other Water Divinities in Africa and the Diaspora*. Bloomington: Indiana University Press, 2008.

Drewal, Margaret T. *Yoruba Ritual: Performers, Play, Agency*. Bloomington: Indiana University Press, 1992.

"The Drilling Fields," a documentary on the Ogoni crisis, produced by the British ITV, 1994.

Dutta, M. J. *Communicating Social Change Structure, Culture, and Agency*. New York: Routledge, Taylor & Francis Group, 2011.

Eagleton, Terry. *Literary Theory: An Introduction*. Minneapolis: University of Minnesota Press, 1983.

Ede, Amatoritsero. "The Arts and Asocial Media: Face Me, I Book You!" (*Maple Literary Supplement*. Issue #10 Sept-Dec 2011, ISSN: 1916–341X).

Egudu, Romanus N. *Modern African Poetry and the African Predicament*. London: Macmillan, 1978.

Epega, Afolabi A. *Ifa: The Ancient Wisdom*. Athelia Henrietta Press, 2003.

Falola, Toyin and Christian Jennings, eds. *Africanizing Knowledge: African Studies Across the Disciplines*. Piscataway, NJ: Transaction Publishers, 2002.

FAMA, Chief. *Practitioner's Handbook for the Ifa Professional*. San Bernardino, CA: Ile Orunmila Communications, 2004.

Finnegan, Ruth. *Oral Literature in Africa*. Oxford: Oxford UP, 1970.

Fox, Robert E. *Masters of the Drum: Black Li/oratures Across the Continuum*. Westport, CT: Greenwood Press, 1995.

Foss, Perkins, ed. *Where Gods and Mortals Meet: Continuity and Renewal in Urhobo Art*, Museum for African Art, New York/ SNOECK, Ghent, 2004.

Furniss, Graham. *The Power of the Spoken Word*. London and New York: Palgrave Macmillan, 2005.

Furniss, Graham and Liz Gunner, eds. *Power, Marginality and African Oral Literature*. Cambridge: Cambridge University Press, 1995.

Garuba, Harry. "Odia Ofeimun," entry in *Dictionary of Literary Biography, Vol. 360: Contemporary African Writers* (Detroit, MI: Gale Research, 2011).

Gbadamosi, Bakare and Obotunde Ijimere. *Not Even God Is Ripe Enough.* London: Heinemann, 1968.

Gedicks, Al. *Resource Rebels: Native Challenges to Mining and Oil Corporations.* Cambridge, MA: South End Press, 2001.

Grayson, Sandra M. "An Interview with Tijan M. Sallah, Poet." *Network 2000: In the Spirit of the Harlem Renaissance,* vol. 4, no. 4 (Fall 1997).

Habila, Helon. *Oil on Water.* London: Hamish Hamilton, 2010.

Hall, Donald. *Death to the Death of Poetry.* Ann Arbor: University of Michigan Press, 1994.

Henige, David. *Oral Historiography.* Harlow, Essex: Longman, 1982.

Hollander, Jack. *The Real Environmental Crisis.* LA: University of California Press, 2003.

Holloway, Joseph H. *Africanisms in American Culture.* Bloomington: Indiana University Press, 1990.

Ifowodo, Ogaga. *The Oil Lamp.* Trenton, NJ: Africa World Press, 2007.

Ipadeola, Tade. *The Sahara Testament.* Lagos: Hornbill House of the Arts, 2012.

Irele, F. Abiola. "Orality, Literacy and African Literature." In *The African Imagination.* New York: Oxford University Press, 2001. pp. 23–38.

———. "The Crisis of Cultural Memory in Chinua Achebe's *Things Fall Apart* 4 (3), 2000: 1 [online] URL: http://web. Africa.ufl.edu/asq /v4/413a1.htm.

Iweala, Uzodinma. *Beasts of No Nation.* New York: HarperCollins, 2005.

Jarosz, L. "Constructing the Dark Continent: Metaphor as Geographic Representation of Africa." *Geografiska Annaler. Series B, Human Geography* 74(2), 1992, 105–15.

Kaiama Declaration, 1998.

Kasfir, Sidney. *African Art and the Colonial Encounter: Inventing a Global Commodity.* Bloomington: Indiana University Press, 2007.

Killam, G. D., ed. *African Writers on African Writing.* London: Heinemann, 1978.

Kunene, Mazisi. *The Ancestors and the Sacred Mountain.* London: Heinemann, 1981.

Kwakye, Benjamin. *The Other Crucifix.* London: Ayebia, 2010.

———. *The Crucifix.* New York: Picador, 2009.

La Guma, Alex. *A Walk in the Night.* London: Heinemann, 1970.

Langa, Mandla. *Naked Song and Other Stories.* Cape Town: David Philip, 1996.

Lankton, J. W., Ige, O. A., and Rehren, T. (2006). "Early primary glass production in southern Nigeria." *Journal of African Archaeology* 4: 111–38.

Larson, Charles. "Writing from the Third World." *World Literature Today* 55.1 (Winter 1981): 57–58.

Launko, Okimba (Femi Osofisan). *Seven Stations Up the Tray's Way.* Ibadan: Mosuro Publishers, 2013.

Lawal, Babatunde. *The Gelede Spectacle: Art, Gender and Social Harmony in an African Culture.* Seattle: University of Washington Press, 1996.

Lister, Julius. *Black Folktales*. New York: Grove Press, 1991.

MacLeod, C. 1997. "Black American Literature and the Postcolonial Debate." *The Yearbook of English Studies* 27: 51–65.

Maja-Pearce, Adewale, ed. *The Heinemann Book of African Poetry in English*. Oxford, UK: Heinemann International, 1990.

Mbiti, John S. *African Religions and Philosophy*. London: Heinemann, 1969.

McEwan, C. *Postcolonialism and Development*. New York: Routledge, Taylor and Francis Group, 2009.

McKean, Erin. *The New Oxford American Dictionary. Second Edition*. New York: Oxford University Press, 2005.

Mda, Zakes. *The Heart of Redness*. New York: Picador, 2002.

Mezlekia, Nega. *The God Who Begat a Jackal*. New York: Picador, 2002.

Moore, Gerald and Ulli Beier. *Modern African Literature*. Harmondsworth, UK: Penguin, 1963.

Moyers, Bill. Interview with Chinua Achebe, Amherst, MA, 1988 in World of Ideas Series.

Mudimbe, V. Y. *The Idea of Africa*. Bloomington, IN: Indiana University Press, 1994.

Mutiso, G-C. M. *Socio-Political Thought in African Literature*. London: Macmillan, 1974.

Nduka, Uche. *Chiaroscuro*. Chicago: Yeti Press, 1997.

———. *The Bremen Poems*. Bremen: New Leaf Press, 1995.

Ngugi wa Thiongo with Micere Mugo. *The Trial of Dedan Kimathi*. London: Heinemann, 1972.

Nixon, Rob. "Environmentalism and Postcolonialism," in Olaniyan and Quayson, eds. *African Literature: An Anthology of Criticism and Theory*. Malden, MA: Blackwell Publishing, 2007.

Nwapa, Flora. *Cassava Song and Rice Song*. Enugu: Tana Press, 1986.

Obi, Jospeph. Private correspondence. September 17, 2011.

Obiechina, Emmanuel. *Culture, Tradition and Society in the West African Novel*. Cambridge: Cambridge University Press, 1975.

Ofeimun, Odia. *Dreams at Work*. Lagos: Hornbill House, 2000.

———. *A Feast of Return/Under African Skies*. Lagos: Hornbill House, 2000.

———. *London Letter and Other Poems*. Lagos: Hornbill House, 2000.

———. *A Handle for the Flutist*. Lagos: Update Publications, 1986.

———. *The Poet Lied*. London: Longman, 1980.

Ogbowei, G. Ebinyo. *Song of a Dying River*. Ibadan: Kraft, 2009.

Ogede, Ode. *Art, Society, and Performance: Igede Praise Poetry*. Gainesville: University Press of Florida, 1997.

Ogoni Bill of Rights, 1990.

Ogunbiyi, Yemi. *Perspectives on Nigerian Literature*, vol. 1. Lagos: Guardian Books, 1988.

Ojaide, Tanure, ed. *Dictionary of Literary Biography Volume 360: Contemporary African Writers*. Detroit: Gale, 2011.

———. *The Beauty I Have Seen and Other Poems.* Lagos: Malthouse, 2010.

———. "The Glocal Monster: Oil, Globalization, the Environment, and Nigeria's Niger Delta." UNC Charlotte, NC. GPS Presentation to Phi Beta Delta, April 2009.

———. *Theorizing African Oral Poetic Performance and Aesthetics: Udje Dance Songs.* Trenton, NJ: Africa World Press, 2008.

———. *Ordering the African Imagination: Essays on Culture and Literature.* Lagos: Malthouse, 2007.

———. *The Tale of the Harmattan.* Cape Town: Kwela Books & Snailpress, 2007.

———. *The Activist.* Lagos: Farafina, 2006.

———. *In the House of Words.* Lagos: Malthouse, 2006.

———. *A Creative Writing Handbook for African Writers and Students.* Lagos: Malthouse, 2005.

———. "How the Urhobo People See the World Through Art," *Where Gods and Mortals Meet: Continuity and Renewal in Urhobo Art,* ed. By Perkins Foss, Museum for African Art, New York/ SNOECK, Ghent, 2004.

———. *Poetry, Performance, and Art: Udje Dance Songs of the Urhobo People*: Durham, NC: Carolina Academic Press, 2003.

———. With Joseph Obi. *Culture, Society, and Politics in Modern African Literature: Texts and Contexts.* Durham, NC: Carolina Academic Press, 2001.

———. "The Niger Delta, Nativity, and My Writing," *Sacred Spaces and Public Quarrels*, ed. by Ezekiel Kalipeni and Paul T. Zeleza, Africa World Press, 1999.

———. *Delta Blues and Home Songs.* Ibadan, Nigeria: Kraft, 1998.

———. *Delta Blues and Home Songs.* Ibadan: Kaft Books, 1997.

———. *Great Boys: An African Childhood.* Trenton, NJ: Africa World Press, 1996.

———. *Poetic Imagination in Black Africa: Essays on African Poetry.* Durham, NC: Carolina Academic Press, 1996.

———. Rev. of *Dreams of Dusty Roads* by Tijan M. Sallah. *World Literature Today* 68.1 (Winter 1994): 188.

———. *The Fate of Vultures.* Lagos: Malthouse, 1991.

———. *The Eagle's Vision.* Detroit, MI: Lotus Press, 1987.

———. *Labyrinths of the Delta.* Greenfield, NY: Greenfield Press, 1986.

———. *The Poetry of Wole Soyinka.* Lagos: Malthouse, 1984.

———. *Children of Iroko & Other Poems.* Greenfield Center, NY: Greenfield Press, 1973.

Ojaide, Tanure and Tijan M. Sallah. *The New African Poetry: An Anthology.* Boulder, CO: Lynne Rienner, 1999.

Okara, Gabriel. *The Fisherman's Invocation.* London: Heinemann, 1975.

———. *The Fisherman's Invocation.* Benin: Ethiope Press, 1972.

———. *The Voice.* London: F. Watts, 1964.

Okigbo, Christopher. *Labyrinths with Path of Thunder.* New York: Africana Publishing Corporation, 1971.

Okigbo, Christopher. *Labyrinths with Poems Prophesying War.* London: Heinemann, 1971.

———. *Heavensgate.* Ibadan: Mbari, 1966.

Okome, Onookome. *Pendants.* Ibadan: Kraft, 1993.

Okonta, Ike and Oronto Douglas. *Where Vultures Feast: Shell, Human Rights, and Oil.* New York: Sierra Club Books, 2001.

Okpewho, Isidore. *Call Me by My Rightful Name.* Trenton, NJ: Africa World Press, 2004.

———. *Once upon a Kingdom.* Bloomington, IN: IUP, 1998.

———. *Tides.* London: Longman, 1993.

———. *African Oral Literature: Background, Character, and Continuity.* Bloomington: Indiana University Press, 1992.

———. *The Oral Performance.* Ibadan: Spectrum, 1990.

———. *The Epic in Africa.* New York: Columbia University Press, 1989.

———. *Myth in Africa.* Bloomington: Indiana University Press, 1983.

———. *The Epic in Africa.* New York: Columbia University Press, 1979.

———. *The Last Duty.* London: Longman, 1976.

Okri, Ben. *Starbook.* London: Rider, 2008.

———. *Dangerous Love.* London: Phoenix House, 1996.

———. *The Famished Road.* London: Jonathan Cape, 1991.

———. *Stars of the New Curfew.* London: Secker & Warburg, 1988.

———. *Incidents at the Shrine.* Oxford: Heinemann, 1986.

Olaniyan, Tejumola and Ato Quayson, eds. *African Literature: An Anthology of Criticism and Theory.* Malden, MA: Blackwell Publishing, 2007.

Omoweh, Daniel A. *Shell Petroleum Development Company, the State and Underdevelopment of Nigeria's Niger Delta: A Study in Environmental Degradation.* Trenton, NJ: Africa World Press, 2005.

ONeil, Tom. "Nigerian Oil, Curse of the Black Gold." *The National Geographic* (February 2007).

Ong, Walter J. *Orality and Literacy: The Technologizing of the Word.* London/New York: Methuen, 1982.

Onwueme, Tess. *Then She Said It!* New York: African Heritage Press, 2003.

———. *Tell It to Women: An Epic Drama.* Detroit, MI: Wayne State UP, 1995.

Opland, Jeff. *Xhosa Oral Poetry.* Cambridge: Cambridge University Press, 1983.

Otobotekere, Christian. *Next to Reality.* Gardena, CA: African Books Network Project, 2011.

———. *Beyond Sound and Voice.* Port Harcourt: Herodotus Publishing Ventures, 2010.

———. *My River.* Gardena, CA: African Books Network Project, 2009.

———. *Playful Notes and Keys.* Port Harcourt: Sadah Printing Press, 1987.

Osondu, E. C. "Waiting" in http://guernicamag.com/fiction/762/waiting.

Osundare, Niyi. *The Eye of the Earth.* Ibadan, Nigeria: Heinemann, 1986.

———. *Songs of the Marketplace.* Ibadan: Spectrum, 1983.

———. *Songs of the Marketplace.* Ibadan: Spectrum, 1982.

Parini, Jay. "The Greening of the Humanities," *The New York Times* Sunday Magazine, October 23, 1995.

Quinones, Ayoka Wiles. *I Hear Olofi's Song: A Collection of Yoruba Spiritual Prayers for Egun and Orisa.* Philadelphia: Oshun Publishing Company, 2010.

Sallah, Tijan M. *Dream Kingdom: New and Selected Poems.* Trenton, NJ: Africa World Press, 2007.

———. *Wolof: The Heritage Library of African Peoples.* New York: The Rosen Publishing Group, 1996.

———. *Dreams of Dusty Roads.* Washington, DC: Three Continents Press, 1993.

———. *Kora Land.* Washington, DC: Three Continents Press, 1989.

———. *When Africa Was a Young Woman.* Calcutta, India: Writers Workshop, 1980.

Sapir, Edward. *Selected Writings in Language, Culture, and Personality.* Berkeley: University of California Press, 1949.

Saro-Wiwa, Ken. *Lemona's Tale.* Burnt Hill, UK: Penguin, 1996.

———. *A Month and a Day: A Detention Diary.* London: Penguin, 1995.

———. *A Forest of Flowers.* Port Harcourt: Saros, 1982.

———. *On a Darkling Plain.* Port Harcourt: Saros, 1978.

Scheub, Harold. *African Oral Narratives.* Boston: G. K. Hall, 1977.

Schmidt, Peter and D. Avery. "Complex iron Smelting and Prehistoric Culture in Tanzania." *Science* 201 (1978): 1085–89.

Schmidt, Peter and Terry Childs. "Ancient African Iron Production." *American Scientist* 83 (1995): 524–33.

Shoneyin, Lola. *The Secret Lives of Baba Segi's Wives.* London: Serpent's Tail, 2010.

Sickels, Amy. "The Critical Reception of *Things Fall Apart.*"

Singh, R. B. *Global Environmental Change.* New York: Taylor & Francis Group, 1995.

Soyinka, Wole. *Sarmakand and Other Markets I Have Known.* London: Methuen, 2002.

———. *Selected Poems: Idanre, A Shuttle in the Crypt, Mandela's Earth.* London: Methuen, 1989.

———. *Mandela's Earth and Other Poems.* New York: Random House, 1988.

———. "The Writer in a Modern African State," *Art, Dialogue and Outrage: Essays on Literature and Culture.* Ibadan: New Horn, 1988.

———. *Death and the King's Horseman.* New York: Hill and Wang/Noonday Press, 1987.

———. *Ake: The Years of Childhood.* London: Rex Collings, 1981.

———. *The Man Died.* London: Rex Collings, 1972; Harmondsworth, UK: Penguin, 1976.

———. *Myth, Literature and the African World.* Cambridge: Cambridge University Press, 1976.

———. *Death and the King's Horseman.* London: Eyre Methuen, 1975.

Soyinka, Wole. *Season of Anomy*. London: Rex Collings, 1973.
———. *A Shuttle in the Crypt*. London: Rex Collings/Eyre Methuen, 1972.
———. *The Interpreters*. London: Andre Deutsch, 1965; London: Heinemann & Deutsch, 1970.
———. *Idanre and Other Poems*. London: Eyre Methuen, 1967.
Spivak, G. C. "Can the Subaltern Speak? Speculations on Widow-Sacrifice." *Wedge* (Winter–Spring, 1985) 7–8: 120–130.
Spyra, Ania. *WLT*, January/February, 2012, vol. 86, no. 1, p. 21.
Suso, Bemba and Banna Kanute. *Sunjata*. New York: Penguin, 1999.
Terry, Olufemi. "Stickfighting Days." *The Guardian* (London), July 6, 2010. http://www.guardian.co.uk/books/interactive/2010/jul/06/stick fighting-olufemi-terry.
Thompson, Robert Farris. *Flash of the Spirit: African & Afro-American Art & Philosophy*. New York: Vintage Books, 1984.
Thompson, Stith. *Motif-Index of Folk-Literature*. Bloomington: Indiana UP, 1989.
Unigwe, Chika. *On Black Sisters' Street*. London: Jonathan Cape, 2009. www.nepad.org.
United Nations Human Development Statistics.
Vambe, Maurice T. ed. *Orality and Cultural Identities in Zimbabwe*. Gweru: Mambo Press, 2001.
Whorf, B. L. *Language, Thought, and Reality*. Cambridge, MA: MIT Press, 1956.
Yeibo, Ebi. *Song for Tomorrow and Other Poems*. Ibadan: Kraft, 2003.
———. *The Forbidden Tongue*. Ibadan: Kraft Books, 2009.
Yerima, Ahmed. *Hard Ground*. Ibadan: Kraft Books, 2006.

INDEX

GPSR Compliance
The European Union's (EU) General Product Safety Regulation (GPSR) is a set
of rules that requires consumer products to be safe and our obligations to
ensure this.

If you have any concerns about our products, you can contact us on

ProductSafety@springernature.com

In case Publisher is established outside the EU, the EU authorized
representative is:

Springer Nature Customer Service Center GmbH
Europaplatz 3
69115 Heidelberg, Germany

www.ingramcontent.com/pod-product-compliance
Ingram Content Group UK Ltd.
Pitfield, Milton Keynes, MK11 3LW, UK
UKHW021914230725
461108UK00007B/74